CRITICAL CHILDREN

RICHARD LOCKE

CRITICAL CHILDREN

THE USE OF CHILDHOOD
IN TEN GREAT NOVELS

COLUMBIA UNIVERSITY PRESS   NEW YORK

COLUMBIA UNIVERSITY PRESS
Publishers Since 1893
New York   Chichester, West Sussex

Copyright © 2011 Richard Locke

Library of Congress Cataloging-in-Publication Data

Locke, Richard, 1941–
Critical children : the use of childhood in ten great novels /
Richard Locke.
    p. cm.
Includes bibliographical references and index.
ISBN 978-0-231-15782-7 (cloth : alk. paper) — ISBN 978-0-231-52799-6 (e-book)
1. Children in literature.   2. American fiction—History and criticism.
3. English fiction—History and criticism.   I. Title.

PS374.C45L63 2011
823.009'3523—DC22

2010053805

Columbia University Press books are printed on permanent and durable acid-free paper.
This book is printed on paper with recycled content.

Printed in the United States of America

c 10 9 8 7 6 5 4 3 2 1

References to Internet Web sites (URLs) were accurate at the time of writing.
Neither the author nor Columbia University Press is responsible for URLs
that may have expired or changed since the manuscript was prepared.

DESIGN BY VIN DANG

FOR WENDY

CONTENTS

———

CRITICAL CHILDREN

INTRODUCTION

——

IN 1876 MARK TWAIN stopped working on the manuscript of *Huck-leberry Finn* and didn't pick it up for three years. He'd written 446 pages and come to the middle of the eighteenth chapter. The fugitive orphan Huck and the runaway slave Jim have been violently separated once again after a steamboat has crushed the raft that is their home and their vehicle to freedom. Huck dives toward the bottom of the river below the thirty-foot steamboat wheel, but when he surfaces he can't find Jim and finally scrambles ashore in the dark. He comes to a backwoods country mansion, a "big old-fashioned double-sized log house" guarded by dogs and armed men in a state of high suspicion and alarm, and after a terrifying interrogation that establishes his status as a castaway and his ignorance of the local war, he is adopted by the "aristocratic clan" of the Grangerfords, who tell him "I could have a home there as long as I wanted it."[1] Huck has survived a rite of passage from river to shore. He has reentered civilization.

At first he is filled with admiration: the family and the house are "so nice" and have "so much style." He describes the design and decoration of the house (a Kentucky Penshurst) with the astonished precision of an explorer in a newfound land, but the family's taste in art and literature begin to "aggravate" him. They maintain a funeral cult of a dead daughter whose "sadful" drawings and verse albums Huck describes for pages on end. Just as we become impatient with his detail, we realize he's going on because these images "always gave me the fan-tods" (121); his catalogue is an attempt at cultural and psychological control. And we recognize that the family's melancholy taste is a comic but perversely plausible response to their death-obsessed ethos of revenge killing. Huck asks the youngest Grangerford son, Buck, who is effectively his "aristocratic" double (he's the same age as Huck—"thirteen or fourteen or along there"—they share clothes, and their names rhyme, of course), to define the word that expresses the central concept that governs this rich, highly civilized, long-established, and utterly paranoid community: "What's a feud?"

It's here that Twain stopped writing. He'd sounded a theme that was large enough to sustain neglect as he moved off toward other literary projects. But when he returned to *Huckleberry Finn* in 1879 he immediately constructed a six-page narrative that ends with one of the most powerful (and celebrated) presentations of the central themes, actions, characters, and images of the entire novel. Twain's creative response to Huck's question is a conspicuous instance of the deepening and enlargement that can result from using the figure of a child as a means of cultural and moral interrogation. Huck's ignorance, vulnerability, and curiosity; his improvisatory mix of candor and deceit, prejudice and fresh perception; his multiple fabricated identities; and his moral bewilderment throw into relief the ferocious self-destructive world of the vainglorious American frontier "civilization," with its Grangerford "clan" and its Shepherdson "tribe," all "high-toned, and well born, and rich and grand" (126).

What Huck is discovering is that the shore is even less safe than the river. A family is not a haven in a heartless world; it makes it even crueler. Men and boys have been killing one another here for thirty years. The transgressive love and elopement of a local Romeo and Juliet (facilitated by Huck's delivery of a message hidden in a "testament" at the church where both families hear sermons every Sunday of "brotherly love, and such-like tiresomeness") precipitates a climactic slaughter. Huck takes refuge in a tree; he has rushed back to nature, from which an agile boy can take a wider view of the human disaster unfolding below. He sees Buck and another boy caught in a skirmish. His description of it begins like a boy's adventure story, but he quickly complicates the narrative and becomes a distraught participant observer:

> All of a sudden, bang! bang! bang! goes three or four guns—the men had slipped around through the woods and come in from behind without their horses! The boys jumped for the river—both of them hurt—and as they swam down the current the men run along the bank shooting at them and singing

out, 'Kill them, kill them!' [Not calling or crying out but "singing out"—exultantly.] It made me so sick I most fell out of the tree. I ain't agoing to tell *all* that happened—it would make me sick again if I was to do that. I wished I hadn't ever come ashore that night, to see such things. I ain't ever going to get shut of them—lots of times I dream about them.

Huck responds to the horror by insisting that he controls the narrative of it but confesses that he can't control the sickening memory that persists even into his current dreams. The trauma isn't "shut." And his story isn't finished:

When I got down out of the tree, I crept along down the river bank a piece, and found the two bodies laying in the edge of the water, and tugged at them till I got them ashore; then I covered up their faces, and got away as quick as I could. I cried a little when I was covering up Buck's face, for he was mighty good to me.

It was just dark, now. I never went near the house, but struck through the woods and made for the swamp.

There he meets Jim, who has fixed the raft, and they "shove off for the big water":

I never felt easy till the raft was two mile below there and out in the middle of the Mississippi. Then we hung up our signal lantern, and judged that we was free and safe once more. I hadn't had a bite to eat since yesterday; so Jim he got out some corn-dodgers and buttermilk, and pork and cabbage, and greens—there ain't nothing in the world so good, when it's cooked right—and whilst I eat my supper we talked, and had a good time.

The banality conveys a return to commonplace security. "I was powerful glad to get away from the feuds, and so was Jim to get away from the swamp. We said there warn't no home like a raft, after all. Other places do seem so cramped up and smothery, but a raft don't. You feel mighty free and easy and comfortable on a raft" (133–34).

Huck says that to be on the river is to be "free," but to be "safe" they must put up the "signal"—they need a cultural artifact to protect them; they can't entirely renounce civilization. He then swerves into a regressive childish account of the food the fatherly Jim provides him—the length of the description somewhat comically conveys Huck's urgent need to eradicate the preceding violent narrative and affirm the comforts of life with Jim. But the chapter ends with Huck's authoritative expression of the balance he perceives between the deadly, social "feuds" and the dangerous, natural "swamp" and with his affirmation of the raft as a "home," not "cramped up and smothery" (so confining that you die for lack of breath, as you would if you drowned). The open easy motion of the concluding sentence—"You feel mighty free and easy and comfortable on a raft"—conveys his happy sense of order recovered at last, even as its boyish hyperbole reminds us ironically that the drifting raft can also be fatally fragile and that it is carrying them deeper into slave territory.

Twain's use of a child—with its fresh perspective; its physical and emotional intensity; its comic, satiric, and melodramatic narrative precision (and distortions); and its intrinsic capacity to arouse the reader's sympathy, nostalgic identification, urgent memories, and ethical alertness—makes much of the greatness of *Huckleberry Finn* possible in a way that an adult-centered novel could not achieve. How novelists employ children is the subject of *Critical Children*. The title is meant to convey both the critical importance of children and their function as critics of their worlds.

The ten great novels in this book all use children caught in violent situations as vehicles of moral and cultural interrogation. Despite many differences of setting, style, and structure, and though they were written in the course of 130 years, from 1838 to 1969, these novels portray these children so vividly that their names are instantly recognizable even by those who have never read the books in which they appear. These fictional characters serve as an index of personal and social health and virtue (or illness and vice). They are icons, figures that are taken to embody fundamental possibilities and problems, even long after their historical contexts have vanished and their authors have died, and like all cultural artifacts they are subject to many kinds of appropriation and misreading. But rather than focusing primarily on the contexts of their creation and reception (then and now), I want to examine how these books about children work as literature, as verbal performances that invite and resist interpretation and support and provoke rereading over many years by many people. I want to convey their variety and continued vitality, to demonstrate the way these great books spring to life from their details— to read them not as a scholar or theorist or social historian but as a writer and close reader, an editor and teacher of literary writers.

It's remarkable that so many classic (or, let's say, unforgotten) English and American novels should focus on children and adolescents not as colorful minor characters who provide some humor and pathos while the heroes and heroines are making their way toward marriage or death, but as the vivid, intense center of attention. And this is relatively recent; scholars tells us that *Oliver Twist* (published in 1838) was the first novel in English "with its true center of focus on a child" and that the opening pages of *Jane Eyre* (published in 1847) "probably represent the first occurrence of first-person narration by a child in English fiction."[2]

Such books enlist a particular child's story in a larger cultural narrative. They invite us to follow the story of a child's imperiled growth and development and thereby to participate in a process of discovery, a dramatic analysis of what Blake called our "mind-forg'd manacles," an attempt at liberation or the restoration of a just order. These books provide us with the vicarious experience of an ultimate recovery of health and virtue or a thrilling sentimental or melodramatic decline. In them the death of a child becomes a sacrifice that effects a revelation. Nostalgia, self-pity, and anger often color the emotional atmosphere and tone of these novels, and religious imagery is never very far away, though these books are essentially post-Christian (no matter what lip service they pay to orthodox belief). In every one a child is used as a means of adult salvation or consolation—including the reader's. Even novels that appear to end in defeat are designed to provide the reader with moral or psychological insight that can comfort or redeem. In this sense, in every one a child is leading us into the kingdom of heaven or its secular equivalent (moral responsibility, psychological maturity, or their opposite: consoling regression).

I begin with Dickens's heroic victims—Oliver Twist, the flat, unchanging saint; David Copperfield, the self-liberating artist; Pip in *Great Expectations*, the deluded loser. I go on to consider Mark Twain's free spirits and slaves in *Tom Sawyer* and *Huckleberry Finn*. I then examine Henry James's demonic lambs—Miles and Flora in *The Turn of the Screw*—and J. M. Barrie's eternal narcissist, Peter Pan, and his chief modern American descendent, J. D. Salinger's saintly dropout, Holden Caulfield in *The Catcher in the Rye*. I then turn to Dolly Haze, the subject of Vladimir Nabokov's *Lolita*, a suave and trembling elegy on an abused girl by a narrator of exceptionally seductive dexterity. I conclude with Philip Roth's performing loudmouth, Alexander Portnoy, American Narcissus extraordinaire.

The children in these ten novels are used for a variety of rhetorical and ideological purposes. Oliver Twist is used to exhort the reader to outrage and social-political reform. Tom Sawyer is used to celebrate American democracy in its centennial year (1876), but nine years later, Huckleberry

Finn is used to lament its betrayal by racial and cultural slavery. Both Peter Pan and Holden Caulfield encourage the reader's sentimental retreat into comforting pathos. David Copperfield and Alexander Portnoy are used to provoke the reader's (presumed) escape from imprisoning, regressive psychological fixations, as Pip in *Great Expectations* is used to provoke escape from childish social delusions and values. In both *The Turn of the Screw* and *Lolita* children are deployed to expose the reader's intellectual and moral vanity, his narcissistic complicity in the cultural use and abuse of children.

In the course of 130 years, the structures and styles of books centered on children have changed as culture and society have changed. Dickens and Twain present linear narratives that express a young pilgrim's coherent progress. Though they may end in empty affirmation or wry defeat, their narratives unfold—they're confidently teleological. With James, the narrative becomes a labyrinthine puzzle that defeats every attempt at coherent resolution. With Barrie, fairytale coherence ("make-believe" order) is a triumph of the highly visible author's regressive will, an expression of melancholia. With Salinger, the newly representative figure of the rebel teenager acts as a voice in the wilderness of phony commercial culture, but the narrative takes the shape of linear rite of passage toward the restoration of natural and cultural order, symbolized by a ten-year-old girl riding a wooden horse on a carousel, an artful circle. Much more problematic is the sly multiplicity of the narratives of *Lolita*, where linear cross-country journeys are at once deferrals, escapes, and quests. The central child is fatally occluded by her lover's crooning confession, and the novel's "reality" ("one of the few words," Nabokov insisted, "which mean nothing without quotes")[3] becomes a crazy quilt of memories, lies, allusions, masks, and mirrors. The nonlinear narrative of *Portnoy's Complaint* is composed of free-associative "blocks of consciousness"[4] that wildly bounce around the Freudian family romance and defeat any possibility of growth and development (let alone a pilgrim's progress) for the raucously static and impotent narrator who is at once desperate and reluctant to escape his childhood. So we've gone from ever-polite Oliver to ever-obscene Portnoy; from a much-abused agent of redemption to a self-abused narcissistic prisoner of guilt and proud rage; from a melodramatic moral allegory affirming the kingdom of Benevolence and Mercy to a vituperative, howling, comic monologue.

But why these particular ten novels? Because I've read and reread them with ever growing admiration and discovery. Because I'm not alone in my enthusiasm—general readers, writers, and students as well as scholars share it. And, as I've said, these characters still command instant recognition, though, of course, some of this may be because eight of the ten novels were turned into movies, often more than once. But it's noteworthy that these characters are recognized not as figures in classic books for children (like *Tom Brown's School Days, Little Women, The Little House on the Prairie, Charlotte's Web*) but as children in classic books for adults. The books by Dickens, Twain, and Barrie were read by Victorian or Edwardian children, and high school adolescents are often assigned *Huckleberry Finn* and *The Catcher in the Rye* as socializing rites of passage: both rebels are ultimately tutelary spirits of American democracy. (That both books are often denounced or banned as well as required confirms their continued cultural centrality.) But these ten books are not primarily for children. And, of course, these characters are not the only great children to be found in novels, nor are these ten novels the only great novels about children—think of *Wuthering Heights, Jane Eyre, What Maisie Knew, A Portrait of the Artist as a Young Man*. Still, these characters command a wider extra-literary force-field in popular consciousness than Cathy or Jane or Maisie or Stephen. And although these characters are fictional, they exert normative authority in ways that rival or exceed that of the nonfictional characters of, say, *Father and Son* or *Black Boy* or *Memories of a Catholic Girlhood* or *The Woman Warrior*. That nine of the eleven central characters are boys, that all are white, and that all of the authors are male and white reflects the race, class, and gender priorities and prejudices of the society that found them—and despite political progress still finds them—so compelling. There are many other books of great distinction that feature nonwhite children, and many by nonwhite and female authors.[5]

Though nineteenth-century literature was extravagantly devoted to boys and boyhood, four of the most celebrated and perpetually controversial Victorian novels presented the triumphs and tragedies of passionate, rebellious English girls from childhood to late adolescence. Dickens's Little Nell in *The Old Curiosity Shop* (1841) is an angelic orphan girl who flees the city pursued by a grotesque sadistic dwarf and finally dies infected by the poisons of industrialism and crushed by the burden of her care for a senile uncle. Emily Brontë's *Wuthering Heights* (1847), Charlotte Brontë's *Jane Eyre* (1847), and George Eliot's *The Mill on the Floss* (1860) share a vivid evocation of anger at adult injustice and a dramatization of romantic sexual appetite and energy that far exceed conventional feminine bounds of the time, and they exhibit a final swerve from protofeminist heroism to pathos. I exclude three of these novels only because their children are no longer iconic, and I exclude *Jane Eyre* only because she is overwhelmingly more a feminist than a childhood icon. The novel's center of gravity is not Jane as a girl but as a woman faced with marriage.

For all their radical interrogation of cultural, moral, and psychological structures, modernists such as Lawrence and Joyce employed children— Paul Morel in *Sons and Lovers* (1913), Stephen Dedalus in *A Portrait of the Artist as a Young Man* (1916)—for traditional purposes, as indices of health and virtue. The modernists' use of childhood as the source of authentic salvation (embodied in the artist's vocation) is notably conservative. One remarkable exception is Richard Hughes's suave pirate tale *A High Wind in Jamaica* (1929), which achieves extreme moral and psychological destabilization with great economy of means. And Henry Roth's *Call It Sleep* (1934) deploys child characters to masterful effect. But despite their great literary distinction, the children in these books are not instantly recognizable—their names are not catchwords. And this is not a comprehensive study of children in English and American literature but a close reading of ten iconic images of childhood.

Despite my insistence on the particular, some general historical background should be of help before we begin with Dickens. The rhetorical use of children as a means of interrogating cultural norms (and thereby contesting or enforcing them) has a history that extends back to classical and biblical times. And this history has continued to exert pressure on the ways children have been portrayed over the past two hundred years. In three of the four Gospels Jesus utters variations of Mark 10:14: "Suffer the little children to come unto me, and forbid them not: for of such is the kingdom of God. Verily I say unto you, Whosoever shall not receive the Kingdom of God as a little child, he shall not enter therein," and Saint Augustine famously employed scenes from his childhood to advance the narrative argument of his *Confessions*. But most cultural historians agree that the origin of the essentially modern use of the figure of the child lies in John Locke's *Some Thoughts Concerning Education* (1693), a series of letters on raising a proper English gentleman that is notable for its tacit erasure of the doctrine of original sin and its expression of a new faith in secular education emphasizing play, tolerance, and reason. In children, writes Locke, "Nine Parts of Ten are what they are, Good or Evil, useful or not, by their Education." Learning should be "a Play and Recreation to Children," and "all their innocent Folly, Playing, and *Childish Actions, are to be* left perfectly free and *unrestrained*, as far as they can consist with the Respect due to those that are present; and that with the greatest Allowance."[6] Locke's *Thoughts* became immensely popular and influential throughout Europe in the eighteenth century.

It was succeeded by an even more powerful book in which a child was deployed as the agent of world-historical change. In 1762 Rousseau published *Emile, or On Education*, at once a novel and a treatise, both narrative and analytical. It is a self-consciously revolutionary book, and its most celebrated modern champion, the political theorist Allan Bloom, argues that it was "meant to rival or supersede" Plato's *Republic* as a foundational document for modern civilization. Kant viewed its publication "as an event comparable to the French Revolution,"[7] and *Emile* is certainly bent on revolution, on eclipsing both the biblical and classical traditions and replacing Christianity and its doctrine of original sin with Enlightened secular humanism. But Rousseau's story of a boy's exemplary education is also a kind of modern Gospel. While the biblical Gospels brought the good news that belief in the story of the sacrifice and resurrection of a spotless child of God will grant redemption and eternal life, *Emile* also proclaims that belief in the story of a perfect child—created through a modern, "natural" education—can save your life. For devout Christians, Rousseau's suggestion that a redemptive revolution should arise from a child's developing heart and mind (without religious instruction) was patent heresy—and a flagrant instance of the sin of pride. But Rousseau prevailed: *Emile* became a central text of the age. Every family became a sacred family; every child, a savior, innocent and ready to wipe our guilt away. Children became divine.

A similar transformation of baby Jesus into a revolutionary Everychild can be seen in the works of two great English romantic poets, William Blake and William Wordsworth. Like Rousseau, they both famously used childhood as a critical criterion from which the fallen state of modern society could be measured and condemned—and as a divine resource through which it could possibly be redeemed. Blake's *Songs of Innocence and of Experience* (1789–1794) and Wordsworth's *Lyrical Ballads* (1798–1805), *Poems in Two Volumes* (1807), and autobiographical *The Prelude, or Growth of a Poet's Mind* (1805–50) contain the classic English literary portraits of childhood. Blake's pathetic, soot-blackened chimneysweeps crying "weep, weep, weep, weep" and his blasted infant in whose "cry of fear . . . the mind-forg'd manacles I hear"[8] are presented in faux-naïve songs, nursery rhymes, and hymns that embody a counter-vailing force to eighteenth-century rationalism and materialism. Blake's children rebuke adult society and culture.

Few literary texts in English history have exerted so powerful and long-lasting an influence as Wordsworth's "Ode: Intimations of Im-mortality from Recollections of Early Childhood" written from 1802 through 1804 and published in 1807. After an epigraph taken from an earlier poem declares the central theme, "The Child is Father of the Man," we soon encounter the memorable cry, "Whither is fled the vi-sionary gleam? / Where is it now, the glory and the dream? / . . . trailing clouds of glory do we come / From God, who is our home: / Heaven lies about us in our infancy! / Shades of the prison-house begin to close / Upon the growing Boy."[9]

This ode is among the most deeply interpreted texts in English lit-erature, and there are those, such as Lionel Trilling, who argue that it enacts a transformation from adolescent nostalgia to adult moral real-ism.[10] But for most nineteenth-century readers it sounded a profoundly seductive, melancholy theme. The nurturing memory of wondrous boy-hood recurs throughout Wordsworth's poetry and is the source of his autobiographical epic *The Prelude*, but he was certainly not alone in such deployment of the figure of the redemptive child. His great American counterpart, Emerson, made a similar use of nostalgia and daringly couched it in theological terms: "Infancy is the perpetual Messiah, which comes into the arms of fallen men, and pleads with them to re-turn to paradise."[11] In both cases a child is used as a source of romantic or transcendental truth and power. But even as the divine appeared to withdraw as the century progressed, the child became the object of in-creasingly sentimental devotion at the same time as it served as an index of ethical maturity (not necessarily grounded in religious belief in any but the most notional sense).

For all his often effusive religious rhetoric, Dickens expanded the romantics' moral and psychological (but not religious) use of the child until its welfare also became the crucial measure of a nation's—indeed an empire's—social and political health, and even its survival. And the other novelists I'll discuss built on his achievement in a variety of ways.

Portnoy is the most recent iconic literary child. The only instantly recognizable fictional child to appear since him, I believe, is Harry Pot-ter, the hero of a series of children's novels that offer the intense delights of Tolkien and C. S. Lewis but steadfastly remain within the generic limits of literature for children and young adults. If we turn to literary fiction and forgo the requirement that the characters be iconic, we find a remarkable use of children in Don DeLillo's *White Noise* (1985) and several novels by Ian McEwan, including *The Child in Time* (1987) and *Atonement* (2001). Steven Millhauser, Marilynne Robinson, Jamaica Kincaid, and Peter Carey have also centered strong books around children. Recent novels by Kazuo Ishiguro, Jonathan Lethem, Francine Prose, A. M. Homes, Roddy Doyle, Jonathan Safran Foer, and Emma Donoghue are conspicuous achievements. Children have also functioned as postmodern epic heroes in English-language novels set in Asia and Africa, such as Salman Rushdie's *Midnight's Children* (1980) and Ben Okri's *The Famished Road* (1991).

Moreover, what would have been autobiographical first novels of childhood fifty years ago are now nonfictional "memoirs" that attract much attention. Frank Conroy's *Stop-Time* (1967) and Maxine Hong Kingston's *The Woman Warrior* (1976) were followed by such books as Richard Rodriguez's *Hunger of Memory* (1982), Mary Karr's *The Liars' Club* (1995), and Frank McCourt's *Angela's Ashes* (1996).

That no instantly recognizable literary child has appeared in the past forty years may be the result of the declining cultural centrality of literature. People are more likely to turn to movies or television, to music or websites as sources of self-definition—these are the media that command the authority once attributed to works of literary art, particularly since the distinction between high and low culture no longer obtains. The power of a childlike Michael Jackson is fully and abundantly expressed in his performances. His phantasmagoric reincarnations of Peter Pan certainly rival and for many may eclipse the Edwardian original.

But with this I have moved toward large questions of cultural history, of the context of creation and reception, of what's been called the political unconscious. Let me return to *Huckleberry Finn* and, in fact, to a detail from the same narrative of meeting the Grangerfords. After assuring them of his innocence and ignorance, Huck spins an elaborate life story of family deaths and disasters that ends with his becoming an orphan, falling off a Mississippi steamboat, and finding himself on their doorstep. He calls himself "George Jackson" to hide his status as a runaway and partner of a fugitive slave. The Grangerfords are moved by his tale (we soon learn how susceptible they are to pathos) and tell him, as noted above, "I could have a home there as long as I wanted it." So Huck has given himself a new life, a new name, and a new family. He even has a kind of brother.

Then it was most daylight, and everybody went to bed, and I went to bed with Buck, and when I waked up in the morning, drat it all, I had forgot what my name was. So I laid there about an hour trying to think, and when Buck waked up, I says:

"Can you spell, Buck?"

"Yes," he says.

"I bet you can't spell my name," says I.

"I bet you what you dare I can," says he.

"All right," says I, "go ahead."

"G-o-r-g-e-J-a-x-o-n—there now," he says.

"Well," says I, "you done it, but I didn't think you could. It ain't no slouch of a name to spell—right off without studying."

I set it down, private, because somebody might want *me* to spell it, next, and so I wanted to be handy with it and rattle it off like I was used to it.

(120)

In this proliferation of self-creation even Huck's false name produces echoes. George is presumably George Washington, the eastern aristocratic Father of Our Country, whom Twain satirized in his own first literary success *The Celebrated Jumping Frog of Calaveras County*: "As a boy, he gave no promise of the greatness he was one day to achieve. He was ignorant of the commonest accomplishments of youth. He could not even lie."[12] And Jackson is not only a memory and a wish for Huck and Jim's Jackson's Island refuge but also presumably Andrew Jackson, the first populist western president and also the name of a stupid fighting bull dog in the title sketch of *The Celebrated Jumping Frog*. So Twain has Huck create an identity for himself that combines a wish for refuge, a father, two presidents, eastern and western America, and a comic pugnacious animal. Quite a feat. But then Huck can't remember or spell this new name.

This short scene is a ceremony or covert catechism of identity, and it dramatizes the role of education in the creation of a social self. Such a scene is only possible by using children. The radical depth of Huck's vulnerability, the scale of his self-creation, the artificiality of socially fabricated identity, the comic twist in which the reader recognizes that Huck (as an ignorant child) can't even spell his fake name correctly and thus remains in a peril he doesn't recognize, all these themes and narrative effects—in all their grandeur—spring from Twain's decision to use a child.

CHARLES DICKENS'S HEROIC VICTIMS

Oliver Twist, David Copperfield, and Pip

OF ALL THE FIGURES in English literature, Charles Dickens is most famous for his children—Oliver Twist, Little Nell, David Copperfield, and Pip in *Great Expectations*. Dickens extended the romantics' moral, psychological, and philosophical use of the child from the realm of lyric and personal epic poetry into that of the encyclopedic Victorian novel so that a child's welfare now also became the crucial index of a nation's—indeed, an empire's—social and political health and even its survival. Throughout the legendary sprawl of his fifteen novels, fourteen volumes of stories, and five collections of nonfiction, Dickens repeatedly explored the theme expressed most memorably in Wordsworth's phrase, "the Child is Father of the Man," with unprecedented ferocity, glee, sorrow, and grandeur.

The fundamental optimism of "the Child is Father of the Man" lies in its Rousseauesque suggestion that a naturally good childhood will ensure a good life, that childhood experiences are a generative resource for one's whole adult life. But, as we've seen, Wordsworth also used the phrase as the epigraph to one of his most famous and powerful poems, "Ode: Intimations of Immortality from Recollections of Early Childhood" (1807), which is filled with profoundly seductive melancholy: "Whither is fled the visionary gleam? / Where is it now, the glory and the dream?" Most nineteenth- and twentieth-century readers have responded strongly to the poem's sense of loss and sorrow, its nostalgia for natural childhood and fear of the "prison-house" of adult culture and society. Many of Dickens's novels begin with childhood and are over-shadowed by various kinds of prisons (as Lionel Trilling and Edmund Wilson noted in celebrated essays).[1] In *Oliver Twist* the workhouse and Newgate Prison are the most conspicuous. In *David Copperfield* there is the sadistic school, the rat-infested warehouse, the King's Bench debtor's prison, and the final progressive penitentiary (which is overtly described as a means of perpetuating the prisoners' criminality). But even more insidious is what Dickens calls the "captivity" of David's fixations on a "child-wife" and a Byronic male friend—which lead to moral, emotional, and physical death.[2] And convicts, criminals, prisons, and imprisoning fantasies are at the center of *Great Expectations*.

OLIVER TWIST

That the child is father of the man is essentially an optimistic truth in *Oliver Twist*. Oliver's unchanging innocence and grace make him an agent of redemption in the fallen world for those who help him save them-selves and England. But in *David Copperfield* and *Great Expectations* we see that a damaged child produces a damaged man. Childhood fantasy is a resource that can comfort one's whole life (like a beloved mother) and serve as the source of a literary career, but childhood loss and abuse can also cripple one's development and destroy one's personal life.

These very different perceptions of childhood lead to the very different narrative forms of each book. The full title of *Oliver Twist* is *The Adventures of Oliver Twist; or, The Parish Boy's Progress*. "Adventures" immediately identifies it with the picaresque tradition of Fielding, Defoe, and Smollett; "Parish Boy" quickly places the central figure in a social-economic-political context that the novel will vigorously criticize and condemn; and "Progress" alludes both to John Bunyan's immensely popular religious and moral allegory, *Pilgrim's Progress* (1678–84)—and therefore identifies Oliver with its allegorical hero, Christian—and to *The Rake's Progress* (1735) by the painter William Hogarth, whom Dickens described in the 1841 preface to *Oliver Twist* as "the moralist, and censor of his age," a "giant," with "a power and depth of thought which belonged to few men before him, and will probably appertain to fewer still in time to come."[3] The book's full title, then, conveys that the novel will be picaresque, political, religious, allegorical, and intensely visual and will unflinchingly encompass even what Dickens calls "the very scum and refuse of the land." As he declares in the preface, "I wished to show, in little Oliver, the principle of Good surviving through every adverse circumstance, and triumphing at last" (3). The book will resemble the life of a saint—an unchanging exemplary sacred essence, a static icon in a violently fallen world. The child will be used to "show" a triumphant "principle." There will be no need for subtle psychology, no personal development. The action and the prose style can and must move toward bold effects, melodrama, and Manichean black and white.

By the time Dickens completed the first edition of *Oliver Twist*, his second novel, in 1838, he had grown from the effervescent comic genius of the *Pickwick Papers* to a far more complex, darker, riskier, but no less virtuosic (if far less charming) writer eager not just to imagine a lost paradise but to reclaim it from the depths of urban hell. Dickens considered the generalizing cant of religion and political philosophy and "the little-regarded warning of a moral precept" (5) either impotent or complicit with the evils of contemporary society. But for him the reader's spontaneous response to fiction—which can combine satire, comedy, pathos, melodrama, romance, and realism—could produce real change on the largest scale. By means of a novel's animated, dramatic particularity and its verbal activity at the highest level of virtuosity, the reader's active sympathy could be awakened and civilization secured. And the most effective and most original device to arouse sympathy was to center a novel on an abused child.

In the first paragraph of the first chapter of *Oliver Twist*, this child is identified as "the item of mortality whose name is prefixed to the head of this chapter" (17). This phrase places narrator and reader at such a remove from the newborn baby that it exists not as a human being, or even a living creature, but as part of a commercial inventory, an object for sale, indeed, as part of the funeral trade with its rhetoric of pious uplift. But there's even more going on in the phrase "whose name is prefixed to the head of this chapter," for it ironically binds the narrator and the reader together in a bibliographical effort, a hermeneutic complicity that asserts the primacy of the text over any (merely human) reality it might refer to and affirms our participation in a community of alienating intellectual control—which is the object of Dickens's satire.

The first eight chapters of the book, in particular, often deploy a sardonic satire of various kinds of official prose that exceeds the virtuosity of Swift and Orwell. Such adult prose crushes children. The circumlocutions, officious hyperbole, spurious erudition, and fatuous moral elevation suggest a cultural-ethical norm—Benthamite utilitarian philosophy and Malthusian political economy—that is being ferociously discredited even as our recognition of its terms conjoins the narrator and reader into one ethos or worldview. As the novel progresses new elements are introduced. Melodrama, pathos, and what Steven Marcus calls "cosmic" coincidences assert a deep compensatory structure,[4] an alternative order more moral than the Benthamite philosophy—epitomized for Dickens in the Poor Law Amendment Act of 1834—that justified cruelty on both a social and individual level.

In the novel's opening pages we read that Oliver's first cry "advertises" that "a new burden [has] been imposed upon the parish" (18). He has trouble drawing breath but "custom has rendered [this] necessary" (18)—as if respiration were a social rather than biological reality. The "parish surgeon who did such matters by contract" (18) refers to Oliver's illegitimacy as "the old story" (19), but lest we follow that phrase into the realm of fable and literature, we read that the baby's faded wrappings define him: "he was badged and ticketed, and fell into his place at once— a parish child—the orphan of a workhouse—the humble half-starved drudge—to be cuffed and buffeted through the world—despised by all, and pitied by none" (19). The sequence of phrases interrupted by dashes dramatizes the discontinuous violence, the fragmentation, of Oliver's existence as a social being, but at the same time the biblical overtones that culminate in "despised by all, and pitied by none" suggest his similarity to the crucified savior.

In the second chapter, the tones and styles available to the narrator continue to multiply. There is the bluff declaration that "for the next eight or ten months, Oliver was the victim of a systematic course of treachery and deception" (19). There is the legalese of "juvenile offenders against the poor law" and the allusion to Milton's hell in *Paradise Lost* in "finding in the lowest depth a deeper still" (20).[5] There is the arch regency gossip of Oliver on his ninth birthday "keeping it in the coal-cellar with a select party of two other young gentlemen, who, after participating with him in a sound threshing, had been locked up therein for atrociously presuming to be hungry" (21)—which combines a tone of social reportage with a moralistic denunciation of the crime of being hungry. This last prepares us for the legendary scene in the dining hall when Oliver (not of his own volition but selected by lot by the starving boys) steps forward. The pacing is spectacular:

The evening arrived; the boys took their places. The master, in his cook's uniform, stationed himself at the copper [pot of gruel]; his pauper assistants ranged themselves behind him; the gruel was served out; and a long grace was said over short commons [food]. The gruel disappeared; the boys whispered to each other, and winked at Oliver; while his next neighbours nudged him. Child as he was, he was desperate with hunger, and reckless with misery. He rose from the table; and advancing to the master, basin and spoon in hand, said: somewhat alarmed at his own temerity:

"Please, sir, I want some more."

The master was a fat, healthy man; but he turned very pale. He gazed in stupefied astonishment on the small rebel for some seconds; and then clung for support to the copper. The assistants were paralyzed with wonder; the boys with fear.

"What!" said the master at length, in a faint voice.

"Please, sir," replied Oliver, "I want some more."

The master aimed a blow at Oliver's head with the ladle; pinioned him in his arms; and shrieked aloud for the beadle.

The board were sitting in solemn conclave, when Mr. Bumble rushed into the room in great excitement, and addressing the gentleman in the high chair, said,

"Mr. Limbkins, I beg your pardon, sir! Oliver Twist has asked for more!"

There was a general start. Horror was depicted on every countenance.

"For *more!*" said Mr. Limbkins. "Compose yourself, Bumble, and answer me directly. Do I understand that he asked for more, after he had eaten the supper allotted by the dietary?"

"He did, sir," replied Bumble.

"That boy will be hung," said the gentleman in the white waistcoat. "I know that boy will be hung."

(27)

A great number of characters and points of view are expertly deployed here. The narrator easily switches between the rapid action of the boys nudging Oliver forward, the omniscient contextualization of "child as he was, he was desperate with hunger," and the inwardness of "somewhat alarmed at his own temerity" in which the grand word "temerity" serves to dignify and interpret inarticulate immaturity. There are the comic role reversals in which the adults are "stupefied" and shriek for assistance; the pell-mell change of scene to the boardroom; the bureaucratese of "the supper allotted by the dietary," which locates responsibility in the realm of spurious public-health policy; and the final comic knell of the deadly "gentleman in the white waistcoat" who pronounces "that boy will be hung." Everything points toward that conclusion—hunger is a capital crime.

To the readers of Dickens's time, Oliver's very name—bestowed upon the nameless orphan according to the alphabetical system of the parish beadle, Bumble—has expressed this from the first: Robert Tracy informs us that to "twist" meant "to eat heartily" as well as "to hang," and that "a twist" was a yarn and, of course, also suggested perversion, as it still does.[6]

Most of the instances of physical child abuse in the novel occur in the first eight chapters. Oliver is repeatedly beaten, kicked, confined. He is spared indenture to a chimney sweep who has already "bruised three or four boys to death" (31) but is apprenticed to an undertaker. He is pushed downstairs into a "stone cell, damp and dark" (40) where he's fed the dog's food and sleeps among the coffins. He is tormented by the "hungry and vicious" (51) older apprentice, and after rising up in protest—for the second time in his life and one of the three times he is active in this way in the entire novel—and striking the boy, he is assaulted by the undertaker, his wife, the cook, and the apprentice, who scratch and "tear and beat" (53) him and lock him in the garbage room in the cellar. The beadle is summoned from the workhouse and "by way of prelude" gives a kick to the closed cellar door and

> then, applying his mouth to the keyhole, said, in a deep and impressive tone,
> "Oliver!"
> "Come; you let me out!" replied Oliver, from the inside.
> "Do you know this here voice, Oliver?" said Mr. Bumble.
> "Yes," replied Oliver.
> "Ain't you afraid of it, sir? Ain't you a-trembling while I speak, sir?" said Mr. Bumble.
> "No!" replied Oliver boldly. . . .
> "He must be mad," said Mrs. Sowerberry [the undertaker's wife], "No boy in half his senses could venture to speak so to you."
> "It's not Madness, ma'am," replied Mr. Bumble, after a few moments of deep meditation. "It's Meat."
> "What!" exclaimed Mrs. Sowerberry.
> "Meat, ma'am, meat. . . . You've raised a artificial soul and spirit in him, ma'am, unbecoming a person in his condition: as the board, Mrs. Sowerberry, who are practical philosophers will tell you. What have paupers to do with

soul or spirit? It's quite enough that we let 'em have live bodies. If you had kept the boy on gruel, ma'am, this would never have happened."

"Dear, dear!" ejaculated Mrs. Sowerberry, piously raising her eyes to the kitchen ceiling: "this comes of being liberal!"

(56)

This takes us from a beadle speaking like the personification of the dungeon itself into the realm of the Malthusian theory of utilitarian starvation that would keep a pauper in his proper, natural condition of having a live body but certainly no soul.

To escape the fatal "liberalism" of his indenture, Oliver takes autonomous action for the third and final time in the book and sneaks out of the house the next morning. He passes the workhouse and sees a frail child he knows weeding the front garden. "They had been beaten, and starved, and shut up together, many and many a time. . . . 'You mustn't say you saw me, Dick,' said Oliver. 'I am running away. They beat and ill-use me, Dick; and I am going to seek my fortune, some long way off. I don't know where'" (59).

Here at the end of the seventh chapter, as he becomes a criminal fugitive, Oliver has reached the summit of his heroism. From this point on he will never initiate any actions. He will react, he will run, he will faint again and again, but he will not "seek his fortune" but simply search for almost any kind of family comfort and affection. Indeed, he will seek passivity—even unconsciousness, as in the nearly dozen scenes where he collapses into a faint or in the three hypnogogic scenes where, half-awake, he is paralyzed by the sight of evil Fagin. In the midst of a novel that will repeatedly propel itself into melodramatic action, theatrical rhetoric, and the most brilliantly particularized scenes teeming with sordid life, Oliver will be the small, still center, the innocent soul, immaculate, emitting an odor of sanctity and effecting by his example the workings of grace: "The sight of him turns me against myself, and all of you," cries the drunken prostitute Nancy, whose self-transformation becomes the main action of the second half of the novel (175). To emphasize Oliver's beneficent effect, Dickens will even permit himself to conclude a chapter with the sentimental lesson: "The blessings which the orphan child called down upon them, sunk into their souls, diffusing peace and happiness" (210).

Perhaps the most conspicuous technique that Dickens uses to convey Oliver's noble innocence and what one contemporary reviewer called his "exquisite delicacy of natural sentiment" is his unwavering genteel diction unpolluted by the vice and misery that surround him.[7] Oliver always sounds like the "little gentleman," as Dickens was called by the other boys in the squalid London warehouse where he slaved at the age of twelve. Oliver's ever-polite speech even spreads to the prostitute as she progresses toward her redemption. Another contemporary reviewer wrote, "May we not ask where she got her fine English? She talks the common slang of London, in its ordinary dialect, in the beginning of the novel; at the end no heroine that ever went mad in white satin talked more picked and perfumed sentences of sentimentality."[8]

Since Dickens was justly celebrated as "the Regius professor of slang"[9] for his expert use and knowledge of low London lingo—which is displayed in full splendor in *Oliver Twist*—Oliver and Nancy's profoundly unrealistic dialogue is clearly the result of choice. I would suggest that it is the equivalent of casting a beautiful actress—Lillian Gish or Garbo—in a lowlife part in a Hollywood movie: her beauty signals her soul. It resembles the virtuoso vocal art of such characters as the prostitute Violetta in *La Traviata*; her heart of gold is proven by her extraordinary arias. Oliver's verbal performances are ostentatiously polite and sentimental—both in the hearts-and-flowers pastoral paradise of the London suburbs where he finds refuge with the Maylies and in the sordid hellish "labyrinth" (108) of London, a "most intricate maze of narrow streets and courts" (87).

It's notable that Oliver is the only child to be seen in the (idyllic) Wordsworthian suburbs but one of many children in the (satirized) workhouse parish and doubled and redoubled in (brutally realistic or melodramatic) London: "A dirtier or more wretched place [Oliver] had never seen. The street was very narrow and muddy; and the air was impregnated with filthy odours. There were a good many small shops; but the only stock in trade appeared to be heaps of children, who, even at that time of night, were crawling in and out at the doors, or screaming from the inside" (64). Children are just items of mortality.

But one central aspect of the originality and genius of the book lies in the way the threatening criminal world not only impinges upon "green" Oliver (as he's called) (62, 65, 69)—trapping, confining, enclosing him— but also incomparably enlarges and enlivens the novel itself. After the first eight chapters of nasty rural opera buffa, with expressionistic caricatures spouting Benthamite slogans and a narrator given to remarks of dark Swiftian urbanity, we enter the outskirts of London with Oliver and suddenly hear a voice from another world: "Hullo, my covey, what's the row?" (62). And soon a "snub-nosed, flat-browed, common-faced boy"—the Artful Dodger—with "all the airs and manners of a man" and wearing filthy oversized clothes, becomes Oliver's Virgil, guiding him into the inferno of criminal London, where he is greeted with more warmth and affection—and food—than he has ever encountered before. Though Fagin is "a very old shriveled Jew, whose villainous-looking and repulsive face was obscured by a quantity of matted red hair" (65) and holds a toasting-fork in his hand (a stereotypical devil complete with pitchfork), he welcomes Oliver with more charm, courtesy, and physical comfort than the boy has ever encountered: "The Jew grinned; and, making a low obeisance to Oliver, took him by the hand; and hoped he should have the honour of his intimate acquaintance. . . . 'We are very glad to see you, Oliver—very,' said the Jew, 'Dodger, take off the sausages; and draw a tub near the fire for Oliver'" (65–66). Here Oliver finds expressions of physical tenderness (the Artful Dodger "smoothed Oliver's hair down over his eyes" [69]), and this man-boy community even offers educational opportunities: the next day's lessons take the form of "a very curious and uncommon game" (69), in which Fagin enacts the role of a possible victim for pickpockets "in such a very funny and natural manner, that Oliver laughed till the tears ran down his face." This is the first time in the book that Oliver has laughed. He is soon "deeply involved in his new study" (69–71).

Fagin is certainly capable of violent outbursts and of striking the boys with his toasting fork, but he also enforces a "stern morality" and insists upon the "necessity of an active life" (71). He is—most ironically—a strict Victorian father. He lectures Oliver on ingratitude ("You've been brought up bad," comments the Dodger [129]), and, like his rural counterpart, the beadle, Fagin spouts utilitarian philosophy: "Number one . . . a regard for number one holds us all together, and must do so, unless we would all go to pieces in company" (289). Like any sentimental gangster, he's given to self-pity: "It's a poor trade . . . and no thanks; but I'm fond of seeing the young people about me; and I bear it all; I bear it all" (260). This last Christian echo can also be heard—but most unironically—in his pupil Nancy's "I have borne all this for you already" (142). Fagin is a fence, a pimp, a "loathsome reptile" (132), and by implication a homosexual pedophile. But from his debut as a most unkosher, sausage-eating

Jew, through a multitude of grotesque (and anti-Semitic) descriptions and melodramatic speeches to his final moments in his condemned cell in Newgate, where he sounds like Lear (he calls himself "an old man, my Lord; a very old, old man" [355]), the sheer variety, flexibility, and warmth of the prose that describes Fagin convey a mythic and nightmarish father figure of far more psychological veracity than the (contrasting) monochromatic cardboard of Brownlow and Maylie. And even Fagin can be redeemed by Oliver; in the death cell Fagin most preposterously whispers into Oliver's ear the location of the inheritance papers and then lapses into the hallucination that Oliver (once again "my dear") can lead him out of prison (356). Their roles are finally reversed.

The decision to use Oliver as a vehicle of what might be called, most anachronistically, an expressionist allegory—"the principle of Good surviving through every adverse circumstance, and triumphing at last"—affects the structure of the narrative and makes possible the conspicuous variety and extremism of the literary styles Dickens employs. Oliver functions like a stone thrown into a pond that changes everything but is itself unchanged. He dominates the earlier chapters but gradually dwindles away as we turn to the ever-widening effects of his exemplary being ("he is a child of a noble nature and a warm heart" says the insufferably "dear, sweet, angel lady," his orphan aunt Rose Maylie—Nancy's alter ego, confidant, and heavenly guide [274, 269]).

In *Oliver Twist*, most paradoxically, the flagrantly reductive depiction of a child, his employment as a device in propaganda, produces a most surprising and daring aesthetic exfoliation. The static, external, voyeuristic use of a child as a conventionally pathetic, essentially prepsychological figure permits extreme structural and stylistic variety—all in the service of a large moral and cultural lesson: if a child's unchanging innocence can be preserved by sympathetic adults, a world of heavenly goodness and mercy will follow. A little child shall lead them. Much-abused and much-rescued Oliver is a useful lamb.

DAVID COPPERFIELD

Dickens uses Oliver to demonstrate that a little child shall lead us into the kingdom of heaven by the example of his being. Dickens uses David Copperfield and Pip in *Great Expectations* to show how powerfully the child is father of the man: a triumphant hero as a man of letters who has escaped the prison of his childhood in *David Copperfield*, and a sor-rowful, chastened victim of childish delusions—a stoic loser—in *Great Expectations*.

The various titles Dickens considered for *David Copperfield* suggest a very different kind of fiction from *The Adventures of Oliver Twist; or, The Parish Boy's Progress*. In his working notes for the first serial install-ment in 1849, he called it *The Personal History and Adventures of David Copperfield* but changed "Adventures" to "Experience" in the notes for the second installment, a turning inward to the subjective, psychological, intimate. In the first edition of the complete book in 1850, he cut the title even further to *The Personal History of David Copperfield*. This cancels any suggestion of picaresque adventure and concentrates entirely on autobi-ography: a work of history that is also personal, that encompasses both public and private, both social and psychological material and, most im-portant, is told in the first person (the first time Dickens used this voice in a novel). "History" also emphasizes the dynamic and developmental nature of the subject. The chapter titles reflect this as they run from "I Am Born" to "A Last Retrospect," going from naïve first-person action (a full sentence) to a larger historical view conveyed in a phrase unmodi-fied by any pronoun. The book begins with a child's perspective and ends with that of a professional writer, indeed, a famous "man of letters."

Unlike *Oliver Twist*, the novel will not "show" a "principle" but show "whether I shall turn out to be the hero of my own life" (11). Unlike Oli-ver, David is not static but changing. Since the child is father of the man, the book must take the form of the story of his growth and development; it is necessarily not a melodramatic allegory but a bildungsroman. It can-not confine itself to the portrait of the artist as a young man but must show how the child became the mature artist who could write this par-ticular "personal history." So the depiction of the child serves the urgent present purposes of the adult. And childhood itself is shown to be both a resource for creativity ("fancy" that leads to a professional career as a famous man of letters) and a curse that the "hero" must overcome.

That a writer's private experience has universal importance, that a writer is the hero of the modern age, had been most famously and vividly articulated ten years before by Dickens's friend Thomas Carlyle in an enormously popular and influential series of public lectures published as *On Heroes, Hero-Worship, and the Heroic in History* in 1841. It clear-ly stands as a powerful cultural source for *David Copperfield* not as its immediate textual source (which is an autobiographical fragment Dickens wrote a few years before starting the novel) but as its urgent philosophical premise.

Carlyle begins *On Heroes* with the famous declaration, "As I take it, Universal History, the history of what man has accomplished in this world, is at bottom the History of the Great Men who have worked here,"[10] and he then devotes four lectures to the Hero as Divinity (Odin), Prophet (Mahomet), Poet (Dante and Shakespeare), and Priest (Luther and Knox). He then describes "The Hero as Man of Letters" (Johnson, Rousseau, and Burns) and concludes with "The Hero as King" (Cromwell and Napoleon), in which the hero is notoriously on the verge of being a protofascist strongman.

Carlyle opens the lecture on "The Hero as Man of Letters" with an emphatic assertion: "Since it is the spiritual always that determines the material, [the] Man of Letters Hero must be regarded as our most important person. He, such as he may be, is the soul of all. What he teaches, the whole world will do and make." This hero may be impoverished and unknown and appear to be what we would call a marginal figure, but "he is the light of the world; the world's Priest;—guiding it, like a sacred Pillar of Fire, in its dark pilgrimage through the waste of Time." Like any hero, the modern writer "must pass through the ordeal, and prove himself. *This* ordeal; this wild welter of a chaos which is called Literary Life: this too is a kind of ordeal!"

These are the echoes that surround the famous first sentence of *David Copperfield*: "Whether I shall turn out to be the hero of my own life, or whether that station will be held by anybody else, these pages must show" (11). The structure of the sentence is that of a formal problem of moral philosophy, but the solution to the problem "must" arise from the result of literary action. The purpose of the "pages" (emphasizing the serial progress, not the final totality of the book) is to "show," prove, demonstrate, test the validity of the two alternative propositions. The emphasis is on urgent process, and throughout the novel the narrator will repeatedly interrupt the past-tense flow of memory to break into the present tense: "I see it now"; "Here we stand, all three, before me now"; "My pen shakes in my hand" (81, 157, 367). This conveys the intensity of the effort, the critical importance of the task, and the power of memory to recover the past if memory is transformed by literary action. The point is not to sink into nostalgia but to evoke and appropriate the past for present use—both personal and professional.

Remembering Carlyle, we understand how grand it is for David to be a "hero" and why being a hero is referred to as a "station," implying his public, professional, social function. But David's curious uncertainty about his role in his own "life"—which, we understand, means both his existence and the record of it, the autobiography that we're reading, which must conform to the formal requirements of its literary genre— raises the obvious question: if he is not the hero, who is? We're invited to keep our eyes open as we read and, of course, by the time we get to the idolized and seductive schoolmate James Steerforth we realize that David must decide whether Steerforth is the hero of his life or whether he must assume the role himself.

There is another, more remotely buried possibility: that insofar as "my life" also means "my being alive," it is David's dead father who in this etiolated sense is the primary agent (almost the hero) of his life. It's notable that in the original magazine installments of the novel, the full title read *The Personal History, Adventures, Experience and Observation of David Copperfield the Younger, of Blunderstone Rookery, which he never meant to be published on any account* (814). The comic garrulity suggests that Dickens was still uncertain what genre the work would conform to, and the past tense of "never meant" implies that the narrator is dead and the document published posthumously—whereas in the final version the book is most definitely a famous writer's public declaration of his heroism. But we should note the formal emphasis of "David Copperfield the Younger." The phase implies an identity distinct from but also derived from an earlier one. To become a self is to distinguish oneself from one's father, even if one's name affirms one's continuity. The opening chapters stress that David's father died six months before his birth and was an impractical, improvident, childish romantic dreamer now living in the "shadowy" realm of the grave and memory. The boy associates him with the cemetery where he lies across the way from Blunderstone—a site that is both pastoral and comforting but also melancholy and even frightening when the boy first hears of Lazarus risen from the dead. David must rise above this deadly but also curiously empowering inheritance.

Two supernatural or superstitious circumstances surround his birth. It occurs on a Friday at midnight: "The clock began to strike, and I began to cry, simultaneously" (11), which suggests that to live is both to be part of time and to cry, that time makes you weep. His "nurse" and some "sage women in the neighborhood" declare that the timing of his birth presages that he will be "unlucky in life" but "privileged to see ghosts and spirits" (11). This will prove true, of course, because, as a novelist, his perceptions go beyond the limits of life into the realm of death. He offers the demurral that "unless I ran through that part of my inheritance while I was still a baby, I have not come into it yet" (11), but this grants that it does exist as an inheritance, a gift he may have squandered unthinkingly (like his profligate father or the comic double of his father, Micawber) or has yet to receive. To write his "life"—which will necessarily evoke the dead—is indeed to see ghosts and spirits. The book is proof of his magical inheritance.

The second supernatural circumstance of his birth is that he was born with a caul, the fetal membrane thought in folklore to protect the child from shipwreck and drowning, both of which images figure powerfully in David's visits to Yarmouth and in the final death by drowning of both Steerforth and his opposite and rival, Ham Peggotty. A caul was also traditionally used in divinations about a child's future and was thought to be good luck and a sign that the child would have second sight and could communicate with the dead, all of which, of course, apply to David.

However, Dickens takes these ancient folk beliefs and fairytale elements and plunges them into the contemporary commercial world. David's caul is immediately commodified, advertised for sale for fifteen guineas, though the ad turns out to be a "dead loss" (11). Ten years later, we read, it was sold to "an old lady with a handbasket" (resembling Fate) who "died triumphantly in bed, at ninety-two" without ever having been on the water, for her repeated injunction was "let us have no meandering." David immediately comments that "meandering" is necessary for the procurement of tea "to which she was extremely partial" (12). This is the first indication of the imperial and, indeed, worldwide context of the book: the life of each character is embedded in commerce and far-flung locations, notably India and, at the end of the novel, Australia. It's noteworthy, too, that David records that at ten he "felt quite uncomfortable and confused, at a part of myself being disposed of in that way" (12)—that part of his body and his inheritance was an object of value sold to another. From the start he was used and his powers diminished.

"Let us have no meandering" is both a literary joke (since the entire anecdote is an example of comic digression) and an important declaration that this "life" will not be an antique picaresque. There will certainly be wandering: David will wander the streets of London and the road to Dover and much later travel through the romantic Swiss alps (a Byronic figure like Steerforth at last). And at the opposite extreme there will be the grim example of old Daniel Peggotty, now dubbed the "Wanderer," searching for the ruined child, his niece Em'ly, with ferocious, mad, incestuous obsession. At the end of the novel, the Peggottys, a redeemed prostitute, and the proliferating Micawbers will all emigrate to Australia, where they will flourish as they cannot in contemporary England, which deals with marginality and crime by confining selected deviants in a hypocritical "progressive" penitentiary that only serves to foster further criminality. Such rich thematic exfoliation from a word like "meandering" exemplifies the triumphant heroic power of our man of letters as he writes his life out of the memories and legends of his childhood.

David resumes the narrative of his birth with his father. "There is something strange to me, even now, in the reflection that [my father] never saw me; and something stranger yet in the shadowy remembrance that I have of my first childish associations with his white grave-stone in the churchyard, and of the indefinable compassion I used to feel for it lying out alone there in the dark night, when our little parlour was warm and bright with fire and candle, and the doors of our house were—almost cruelly, it seemed to me sometimes—bolted and locked against it" (12). The Wordsworthian "childish associations" of the fiery, bright interior realm of mother and child and the stony, dark, cold realm of the "cruelly excluded" father, who arouses "compassion," prepare us for the coming exile of the boy who will himself eventually become a master of the "shadowy" realm of "fancy," or literary imagination, which is part of his father's posthumous gift to him.

This "inheritance" is transmitted through the "small collection of books" that his father "had left in a little room up-stairs, to which I had access." After his mother's marriage to the repressive ("gloomy," "austere," "wrathful," "tyrannical") but sexually attractive Murdstone, we read, "From that blessed little room, Roderick Random, Peregrine Pickle, Humphrey Clinker, Tom Jones, the Vicar of Wakefield, Don Quixote, Gil Blas, and Robinson Crusoe, came out, a glorious host, to keep me company. They kept alive my fancy, and my hope of something beyond that place and time,—they, and the Arabian Nights, and the Tales of the Genii,—and did me no harm." He would "console" himself "by impersonating my favorite characters" and "putting . . . Murdstone into all the bad ones." He speaks of his "greedy relish for a few volumes of Voyages and Travels. . . . This was my only and my constant comfort. When

I think of it [note present tense], the picture always rises in my mind [like Lazarus or his father], of a summer evening, the boys at play in the churchyard [where his father lies], and I sitting on my bed, reading as if for life"—meaning "to stay alive," "to gain life," and "for the rest of my life" (59–60). Dickens took these famous passages nearly verbatim from the autobiographical fragment he wrote a few years before launching into *David Copperfield*.

The power of these "childish associations" is intensified by their being immediately followed by the contrasting narrative of his flogging, his biting Murdstone's hand ("it sets my teeth on edge to think of it" he writes in the present [62]), his five-day incarceration in his room, and his exile to the brutal Salem House school, where he is forced to become a kind of walking book by wearing a sign reading (with wonderful double meaning of both plea and warning) *"Take Care of Him. He Bites"* (81). Even here, in an institution devoted to beating its student prisoners, David's memory of his father's books will serve him well. For at night he retells their stories in a shadowy moonlit dormitory room to his glamorous, idolized, and apparently nurturing friend, Steerforth (who quickly tells him, "I'll take care of you" [89]). Later, after David's mother's death, "the old books . . . were my only comfort" (147). Ultimately, his father's legacy—telling stories—will save his life. When he is abandoned and enslaved in his stepfather's London warehouse, "I fitted my old books to my altered life, and made stories for myself, out of the streets, and out of men and women; and . . . some main points in the character I shall unconsciously develop, I suppose, in writing my life, were gradually forming all the while" (164). When he runs away from the warehouse, it is in order "to tell my story to my aunt" (170), which does indeed give him a "new life, in a new name, and with everything new about me" (206). And his father's creative literary legacy is most apparent when David finally creates himself as a professional writer (first of short-hand parliamentary reports, then of novels) despite the disastrous fatal "contagion" of his first marriage to a sexy childish girl strikingly like his dead mother.

The novel is full of instances of child abuse. Murdstone flogs David "as if he would have beaten me to death" (62) and exiles him to his room for five days of separation from his mother. Even worse than the physical pain is David's guilt at having become "an atrocious criminal" who might be hanged. In this, he becomes his own jailer. At the sadistic school, the headmaster Creakle resembles "a giant in a story book surveying his captives. . . . 'I'm a Tartar,'" he declares (90, 85). "He had a delight in cutting at the boys, which was like the satisfaction of a craving appetite. I am confident that he couldn't resist a chubby boy, especially; that there was a fascination in such a subject, which made him restless in his mind, until he had scored and marked him for the day. I was chubby myself, and ought to know" (91). (Thus, one of David's very few physical self-descriptions is stimulated by the memory of flogging; another is of lying self-consciously, picturesquely, on his mother's breast. These polar extremes of bodily experience produce acute self-consciousness, expressed in conspicuously rare and overtly literary effects.) The psychological effect of this reign of terror is that "I am morbidly attracted to [Creakle's eye] in a dread desire to know what he will do next, and whether it will be my turn to suffer, or somebody's else's. . . . He makes dreadful mouths as he rules the cyphering-book; and now he throws his eye sideways down our lane [of small boys], and we all droop over our books and tremble" (91).

Throughout the book, adults steal from children. A waiter in a pub ends up eating David's meal—a scene that is brilliantly doubled when the glamorous, six-years-older schoolboy Steerforth appropriates David's seven shillings on the first day of school and uses them to throw a night-time "feast" laid "out on my bed in the moonlight," a "royal spread" for the boys in their dorm room (88). (This is altogether superb foreshadowing of Steerforth's expropriatory hedonism and charm.) In London on the day David is about to run away from the warehouse, a teenager with a donkey-cart steals his clothes box and the half-guinea he'd put in his mouth for safekeeping. On the road down to his aunt's in Dover, he hides from tramps and is terrified by a tinker who calls out, "Come here, when you're called . . . or I'll rip your young body open" (180). Most frightening is the "drunken madman" who owns a marine-store shop where David hopes to get some pennies for his clothes (his escape from London necessitates his stripping himself down to the barest covering— a social and infantile reduction). This old ogre keeps howling "goroo, goroo . . . oh my lungs and liver" like a creature from a fairy tale (178).

But the most famous instance of child abuse is not physical so much as social and psychological: David's slave labor in his stepfather's rat-infested warehouse at the decaying edge of the river. The opening lines of the description, which are close to those Dickens used in his autobiographical fragment a few years before, are extraordinary: "It is a matter of some surprise to me, even now, that I can have been so easily thrown away at such an age. A child of excellent abilities, and with strong powers of observation, quick, eager, delicate, and soon hurt bodily or mentally, it seems wonderful to me that nobody should have made any sign in my behalf. But none was made; and I became, at ten years old, a little laboring hind in the service of Murdstone and Grinby" (150).

Apart from the multiple puns in the owners' names (murderer, grindstone, grin and bear it, *merde*), what first strikes a reader is the determinedly literary, remote, but thereby self-controlling tone and the ironies in the phrase "it seems wonderful to me that nobody should have made any sign on my behalf," in which the "wonder" is the lack of any kind of symbolic gesture or communication (such a "sign" would function as the opposite of the animalizing placard *"Take Care of Him. He Bites"*). The literary self-pity of "a little labouring hind" makes him not a boy but a female deer (again, not a dog who bites) in an archaic pastoral fantasy. But "thrown away" is the most impressive phrase, since it conveys that the boy is a piece of refuse tossed down at the edge of the grimy river—the same filthy river that the prostitute Martha will try to drown herself in, and the same that will at the end of the novel serve as the means of escape for the ruined and rejected—the prostitute, the Micawbers, the Peggottys—who are doomed in England but will thrive at the extreme of its empire, Australia.

The theme of childish erotic fixation is central to the book. David's mother is a "childish widow and . . . childish mother," "a very Baby," a "wax doll," a "weak, light, girlish creature," "much too pretty and thoughtless," "who had been used to wind her bright curls round and round her finger, and to dance with me at twilight in the parlour" (14, 13, 54, 131). Her sexual attraction to Murdstone is clearly perceived by the resentful boy ("confound him and his complexion, and his memory!" he writes in the present [30]). Her inability to manage her household (or even have charge of the keys) and even more "improvident" failure to protect her son from his stepfather (not only physically and emotionally but even economically—since no "provision" was made for the boy after his father's death) amount to almost fatal neglect. But not always. The key to David's self-transformation lies in his relationship to his mother, who both adores and rejects him. The fundamental power of their primary connection can be felt in one of the most intense emotional moments in the book—when nine-year-old David returns on holiday from his school:

God knows how infantine the memory may have been, that was awakened within me by the sound of my mother's voice in the old parlour, when I set foot in the hall. She was singing in a low tone. I think I must have lain in her arms, and heard her singing so to me when I was but a baby. The strain was new to me, and yet it was so old that it filled my heart brim-full; like a friend come back from a long absence.

I believed, from the solitary and thoughtful way in which my mother murmured her song, that she was alone. And I went softly into the room. She was sitting by the fire, suckling an infant, whose tiny hand she held against her neck. Her eyes were looking down upon its face, and she sat singing to it. I was so far right, that she had no other companion.

(109)

At this juncture, there is every reason to expect David to be stunned and then burst into tears of abandonment, jealousy, and rage, which makes what comes next all the more crucial to the largest themes of the book:

I spoke to her, and she started, and cried out. But seeing me, she called me her dear Davy, her own boy! and coming half across the room to meet me, kneeled down upon the ground and kissed me, and laid my head down on her bosom near the little creature that was nestling there, and put its hand up to my lips.

I wish I had died. I wish I had died then, with that feeling in my heart! I should have been more fit for Heaven than I ever have been since.

"He is your brother," said my mother, fondling me. "Davy, my pretty boy! My poor child!" Then she kissed me more and more, and clasped me round the neck.

(109–10)

His mother has immediately granted him both infantile regression to her breast and encouragement to be her partner in raising the baby. He is able to be both baby and boy, both suckling and mate, brother and lover. This is developed even more powerfully later in the scene when David tells the story of his life at school to his mother and her double, the nurse Peggotty (whose name, like his mother's, is Clara):

We sat round the fire, and talked delightfully. I told them what a hard master Mr. Creakle was, and they pitied me very much. I told them what a fine fellow Steerforth was, and what a patron of mine, and Peggotty said she would walk a score of miles to see him. I took the little baby in my arms when it was awake, and nursed it lovingly. When it was asleep again, I crept close to my mother's side according to our old custom, broken now a long time, and sat with my arms embracing her waist, and my little red cheek on her shoulder, and once more felt her beautiful hair drooping over me—like an angel's wing as I used to think, I recollect—and was very happy indeed.

While I sat thus, looking at the fire, and seeing pictures in the red-hot coals, I almost believed that I had never been away . . . and that there was nothing real in all that I remembered, save my mother, Peggotty, and I.

(112–13)

This memory connects storytelling, a double identification with both the baby and the mother, and paradise regained. It prepares us for the final scene of separation—the last time David sees his mother. The holiday is over, and the boy has been restored to enough health to want to resume his independent life:

I was not sorry to go. I had lapsed into a stupid state; but I was recovering a little and looking forward to Steerforth, albeit Mr. Creakle loomed behind him. . . . I kissed [my mother], and my baby brother, and was very sorry then; but not sorry to go away, for the gulf between us was there, and the parting was there, every day. And it is not so much the embrace she gave me, that lives in my mind, though it was as fervent as could be, as what followed the embrace.

I was in the carrier's cart when I heard her calling to me. [Note the return to the sound of her voice.] I looked out, and she stood at the garden-gate alone, holding her baby up in her arms for me to see. It was cold still weather; and not a hair of her head, or a fold of her dress, was stirred, as she looked intently at me, holding up her child.

So I lost her. So I saw her afterwards, in my sleep at school—a silent presence near my bed—looking at me with the same intent face—holding up her baby in her arms.

(121)

His mother holds up her baby for him to see in an affirmation of her maternal identity and as an invitation to David, again, both to identify himself with the baby and, as its brother and her partner, to help her raise it. The immobility of the scene in the "cold still weather" in which her usually mobile hair is not stirred suggests a funerary picture and anticipates her death. But given the images and themes of the book, we must also note that both the suggestion that she resembles a work of church art and the emphasis on her gesture of "holding up" anticipate David's second wife Agnes's resemblance to a "stained glass window" (213, 471, 708) and her iconic gesture of one hand "pointing upward" (706, 774–75). David's last sight of his mother foreshadows the ultimate paradise regained of his marriage to Agnes.

But there are two other objects of childish erotic fixation from whom David must free himself: Steerforth, the beloved older boy at school, and Dora, David's seductive first wife, whom he calls his "child-wife" (594–95). The similarities between the erotic descriptions of Steerforth and Dora reflect their function as two adolescent possibilities, one homosexual, the other heterosexual, but both profoundly regressive. Though David is fully capable of Victorian denunciation of Steerforth as a Byronic glamour boy and seducer, David is also capable (right to the end) of unmoralistic, loving descriptions of Steerforth's charms. For some readers, like Martha Nussbaum, this represents David's final achievement of nonjudgmental novelistic wisdom;[11] for others, David's failure to portray an erotic marriage with Agnes—never describing her with the erotic charge that marks his descriptions of his Dora—implies that his heart belongs to Steerforth, which it does, but not because he favors queer love over straight. For his heart also belongs to Dora.

It's certainly clear that Steerforth and Dora share "captivating power" (403). At seventeen, David thoroughly enjoys Steerforth's calling him "my dear Daisy" and "you romantic Daisy" (274–75) and confesses that the "dashing way he had of treating me like a plaything, was more agreeable to me than any behavior he could have adopted" (283). Steerforth is the Byronic beauty and regency gent whose seductive charms always troubled Victorian notions of the respectable British gentleman. "There was an ease in his manner—a gay and light manner it was, but not swaggering—which I still believe [note present tense] to have borne a kind of enchantment with it. I still believe him, in virtue of this carriage, his animal spirits, his delightful voice, his handsome face and figure, and, for aught I know, of some inborn power of attraction besides (which I think a few people possess), to have carried a spell with him to which it was a natural weakness to yield, and which not many persons could withstand. . . . they seemed to open their hearts to him in a moment" (105).

"'If you had [a sister]'" Steerforth tells David at school, with barely disguised homosexual overtones, "'I should think she would have been a pretty, timid, little, bright-eyed sort of girl. I should have liked to know her. Good night, young Copperfield.' 'Good night, sir,' I replied. I thought of him very much after I went to bed, and raised myself, I recollect, to look at him where he lay in the moonlight, with his handsome face turned up, and his head reclining easily on his arm. He was a person of great power in my eyes" (90).

David's later attraction to Dora is the next step in his development. Like so many abandoned children, he has clung to the memory of his "affectionate" mother and rediscovers her when he falls into the "captivity" of his love for "girlish, bright-eyed lovely" Dora: "All was over in a moment. I had fulfilled my destiny. I was a captive and a slave" (362). "I was charmed with her childish, winning way. . . . [Though] I felt she was a little impracticable" (500). Still, "It was all Dora to me. The sun shone Dora, and the birds sang Dora" (447).

So, like his father, he makes a "fairy marriage" to a hopelessly regressive, narcissistic, but intensely sexy child. Despite Victorian conventions, if one reads slowly enough, the sex that their relationship is "steeped" in (enough to "drown" others, writes this undrownable boy) comes vividly through: With "her bright eyes shining very brightly, and her little right hand idly busying itself with one of the buttons of my coat . . . I wondered what she was thinking about, as I gazed in admiring silence at the little soft hand traveling up the row of buttons on my coat, and at the clustering hair that lay against my breast, and at the lashes of her downcast eyes, slightly rising as they followed her idle fingers. At length her eyes were lifted up to mine, and she stood on tiptoe to give me, more thoughtfully than usual, that precious little kiss—once, twice, three times—and went out of the room" (565). But for all this "enchantment," his marriage still leaves him with the feeling of a "void which somewhere seemed to be about me" (597). And eventually his "child-wife" Dora miscarries, weakens, and dies just as his childish mother and her infant had died when David was nine some fourteen years before.

The overt alternative to his mother's and Dora's girlish eroticism is the loving intimacy born of a "disciplined heart" (643) and associated with his childhood "sister," Agnes, not an erotic child but a responsible woman. "She was so true, she was so beautiful, she was so good . . . with her own sweet tranquility, she calmed my agitation." She is "the better angel of my life!" (771). "Whenever I have not had you, Agnes, to advise and approve in the beginning, I have seemed to go wild, and to get into all sorts of difficulty. When I have come to you, at last (as I have always done), I have come to peace and happiness. I come home now, like a tired traveler, and find such a blessed sense of rest!" (524). Her "placid sisterly manner; with her beaming eyes; with her tender voice; and with that sweet composure . . . had long ago made the house that held her quite a sacred place to me" (524–25). Agnes is not a fairy figure, but, like the "stained glass window in the church," "she was like Hope embodied to me" (471).

She is frequently seen carrying keys (pointedly unlike David's mother or Dora, who can't handle them), which suggests the figure of Fidelity or of St. Martha, the housewife saint. The name Agnes, of course, suggests (in Latin) the lamb of God—even as Dora (in French, which the novel always associates with childish irresponsibility) suggests adoration as well as gold. Agnes is most emphatically and repeatedly identified with the hieratic gesture of "pointing upward"—"ever pointing upward, Agnes; ever leading me to something better; ever directing me to higher things!" (774)—most vividly when she gestures to indicate Dora's death and in the last two words of the novel. But most unfortunately for the intended symbolic scheme, the upward pointing gesture inevitably suggests that Agnes is also the angel of death.

In Dora and Agnes, Dickens is contrasting eros and agape; one leads to the grave, the other, to the kingdom of heaven. But even contemporary readers found the figure of Agnes "stiff," and for modern readers she is the very epitome of the repressive Victorian feminine ideal. Despite his operatic insistence on the attractions of her "sweet tranquility," she seems a patently sexless figure—though, of course, David loudly proclaims the triumph of his mature love, marriage, and final multiple fatherhood. There's no doubt that Dickens fully intended to portray David's long denial of Agnes's sexuality and marital availability as a moral and psychological failure, as part of his dangerous immaturity: "I had perversely wandered away from the voice of my own heart" (524). In his working notes Dickens emphasizes that "he *made* her his sister!" (853). But the prose never dances and plays for her as it does for Dora.

Readers never believe in Agnes or that final happy marriage because David has devoted so much attention to the erotic-child aspects of his mother as they are reproduced in Dora. The key recurrent image is of his mother's and Dora's seductive hair. But in what I quoted earlier there is one potential link between David's mother's eroticism and Agnes's heavenly goodness: "When [the baby] was asleep again, I crept close to my mother's side according to our old custom, broken now a long time, and sat with my arms embracing her waist, and my little red cheek on her shoulder, and once more felt her beautiful hair drooping over me—like an angel's wing as I used to think, I recollect—and was very happy indeed" (112–13). His mother's hair both arouses him and comforts him. She is an erotic angel.

In this one instant lies everything Dickens cannot successfully achieve later, no matter how clearly he has David denounce his "perverted" boyish rejection of Agnes in turning her into an angelic sister rather than an angelic lover. For Dickens never conveys David's perception of Agnes as an erotic angel wife—only of Dora as an erotic child-wife.

This is a result of literary technique. Dora is always vividly, actively alive in action, speed, feeling. She is presented dramatically, in scenes more than speeches. Agnes is presented through David's assertions and unironically fulsome declarations (so different from his comic effusions about Dora). In sum, Dora is theater; Agnes is pageant. Dora even has more inner life than Agnes. We do spend a lot of time with Agnes, but she is so severely confined within David's repeated insistence on her tranquil moralistic uplift that we have almost no sense of her desires, needs, or capacities as anything other than a caretaker of her alcoholic father and "better angel" for David (771).

However, there is one hint, unfortunately never developed, that Agnes, too, is a captive of her damaged childhood. In the scene in which David visits her upon his return from his three-year period of mourning and European pilgrimage, he notices that much of her house is exactly as it had been when they were children:

> "I have found a pleasure [she says] . . . while you have been absent, in keeping every thing as it used to be when we were children. For we were very happy then, I think."
>
> "Heaven knows we were!" said I.
>
> "And every little thing that has reminded me of my brother [i.e., David]," said Agnes, with her cordial eyes turned cheerfully upon me, "has been a welcome companion. Even this," showing me the basket-trifle, full of keys, still hanging at her side, "seems to jingle a kind of old tune!"
>
> She smiled again, and went out at the door by which she had come.
>
> It was for me to guard this sisterly affection with religious care. It was all that I had left myself, and it was a treasure.
>
> (772)

This last line alludes to how earlier "in my wayward boyhood I had thrown away the treasure of her love" (752). The fetishized "basket-trifle, full of keys" not only reiterates her practicality with household and heavenly keys but recalls the "hand-basket" of the old lady (Fate) who bought David's caul.

Despite the clarity of the larger narrative scheme—to become a hero David must escape the prison of his childhood and childish fixation on Steerforth and Dora—and despite David's many asseverations, Agnes is not convincingly his wife so much as the responsible nurturing mother he never had, and this second regressive marriage is won at the cost of any convincing erotic life or any mature autonomy for Agnes. For all of David's fervent expostulations—"O, we were happy, we were happy!" (793)—there is nothing in the prose of the final three chapters that conveys the spontaneous dramatic warmth of his interplay with Dora or the glamorous romantic glow of his image of Steerforth asleep in the moonlight. All we get is the Victorian religiosity of "one face, shining on me like a Heavenly light, by which I see all other objects. . . . O Agnes, O my soul, so may thy face be by me when I close my life indeed [not just the book]; so may I, when realities are melting from me like the shadows which I now dismiss [shades of father and of Prospero], still find thee near me, pointing upward!" (805–6). Not a beloved wife and mother of his children but the angel of death. For all the dexterity of the loving erotic vigor that marks his depictions of Dora and Steerforth, he evidently cannot portray eroticized goodness and must fall back on religious clichés.

There is nothing here or at any other moment in the book to suggest that Dickens intends David, the mature man of letters, to be perceived as an unreliable narrator—that this literary failure is Dickens's own deliberate irony at his narrator's expense. Dickens is not Henry James. And we know Dickens admired a child's ability to hold on to Christian pieties, to deny the finality of death, come what may. His favorite poem of Wordsworth's was "We Are Seven," in which a "little Cottage girl" of eight unwaveringly affirms (in Blakean sing-song) that her dead brother and sister, though lying in the graveyard next to her house, are still alive. Wordsworth asks, "A simple Child, / That lightly draws its breath, / And feels its life in every limb, / What should it know of death?"[12] The phrase "a simple Child" both identifies the girl with baby Jesus and suggests she may be retarded, but Dickens never permitted

himself such dark ambiguities about his "favorite child," David Copperfield. Such territory lay ahead in his later novels.

Still, if Dickens fails to portray a final triumph of sexual growth
and development culminating in a marriage of lust and love, he does
show with remarkable care—and in a great thematic enlargement of the
novel—how David's marriage to Dora not only trapped him but provoked him into a surprising change. As David matures he comes not
only to see and regret Dora's dangerous immaturities but also to give
up all hope of "forming her mind"—without rejecting her, indeed, with
redoubled determination to support her (640). His childish erotic love
leads him into the world of professional activity, competence, growth,
and finally fame. To achieve this, David must learn to draw for both his
personal "comfort" and his professional literary work on the "shadowy
world" of his father's books and also on the fairytale and romantic dream
realm in which the enchantments of Dora and Steerforth are vividly
present—without becoming trapped in the prison of romantic regression.
The disasters of his first marriage and of his bedazzled friendship with
Steerforth—both of which lead to death—can only be survived by the
rigorous, "earnest" professional activity as a writer that he develops out
of economic and personal necessity (560). "I had no idea you were such
a determined character, Copperfield!" says his exemplary school friend
Traddles when David embarks on learning short hand (488). And David
himself trumpets his heroic capacity for work: "a patient and continuous
energy . . . [there] I find the source of my success" (560). He praises his
"habits of punctuality, order, and diligence. . . . Whatever I have tried to
do in life, I have tried with all my heart to do well . . . in great aims and
small, I have always been thoroughly in earnest . . . there is no substitute
for thorough-going, ardent, and sincere earnestness" (560).

What makes this self-advertisement more than conventional Victorian bombast—Carlyle's gospel of work—is how precisely and powerfully David distinguishes the intense professional discipline required for
literary work, which encompasses both romance and reality, from the
brutal Evangelical "realism" and criminal hypocritical "respectability" of
Murdstone and Uriah Heep. David's determination is different from
that of the cruelly repressive schoolmaster Creakle, who boasts, "I am
a determined character . . . I do my duty" (85). Rather than making the
usual opposition between irresponsible, dreamy, romantic literary fancy
and hard, realistic, Victorian practical material action, David describes

his literary vocation as the ultimate—and heroic—civilizing force in modern England and its empire.

And yet, with admiration and regret, I believe we must conclude that, despite Dickens's own heroic efforts in delivering this "favorite child" from the shadowy realm of his own autobiography and developing him into a representative man on the grand Victorian scale, there is a final turn of the screw. David is indeed the hero of his own life, a father and a famous novelist, but in his marriage, if not his professional life, he is still a damaged child. The child is father of the man.

PIP IN *GREAT EXPECTATIONS*

Eleven years and four novels later, Dickens returned to the autobiographical mode and produced his darkest, most ambitious, and most accomplished book, *Great Expectations* (1861). Here instead of the orphan David Copperfield's triumphant self-creation, we follow the orphan Pip's desperate, deluded self-destruction. His childish faith in a fairytale destiny of love and wealth utterly corrupts him, and it is only by overcoming narcissism born of abuse and risking his life to care for the true source of his social identity—a fugitive criminal—that he can dwindle into a bleak but genuine maturity.

Dickens was urgently aware of the need to differentiate this autobiographical novel from *David Copperfield* and told a friend that he had carefully reread the earlier book to ensure that there were "no unconscious repetitions."[13] He was equally aware of the aesthetic originality of the book, of the tension between the symbolic (or fairytale) and realistic elements. Using the first person for only the third time in his fifteen novels, Dickens simultaneously employs and subverts Pip's (and the reader's) great expectations of a fairytale or bildungsroman narrative of wisdom finally achieved and ultimately rewarded socially, professionally, and personally. For as Dickens wrote his friend, it was "the grotesque tragic-comic conception that first encouraged me" (533).

David Copperfield began with a declaration of purpose—David was writing his autobiography to prove whether he was the hero of his own life. *Great Expectations* abruptly begins with a traumatic memory. No purpose is articulated. No literary form, no "story of my life," is evoked. The opening chapters of *David Copperfield* gave the circumstances of David's birth in great detail—information he can only have learned from his loving mother and nurse—and great emphasis was placed on his having the same name and possibly the same impractical, dreamy nature as his dead father. David's identity is emphatically established by his social and family context, and it is only after the first chapter and only in the midst of an ongoing, enclosing family narrative that he comes to his earliest memories.

Pip, on the other hand, is self-named. In the very first sentence he informs us that his childhood inability to pronounce his given name has led to his calling himself—and being called by all others—Pip. Thus, he always will be self-defined (which suggests both a possibly heroic freedom and a dangerous, childish grandiosity) but also confined by the limited powers of his "infant tongue" (9). The name Pip (like his surname Pirrip) is a palindrome, and its meanings include a seed, a spot, a speck, a disease of birds or children, to be unwell or depressed, to annoy or irritate, to chirp or peep like a bird, and to puncture or crack an egg shell as chick does upon hatching. The importance and inescapability of this first identity are reemphasized when Pip learns (at seventeen, ten years later) that he is to become a rich gentleman of great expectations but must always maintain one part of his otherwise totally transformed social identity—he must always "bear the name of Pip" (109). And bear it he will.

Pip begins his narrative with a memory of standing in a wasteland, a cemetery in a marsh, trying to decode his ancestry from the typography of the inscriptions on the gravestones of his parents and siblings. It is here that he is startled into traumatic self-awareness—on Christmas Eve, no less—as a "small bundle of shivers growing afraid of it all and beginning to cry." Suddenly "a terrible voice" responds and a man "started up from among the graves" (10). This ferocious resurrection of an angry, Abrahamic godlike figure—a starving escaped convict who threatens to cut Pip's throat if he's not silent—is described (in the first sentence fragment to occur in the book, to convey shock and disorientation) as "a fearful man, all in coarse grey, with a great iron on his leg. A man with no hat, and with broken shoes, and with an old rag tied round his head." But in the very next sentence he is "a man who had been soaked in water, and smothered in mud, and lamed by stones, and cut by flints, and stung by nettles, and torn by briars" (10). This echoes Isaiah's premonitory description of the Messiah as "the suffering servant," "the man of sorrows . . . acquainted with grief . . . despised and rejected."

The escaped convict immediately demands what Pip has just come to understand for the first time—his own name. "'Tell us your name!'

said the man. 'Quick!' 'Pip, sir.' 'Once more,' said the man, staring at me. 'Give it mouth!' 'Pip. Pip, sir'" (10). The repetitions convey chirping, of course, and this fledgling is indeed about to be "pipped"—the convict immediately turns him upside-down, shakes him, and places him on a gravestone. In this birth, Pip and his world have been turned topsy-turvy. What he first sees from his new perch is the agent of this transformation "ravenously" eating a bit of bread that has dropped out of Pip's pocket. So for the convict to alter Pip's condition, to raise him, is also for the convict to be fed, kept alive, and soon delivered from bondage. The emphasis in these first moments of their encounter is entirely on starvation, cannibalism, and violent birth, on infant needs, greed, and terror. Yet in this muddy graveyard in a marsh at the mouth of a river, out of this orphan boy's fearful but also sympathetic and generous response to the convict's cry for help, there arises the theme of transformative reciprocity—fellow feeling, nurture, empowerment, love.

Pip is an abused child: beaten by his surrogate mother, his twenty-years-older sister; comforted in infantilism by her henpecked and beaten childlike husband, the blacksmith Joe (who himself had been abused by his drunken father); and denounced by the village community sitting around the Christmas Day feast as an ungrateful sinner, "naterally wicious" (26). When Pip is summoned three years later to the ruined mansion of eccentric rich Miss Havisham to be a playmate for her adopted daughter, Estella, we understand that his grandiose childish fantasy that he has been magically elevated by a fairy godmother to marry a fairy princess arises in large part from his condition as an abused child. Pip is indeed "morally timid and very sensitive" (54), and he responds to Miss Havisham's and Estella's abuse—not only their insults but even Estella's slapping his face—with abject idolization. He imagines he is the hero of a fairytale, but he is in fact the dunce—the antihero (we'd say) of a profoundly secular modern novel.

As a child, far from basking in Wordsworthian rural bliss (though there are a few moments of lounging in the sunlit marsh with Joe and talking with the sisterly schoolteacher Biddy), Pip is generally frightened, guilty, self-accusatory, remorseful. Forced to help the convict, he becomes a thief (stealing part of Christmas dinner). When his sister is mysteriously attacked and beaten with a convict's leg-iron, he imagines himself to be her murderer. His obsessive guilt conveys his repressed rage, and this makes him especially prone to compensatory, grandiose fantasies of deliverance and elevation to social and romantic power.

In a wonderfully tender scene after he has returned from his first visit to Miss Havisham and, like "a reckless witness under the torture" (57), tells everyone huge splendid lies about it all, Pip confesses the truth to Joe ("I wished I was not common . . . the lies had come out of it somehow"). Joe attempts to comfort him—"You are oncommon in some things. You're oncommon small. Likewise, you're an oncommon scholar"—and to correct him in a most fatherly way: "that's all, old chap, and don't never do it no more" (59–60). But Pip needs more than Joe, and the golden lure of Miss Havisham and beautiful Estella entraps him.

Pip tells us that he had at first "believed in the forge as the glowing road to manhood and independence" (86), but after his great expectations are aroused by Miss Havisham's and Estella's attentions, he sees himself as "coarse and common" (111), is filled with self-hatred, and declares he "wants to be a gentleman" (101). From ten to fourteen he serves Miss Havisham and worships icy, sadistic Estella, though "I never was happy with her, but always miserable" (207). At fourteen he is apprenticed to Joe, but at seventeen, he imagines (with considerable encouragement from Miss Havisham and the tacit collaboration of her lawyer, Jaggers) that a sudden gift of money from an unknown benefactor, which brings an end to his apprenticeship as a blacksmith, and the invitation to move to London to be educated as a gentleman, are the fulfillment of magical destiny: "Farewell, monotonous acquaintances of my childhood, henceforth, I was for London and greatness: not for smith's work in general and for you!" (115). The immediate moral and psychological consequences of this apparently gratified fantasy are the cruel denial, neglect, and desertion of his immediate family. As he is borne away from the village by coach, "the mists had all solemnly risen now, and the world lay spread before me" (125)—an echo of the expulsion from Eden in *Paradise Lost* and also of Coriolanus's deluded belief that he could pursue a heroic life away from Rome ("there is a world elsewhere").

The gap between Pip's adolescent expectations of London and the city's grim reality is dramatically palpable in the opening pages of the "second stage of Pip's expectations," chapter 20. He wanders the chartered streets and discovers them to be "ugly, crooked, narrow, and dirty" (129). His guardian, the violent lawyer Jaggers, lives in the hideous microcosm of "Little Britain," among the courts, Newgate prison, the "black dome" of St. Paul's, and the Smithfield butcher's market: "the shameful place, being all asmear with filth and fat and blood and foam, seemed to stick to me" (131). Pip's roommate turns out to be the ineffectual if charming and amiable gentleman Herbert Pocket, and they soon drift into a life of conspicuous consumption, manic sociability, drunkenness, and debt. Herbert and Pip float along, their feckless passivity in contrast to the ferocious criminal activity of Jaggers's realm.

The only other alternatives to Little Britain are the suburban folly of Herbert's family (a "tumbling" [146] chaos of maternal inattention—the mothers in this novel are uniformly destructive) or the precious theatricality of the domestic refuge (a moated castle in miniature) of Jaggers's law clerk, Wemmick, who maintains a strict barrier between professional and personal life, unlike Jaggers, who is all deadly business. In this world of Hobbesian self-interest, Wemmick does care for his deaf, aged father, but it is characteristic of Dickens's dark realism that Wemmick is also seen moving among the wretched prisoners of Newgate "as a gardener might walk among his plants" (199). Thus Wemmick fosters and thrives on punition. His private personal virtue does not erase his professional complicity in a cruel social system. And the secrecy with which he surrounds his private life taints it with something of Jaggers's paranoia. Wemmick goes so far as to conceal his careful wedding arrangements from Pip, who is told he is to be the best man just as they enter a church. The lower-middle-class domestic comedy of the wedding is qualified by the underlying suggestion of eccentricity approaching mental illness.

Pip does visit his old village a few times, but he is deeply uncomfortable there, insulting to his family, still fawning on Miss Havisham, and noodling about Estella. On these visits home he is brilliantly mocked by one of Dickens's great minor characters, known only as "Trabb's boy"— the shop assistant to the tailor who made Pip's first new fancy clothes (118). The boy is depicted as the ubiquitous strutting personification of hooting teenage rage at Pip's presumption that he had ever really escaped his lower-class country identity. His jeers and street pantomime mock Pip's fine airs, and it's notable that it will be Trabb's boy who— at the very end—serves as the agent of Pip's deliverance from death at the hands of another resentful country servant, Orlick, Pip's psychotic double throughout the novel, whose own great expectations lead to murder and criminal predation.

After four years in London, Pip comes into his majority and full allowance of five hundred pounds a year. With this he performs the only generous act of his late adolescent life—he becomes Herbert's secret benefactor and sets him up in a business career. But two years after this identification with the benevolent powers of the unseen hand of a magical god, Pip's benefactor reveals himself to be the convict he had met in the graveyard. "I'm your second father," cries the fugitive (241), a self-made millionaire in Australia who has secretly come back to London (a capital offence) to see the puppet gentleman he has "made." The "hunted dunghill dog wot you kep life in, got his head so high that he could make a gentleman—and, Pip, you're him" (241). In a dark ironic symmetry, the convict and Pip have both imagined (and staked their lives) on the belief that moral virtue can result in social elevation. But a noble act does not create a nobleman. Pip's only true nobility is moral—"you acted noble, my boy" says the convict, "Noble, Pip. And I have never forgot it" (238). But neither of them understands the gap between private virtue and social status until the end of the book, and the convict never really grasps it all. (Pip is careful to maintain the convict's belief in happy endings by telling him on his deathbed that he loves the convict's daughter, Estella.)

With the convict's return and revelation, Pip must recognize who he really is, how deluded and cruel toward his family he has been ("I had deserted Joe" [243]), how utterly unprepared for "real life" he is ("I am fit for nothing" [256]), and how urgently he must take charge of the fugitive, who is being stalked. The criminal he had fed when he was seven is now his dependent for life.

The last third of the novel, chapters 40 to 59, is devoted to Pip's sudden maturation: his remorse toward his family; his acknowledgment of Miss Havisham's manipulation (and forgiveness of her, even to the point of burning his hands as he attempts to save her life in a fire); his refusal to take any money from Miss Havisham or to spend any more of the convict's money; his new, active, practical skills in devising and executing a complex plan for the convict's escape; and, most important (and exquisitely dramatized by Dickens through Pip's first-person account), the slow and utterly believable evolution of his feelings toward the convict from repulsion to concern to pity to a species of courageous filial love. In the end, although the convict is recaptured and dies and the money is lost, Pip has gained a father and become a loyal son: "For, now, my repugnance to him had all melted away, and in the hunted wounded shackled creature who held my hand in his, I saw a man who had meant to be my benefactor, and who had felt affectionately, gratefully, and generously toward me with great constancy through a series of years. I only saw in him a much better man than I had been to Joe" (332).

It is now Pip who must leave England ("I had no home anywhere" [335]) to join Herbert in the Cairo office of his firm just as the convict had once gone to Australia. Only abroad can Pip come into his true maturity not as a glamorous and powerful romantic gentleman but a modest businessman: "I must not leave it to be supposed that we were ever a great House, or that we made mints of money. We were not in a grand way of business, but we had a good name, and worked for our profits, and did very well. We owed so much to Herbert's ever cheerful industry and readiness, that I often wondered how I had conceived that old idea of his inaptitude, until I was one day enlightened by the reflection, that perhaps the inaptitude had never been in him at all, but had been in me" (355). The moral realism and unblinking if mordant self-knowledge of this are wonderfully conveyed by the motion of the prose here—without any sentimental or melodramatic fairytale flourishes or self-pity or resentment.

I've suggested that Dickens chose to use the figures of children to arouse in readers the sympathy that would effect personal and social transformation and reform. But in a little-noticed passage near the end of *Great Expectations*, Dickens subverts even this belief in the salutary power of sympathy for children. The one figure in the novel who knows the whole story—and does nothing to correct Pip's misunderstandings of it—is his guardian, the violent Jaggers, who thrives at the center of the modern hell of Little Britain. In his last major appearance in the novel, Jaggers finally tells Pip why he has arranged the plots of so many lives the way he has and why their whole story must never be told. The cause of all his plotting, he says, was his feeling of sympathy for a girl of two or three (Estella) who was the daughter of two of his criminal clients, a thief and a murderess, the convict and the woman who would become Jaggers's housekeeper.

Jaggers narrates his story in the third person as if it were no more than a case study or he himself were no more than a figure in a draft of a legal deposition that can be immediately destroyed: "Mind! I admit nothing" (307). This ostentatious depersonalization (masquerading as strength of character, professional habit, and scrupulous concern for all parties) is one of Jaggers's defining traits ("I'll have no feelings here" [309]), but it's also important to recall that Pip has already censured Estella's tendency to "speak of yourself as if you were someone else" (203). Dickens is suggesting there's something innately mad, self-alienating (we'd say schizoid) in such verbal actions.

"Put the case," Jaggers begins,

> that he [Jaggers himself] lived in an atmosphere of evil, and that all he saw of children, was, their being generated in great numbers for certain destruction. Put the case that he often saw children solemnly tried at a criminal bar, where they were held up to be seen; put the case that he habitually knew of their being imprisoned, whipped, transported, neglected, cast out, qualified in all ways for the hangman, and growing up to be hanged. Put the case that pretty nigh all the children he saw in his daily business life, he had reason to look upon as so much spawn, to develop into the fish that were to come to his net—to be prosecuted, defended, forsworn, made orphans, be-devilled somehow.

> (307)

Jaggers is accusing himself here of using and abusing children.

"Put the case, Pip," continues Jaggers, "that here was one pretty little child out of the heap, who could be saved; whom the father believed dead, and dared make no stir about; and to whom, over the mother, the legal adviser [Jaggers] had this power: 'I know what you did [murdered a rival], and how you did it. . . . Give the child into my hands, and I will do my best to bring you off. If you are saved, your child is saved too; if you are lost, you child is still saved.' Put the case that this was done, and the woman was cleared" (307). Jaggers then relates that he also "held a trust to find a child for an eccentric rich lady [Miss Havisham] to adopt and bring up" (307) and gave the child to her. The child, of course, is Estella.

Jaggers's narrative affirms his powers as a secretly benevolent father (analogous both to the convict and to Pip as benefactor of Herbert), but it also shows Jaggers to be as cruelly self-deceived and as emotionally and morally self-serving as Pip. Pip had his fairytale; Jaggers, his secret history. Neither understands how fatal such narratives can be. Jaggers's plot manipulations have brought destruction to all his characters—including the child Estella, who was emotionally deprived, perverted, and abused by her adoptive mother (who made her an unfeeling "puppet" [204] to be used in a revenge plot) and who we learn is now the victim of a violently abusive husband, a rich "gentleman" she coldly married for money and social status.

What Dickens is suggesting here is that to imagine that you have the divine, omniscient, benevolent power of plot—as Jaggers or presumably the novelist does—or that you can deduce a magical fairytale plot from the shape of your life—as Pip does—is to wreak havoc. For all plot is a childish fantasy. All novelists—and readers—are wishful, dreaming children. The ultimate meaning of this last and greatest of Dickens's novels of childhood and its consequences is not a Victorian affirmation of order and progress but that no child can save us.

The final chapter of *Great Expectations* has occasioned years of critical debate that began with some of the first reviews. The last of Pip's expectations to be blasted is of a marriage to the faithful sister figure Biddy, who is wed to the blacksmith Joe on the very day Pip comes down from London to make amends and resume a simple village life. Pip learns that this last fairytale (of the prodigal son come home at last to be feted and married) must also go up in smoke. There will be no family life, no haven in a heartless world, no future generations for this broken dreamer. He leaves England to join Herbert in Cairo, and when he returns on a visit after eleven years abroad, he discovers that Joe and Biddy now have two children and that their little boy is called Pip—a seeming return to the start of the story and a new beginning. But Pip himself has no wife, no son, and no home in England. Like the convict, he can only become a good man away from the "labyrinth" (179), and he knows he must always "must live a bereaved life" (306).

In the final scene, Pip visits the ruined garden of Miss Havisham's mansion, and there by happy chance discovers Estella, also visiting the garden for the first time in many years. She is now a widow and theatrically declares herself to be a changed woman. She says she has been "bent and broken, but—I hope—into a better shape." The last sentence of the novel conveys the suggestion of their future marriage: "I took her hand in mine, and we went out of the ruined place; and, as the morning mists had risen long ago when I first left the forge, so the evening mists were rising now, and in all the broad expanse of tranquil light they showed to me, I saw the shadow of no parting from her" (358).

Thirteen years after *Great Expectations* appeared in book form, and four years after Dickens's death in 1870, his friend and biographer John Forster published another version of the ending and reported that Dickens had rejected it following the advice of the novelist Edward Bulwer-Lytton. The original ending had the final encounter between Pip and Estella take place by accident in Piccadilly Circus (in the center of the center of the empire, not in a scruffy Edenic paradise lost) where they exchange a few words and Estella places a kiss on the cheek of the little boy Pip whom the older Pip has brought to London on an excursion. We know this second Pip is his namesake, not his son, but Estella doesn't, and it is only he who gets a kiss from Estella. We're meant to recall, of course, that she had let Pip kiss her only once—when she had been thrilled by his beating up a boy (young Herbert Pocket) in the garden (75)—and that she was eventually to marry a brutal wife-beating "gentleman." This original ending emphasizes her "most unhappy life," her separation from her husband, who dies, and her second marriage to a country doctor who is "not rich." "I am greatly changed, I know," she says, "but I thought you would like to shake hands with Estella too." We note the self-alienating use of the third person. "'Lift up that pretty child [an elevation] and let me kiss it!'" she says, and Pip comments, "She supposed the child, I think, to be my child"—another false narrative (359).

So in the original version, this novel of childhood ends with a child held up to receive a woman's gesture of love. Estella's treatment of this little boy is an index of her redemption and closes the circle of Pip's childhood story, but her act is based on a self-comforting sentimental misunderstanding about the boy's identity and its significance. The elder Pip must carry on abroad, alone.

The last sentence of the original ending reads, "I was very glad afterwards to have had the interview; for, in her face and in her voice, and in her touch, she gave me the assurance, that suffering had been stronger than Miss Havisham's teaching, and had given her a heart to understand what my heart used to be" (359). Not "was" but "used to be"—to emphasize the loss. The prose is significantly less theatrical, lyrical, and imagistic, of course, than that of the published second version. It conveys what Q. D. Leavis called the "wry" not "bitter" attitude of Pip's entire retrospective narrative.[14] But Dickens rejected this dry four-paragraph version (half a page) and composed the more operatic thirty-three-paragraph (two-page) version we know.

His decision to rewrite the ending has aroused more than one hundred critical responses (overwhelmingly negative), and most readers today concur that the extremely modern, anti-sentimental, downbeat London ending seems much more consistent with the sorrowful wisdom Pip at last achieves. It is worth acknowledging that, in the published version of the novel, the arc of images from wasteland and graveyard to wasted garden (from which this chastened Adam and Eve must now take their solitary way) has classic coherence. But most readers would

probably reply that the whole point of the book has been that such coherence is just whistling in the dark. And Pip himself, in retrospect, has
spoken of being "lost in the mazes of his future fortunes" (111) and of his
life as "a blind and thankless one" (297–98).

AT THREE MOMENTS in his literary career—using the different tech-
niques of his early, middle, and late styles—Dickens created the abused
orphans who would become some of his most famous and enduring
characters. Oliver Twist was an unchanging saintly victim, a two-dimensional, pre-psychological essence, the principle of Good. Dickens used
him as an icon who could reform criminally negligent society by arousing
sympathy in others. Like so many children before (and after) him, Oliver
was an ideological object. David Copperfield was a three-dimensional,
late-maturing "Hero as Man of Letters" and proper Victorian family
man. Dickens used him to construct (with the tools of a first-person,
realistic, historical, and psychological novel) an exemplary case of child
development, of hard-won personal and professional self-creation. But
in *Great Expectations* Dickens portrays Pip as a sterile disillusioned exile.
The first-person vividness of David Copperfield's childhood prepared us
for his happy transformation, however skeptical we are about his second
marriage. The first-person vividness of Pip's childhood prepares us for his
utterly believable "miserable" end. His fairytale fantasies have destroyed
him and exposed the wasteland that is British culture and society. Pip's
ultimate duty is to forgive others and to refuse both resentment and self-
pity. He must go beyond the two defining characteristics of the conventional Victorian novel: melodrama and sentimentality. Despite the
anxious optimism of the final published ending, the book as a whole
conveys a repudiation of the novel of childhood growth and development. That "small bundle of shivers growing afraid of it all and beginning
to cry" is never to come to a happy or merely tragic (and thus consoling)
ending. This most adroitly constructed and most narratively vigorous of
Dickens's novels turns the bildungsroman inside out: it shows not a triumphant progress but a decline into stoic moral realism.

2

MARK TWAIN'S FREE SPIRITS AND SLAVES

Tom Sawyer and Huckleberry Finn

ONE HUNDRED YEARS after America declared its independence, Mark Twain published the first of his two quintessential American novels, fictions that use children to explore and define national identity and possibility. *The Adventures of Tom Sawyer* (1876) masquerades as a children's entertainment, but in fact it addresses a grand centennial theme—can the promise of America as a new beginning for human society, dedicated to life, liberty, and pursuit of happiness, be fulfilled? Or was it only possible to fulfill it thirty or forty years before, in a small town in a provincial Western state, and only possible for boys—indeed only a chosen few of them—up to the age of fourteen or so? Were these few white boys, with "adventurous, troublesome ways,"[1] living in the slave state of Missouri back in the 1840s the last truly free American beings? And when these boys aged into men did the promise of America vanish with their childhood? Did Wordsworth's archetypal description of the loss of childhood powers—"Whither is fled the visionary gleam? / Where is it now, the glory and the dream?"—apply not only to individuals but also to nations? In a century that worshipped progress, this nostalgic, counterevolutionary idea also haunted European and American thought and feeling: adults are shrunken children.

In *The Adventures of Tom Sawyer*, almost all the adults of the town of St. Petersburg—a town named for the rock on which the church was built—are conspicuously compromised, diminished figures, twittering women, feminized men, snobbish, vindictive cliques, and though there are one or two responsible male authorities at the edges of the action (a judge, a Welshman), most of respectable society is composed of eunuchs and biddies. The only adult men with any personal force are deviants—dangerous tricksters, drunks, criminals, murderers. The most powerful man is the "murderin' half-breed" Injun Joe (74), who starves to death in the prison of his underground lair, McDougal's cave. Tom's longed-for stature as "a glittering hero" (173) is established by his escape from that cave, and he is abundantly rewarded by his discovery of Joe's hidden treasure, $12,000, which ensures his economic security and that of his more primitive comic sidekick, Huckleberry Finn.

But by the time Twain finally published *Adventures of Huckleberry Finn* nine years later, in 1885, after many fits and starts and interruptions, his vision of American possibility had darkened, and the characters of the boys and their defining tasks had changed. Compare the endings of the two books. *The Adventures of Tom Sawyer* ends with the boys defeating Injun Joe, a melodramatic, terrifying, almost Gothic figure of evil, fiendishly inventive, murderously violent, drunk, greedy, bent on revenge. The villainy of this swarthy criminal Goliath is ontological, apparently intrinsic to his mixed race, and there are deliberate echoes of Milton's Satan in his intelligence and hurt pride. He dies when his refuge in the natural "labyrinth" of the cave is sealed (204).

At the end of *Adventures of Huckleberry Finn* the corresponding and contrasting figure to Injun Joe is the benign, loyal, and nurturing black slave, Jim (who is never called "Nigger Jim" in the actual text).[2] The boys must free this fugitive slave from his confinement not in a cave (a natural phenomenon) but a flimsy shack (a cultural construction). The dark adult male figure is not a villain but an innocent, something of a noble savage, a loving father of two children, the patient companion of Huck in their journey of escape down the river, and often presented as the victim of an unjust society. His criminality is not innate (racially "natural" like Joe's, Satanic) but imposed by social fictions. His only crime lies in his escape from slavery, but at the end he, too, is imprisoned. In the first book, the containment of an evil half-breed was an essentially defining task for an American hero; now it's the liberation of an innocent black slave.

Despite the books' reputations as exuberant declarations of independence, both *Tom Sawyer* and *Huckleberry Finn* are more about confinement and enclosure than freedom. Twain imagines freedom in these books more as a resistance to various kinds of incarceration than as a state of being to be explored and affirmed in itself. Almost all the adults are agents of confinement—schoolmasters, ministers, and repressive spinsters and widows. The few who resist are deviants, drunks, criminals, con men, and the racially inferior. This is not to deny that there are moments of play and delight in the idyllic or romantically thrilling natural world, but even these are more reactive than self-affirming, self-perpetuating, or expanding, and, in any case, they are attainable only briefly, fleetingly, by boys. So the books are deeply and memorably colored by nostalgia for a childhood paradise lost. American freedom is only possible for boys at play.

But in the notoriously problematic final chapters of *Adventures of Huckleberry Finn*, we discover a Tom Sawyer so obsessed with European literary conventions of prisoner escapes (modeled not on the melancholy, moralistic American kitsch that Twain always gleefully lampoons but on Dumas's French swashbucklers—not even on the English Robin Hood stories that had figured in *Tom Sawyer*) that he not only prolongs the slave's confinement—keeping him in chains and demanding foul food, infestations of rats, and messages in blood—but in fact jeopardizes the entire effort of escape by leaving anonymous notes betraying it. Moreover, in an especially cruel twist, it turns out that Tom has known that the slave had been granted his freedom long before. Tom is so captivated by the rules and rituals of adult culture that he has become complicit in its injustice. His obsessive conventionality confines, imperils, indeed enslaves. At the end of the book, the free American hero has become a narcissistic jailer, and all of American society, a corrupt jail. At first this seems to suggest that even Tom must be left behind, that only the westward-moving solitary Huck can be free. He must escape civilization and "light out for the Territory,"[3] but on closer reading even this seems problematic since Huck expects to be joined in the near future by Tom and the newly freed Jim (suddenly more interested in the boys' fun and games than in joining and freeing his wife and children) so they can pursue new adventures among the Indians. And in fact Twain began this sequel but never completed it.

Still, the famously labored comedy of Tom's rules of escape (or "evasion" as he styles it, following Dumas's *The Count of Monte Cristo*)—which has been universally deplored, except by those critics, such as T. S. Eliot and Lionel Trilling, who have chosen to finesse it—is not so purposeless or careless as it may at first appear.[4] It does serve to dramatize Tom's limited vision and essential complicity in slavery. The prevailing literary style of the concluding chapters becomes closer to Tom's conventional bookish idiom than to Huck's spontaneous local speech. Tom—the charming epitome of small-town juvenile gumption in the first novel—has become ever more a creature of his culture, indeed, almost an adult (which his romance with Becky Thatcher had anticipated), and the results are utterly disastrous. Jim's freedom may be finally ensured, but Huck must try to escape.

What I'm suggesting is that Twain was driven to break the form and style of the book, to upstage Huck, to encumber the narrative with apparently frivolous literary satire, to transform Tom into an unsympathetic snob and Huck into his helpless lackey (straining the reader's patience to its utmost limit) in order to establish and underscore the contrast between two types of boy, two types of literary style (bookish and demotic), between false and true freedom—to force the reader to experience how comedy and narrative frustration can divert attention from the larger, darker theme of collaboration in slavery. The only—intrinsically insoluble—problem in this most generous interpretation is whether the many different kinds of evasion in the last twelve chapters are the result of authorial design (however flawed) or self-deception or bad faith.

In any case, Huck, in fact, even at the end, is hardly free. Although decades of commentary have praised him as the living essence of American freedom and moral heroism, some critics (including Perry Miller, W. H. Auden, Toni Morrison, Jane Smiley, and Jonathan Arac) have demurred. They argue, as would I, that Huck's freedom (and racial tolerance) is sporadic, less creative or self-expressive than reactive to social norms, primarily a regressive and verbal (rather than political) act, and always secured by his considerable trust fund arising from the treasure discovered in the labyrinth in the first novel. For Twain, there's no way out, after all, besides talk. That's the only treasure that sustains the memory of American possibility: a boy's colloquial voice, an aesthetic echo of a lost political and moral ideal.

TOM SAWYER

Tom Sawyer begins not with the town or the river, and not even in the narrator's voice, but with an abrupt cry.

"TOM!"
No answer.
"TOM!"

No answer.

"What's gone with that boy, I wonder. You TOM!"

No answer.

The old lady pulled her spectacles down and looked over them, about the room; then she put them up and looked out under them. She seldom or ever looked *through* them for so small a thing as a boy; they were her state pair, the pride of her heart, and were built for "style," not service;—she could have seen through a pair of stove lids just as well. She looked perplexed for a moment, and then said, not fiercely, but still loud enough for the furniture to hear:

"Well, I lay if I get hold of you I'll—"

She did not finish, for by this time she was bending down and punching under the bed with the broom—and so she needed breath to punctuate the punches with. She resurrected nothing but the cat.

(1)

The novel begins with a summons—an adult is calling a boy's name—but the call is unanswered, ignored, rejected, defied. The very first word of the book is the hero's name; the first action is a vain, ineffectual old lady's attempt to control him, to threaten him. A boy is "a small thing," but this adult can't see him because her eyes are weak and her glasses "built for 'style,' not service." That is, a cultural artifact designed to empower the aging body is used as a theatrical prop, a deluded status symbol. The opposition or conflict of "style" and "service" will, in fact, turn out to be a major theme in both this book and its successor.

So we open with a staccato call and a fragmentary response from the narrator—"no answer." Neither can be sustained. The woman's abrupt verbal gestures function like the "punches" of her broom, and soon she's short of breath. The first action of the book dramatizes adult society's vain attempt—in words and physical gestures embodied in the rapidly changing movement of the omniscient narrator's prose—to capture and control a boy. So the boy is defined, first of all, as one who has escaped an old lady's domain. It quickly turns out that our hero, the archetypal all-American small-town boy, has been hiding in the closet eating jam—a regressive retreat. Throughout the novel he will be scrambling over fences, squirming through windows, and at the end he will discover treasure at the bottom of a cave. But eating jam in a closet is where he begins. Likewise, he will soon prove himself a master of the verbal arts, but his first word is just "nothing." He negates.

There is one especially conspicuous phrase in these first few lines: "She resurrected nothing but the cat." This is Twain's familiar American anti-clericalism, his cracker-barrel atheism, a cosmopolitan jibe at small-town religion. But in *Tom Sawyer* the cat is a more powerful symbol than Jesus, and Tom himself is a kind of cat. Cats figure throughout the novel as totemic figures, the animal spirit of free boyhood. When we first encounter Tom's alter ego, Huckleberry Finn, he is holding his sacred object, a dead cat; the boys' secret signal for escape into night adventures is the meowing of cats. As for "resurrected," both novels are famous for the boys' various risings from the dead. In *Tom Sawyer* the boys even attend their own funerals; Tom and Becky spend three nights in the cave before they climb out; and *Huckleberry Finn* is drenched in death and resurrection imagery.

From the first pages of the earlier novel, Tom embodies virtuosic energy. He is not like the "Model Boy of the village," the conventional genteel paradigm of feminized respectability that he "loathes," but for Twain he is another, grander model of boy: "Within two minutes, or even less, he had forgotten all his troubles. Not because his troubles were one whit less heavy and bitter to him than a man's are to a man, but because a new and powerful interest bore them down and drove them out of his mind for the time—just as men's misfortunes are forgotten in the excitement of new enterprises." Note the economic expansionism implied by "new enterprises"; Tom is engaged not merely in play but in growth and discovery. And what is discovered is, in fact, exultant art and harmony with nature—both learned from a black man: "This new interest was a valued novelty in whistling, which he had just acquired from a negro [*sic*], and he was suffering to practice it undisturbed. It consisted in a peculiar bird-like turn, a sort of liquid warble, produced by touching the tongue to the roof of the mouth at short intervals in the midst of the music—the reader probably remembers how to do it if he has ever been a boy." This last is one of the few direct addresses from author to reader and is clearly driven by a desire to establish the universality of the powers of boyhood (not girlhood, of course).

The paragraph continues by establishing connections between these virtuosic cultural skills and natural, indeed, divine harmonies: "Diligence and attention soon gave him the knack of it, and he strode down the street with his mouth full of harmony and his soul full of gratitude." And the paragraph ends with an even larger claim: "He felt much as an astronomer feels who has discovered a new planet. No doubt, as far as strong, deep, unalloyed pleasure is concerned, the advantage was with the boy, not the astronomer" (5).

In this, pleasure confirms the new fullness of authentic being that the act of discovery brings, and the literary allusion that sounds behind the reference to the astronomer confirms the heroic and romantic scale of Tom's achievement. It is Keats's "On First Looking into Chapman's Homer" that echoes here: Keats writes that when he first read Chapman's translation of Homer, "Then felt I like some watcher of the skies / When a new planet swims into his ken." But Keats immediately enlarges the comparison by extending it from science to heroic discovery: "Or like stout Cortez when with eagle eyes / He star'd at the Pacific—and all his men / Look'd at each other with a wild surmise— / Silent, upon a peak in Darien."[5] By this echo Twain is calling upon an extremely familiar English romantic poem to establish the scale of Tom's achievement and to connect it to scientific progress and the heroic explorations of a bold conquistador. Tom's new powers reconcile nature and culture, past and present, the old world and the new, science, physical adventure, and art. And all learned from a black man—as ever the secret source of American cultural strength, as Twain famously explores in *Huckleberry Finn*.

Another example of boyhood virtuosity has become the most iconic sequence in the entire novel, the fence-painting scene in which "the far-reaching continent of unwhitewashed fence" (10) becomes the field of artistic and social conquest. Tom begins his attempt to escape his task by bribing a childlike black slave who comes "skipping out at the gate with a tin pail, and singing 'Buffalo Gals'" (10–11), but Tom soon realizes that by comporting himself with the absorption and critical discrimination of an artist, he can seduce one boy into painting some of the fence for him. And, of course, other boys soon follow and offer Tom "treasures" to let them paint for him. Tom's skill is clearly social and psychological here, but the achievement is played out upon an aesthetic, cultural field: he converts a chore into a work of art.

Tom's art is both visual and verbal. It transforms the maintenance of a social and physical barrier into a game and the fence itself into a decoration. In the large imagistic structure of the novel, the fence and the cave are the complementary sites of Tom's heroic virtuosity. The fence is a bright, two-dimensional social enclosure; the cave is a dark, three-dimensional, natural labyrinth. Tom triumphs in both arenas, as an artist and comic trickster in the first and as explorer and romantic savior in the second.

So in the first novel Tom epitomizes a vibrant harmony between nature and culture. He is a small-town Missouri Odysseus, ever cunning, inventive, able to defeat his rivals, responsive to the lures of romance both sexual (with Becky Thatcher, however muted) and adventurous, as in the excursion to Jackson's Island, where he plays at being a pirate ("the Black Avenger of the Spanish Main" [65]), and in the exploration and escape from McDougal's cave, which he associates with a career as a Robin Hood. The imagery of the cave, of course, also suggests the myth of Theseus and the Minotaur as well as Jesus' resurrection.

But we should note how Tom's harmony of nature and culture rebukes the official, conventional culture of the town. Tom is relentlessly literary, of course, but the English swashbuckling models he invokes are very different from those of provincial America. For example, in the description of the climactic "Examination Evening" ceremony marking the end of the school year, Twain, the ferocious literary and cultural critic, lets fly at everything that the figure of Tom and the literary style of the novel are meant to oppose:

> A prevalent feature in these compositions was a nursed and petted melancholy; another was a wasteful and opulent gush of 'fine language;' another was a tendency to lug in by the ears particular prized words and phrases until they were worn entirely out; and a peculiarity that conspicuously marked and marred them was the inveterate and intolerable sermon that wagged its crippled tail at the end of each and every one of them. No matter what the subject might be, a brain-racking effort was made to squirm it into some aspect or other that the moral and religious mind could contemplate with edification. The glaring insincerity of these sermons was not sufficient to compass the banishment of the fashion from the schools, and it is not sufficient to-day; it never will be sufficient while the world stands, perhaps. . . . But enough of this. Homely truth is unpalatable.
>
> (156)

Just how "homely" the truth must be will be explored even further when Twain invents the very different literary style of *Huckleberry Finn*.

The "school-girl pattern" is what Tom resists. Its repression extends to the realm of the body, for when Tom is dressed for Sunday school, his natural shape is encased and distorted; he is "improved and uncomfortable" (29), "straight and pretty" (32). He is praised as "a good boy. Fine boy. Fine, manly little fellow" (36) by the eunuchs that rule the school, and so it's hardly accidental that when asked to name Jesus' first two disciples, he blurts out instead David and Goliath, a youthful, diminutive Old Testament warrior and the giant he defeated.

Although misogyny and stereotypical sexist condescension mark Twain's descriptions of women and girls, part of Tom's education lies in the growth of his responses to Becky Thatcher and in his final assumption of the role of the mythic hero who delivers her from darkness and death in the cave. Even before the climax, Tom's assumption of Becky's guilt in tearing an anatomy book (he startles her by looking over her shoulder at the frontispiece depicting "a human figure, stark naked" [148]) does indeed make him "noble." Looking at the anatomy book, they had been a childish Adam and Eve surprised by the guilty knowledge of the human body; he is then whipped by the teacher to atone for Becky's sin and so receives her blessing, which ends the chapter: "Tom, how *could* you be so noble!" (152).

The full scale of Tom's heroism is established by his victory over the terrifying Injun Joe, "that murderin' half-breed" (he's killed five men, we're told) (74, 241). Joe anticipates some of the frightening excesses of Pap, Huckleberry Finn's cruel father (Pap gets no more than a passing reference in *Tom Sawyer*). Like Pap, Joe is a violent drunk, but even more horrific. He murders a man and persuades a confederate that he, not Joe, is guilty of the crime. Joe later escapes from a crowded courtroom, reappears in town disguised as a "deef and dumb Spaniard" (187), finds a treasure chest, and hides it in his lair deep in McDougal's cave. Joe is Tom's fantasy pirate sprung to extraliterary life—a murderous, shape-shifting criminal with a hoard buried deep in a labyrinthine cave, a dragon figure out of German folklore, even a minotaur. Injun Joe's asocial, male ferocity is clearly even more threatening to Tom than feminized respectability.

It is true that Twain permits Injun Joe some Satanic pride, for example, when he declares he is bent upon revenge for being "horsewhipped . . . like a nigger!" when he had begged for food (208). But Joe's rage at the Widow Douglas conveys a misogynistic rhetorical glee that suggests the narrator himself is running out of control: Joe wants to mutilate the widow with a knife: "When you want to get revenge on a woman you don't kill her—bosh! you go for her looks. You slit her nostrils—you notch her ears, like a sow's!" (208). This outburst of rage by a humiliated, starving, half-breed murderer lets slip a note of deeper rage at feminine vanity and the female body.

But for all the cartoonish, overdetermined melodrama of Joe's villainy, his death produces a surprising change of tone in the narrator. Joe has personified the dangers of miscegenation and true (not literary) male criminality, but he is finally described as a "wretch," "captive," and "poor unfortunate" (238–39). Injun Joe's rejection of society has gone so far that he must die alone, of starvation, eating bats and candle wax and drinking drops of water collected from a dripping stalagmite. Joe expires at the very edge of the cave, just behind the mighty wooden door that has been sealed to contain the dangerous realm. And his one defining cultural artifact, his bowie knife, lies broken. In a particularly prescient twist, Twain describes how Injun Joe has become a cultural commodity—the stone cup in which he caught his last drops of water is now a tourist attraction. The Gothic villain has suddenly become pathetic, his lost powers a rebuke to toothless contemporary commercialism.

HUCKLEBERRY FINN'S FIRST INCARNATION

But there is, of course, yet another alternative to Injun Joe, another misfit, another kind of boy for Tom to consider: Huckleberry Finn. While Joe is described as "the bloody-minded outcast" (238), Huck is "the romantic outcast" (49). In *Tom Sawyer* Huck is portrayed as a credulous innocent in cast-off rags—a much simpler and smaller figure than he was to become when he begins to tell his story himself. In the first book the narrator is most anxious to pass an explicit diminishing judgment on Huck from his very first appearance: "Shortly Tom came upon the juvenile pariah of the village, Huckleberry Finn, son of the town drunkard. Huckleberry was cordially hated and dreaded by all the mothers of the town, because he was idle, and lawless, and vulgar and bad—and because their children admired him so, and delighted in his forbidden society, and wished they dared to be like him" (47–48). As that third sentence runs on, one feels the narrator discovering the antinomian possibilities of the character. "Tom was like the rest of the respectable boys," Twain continues, thus labeling Tom with a particularly problematic adjective, "in that he envied Huckleberry his gaudy outcast condition, and was under strict orders not to play with him. So he played with him every time he got a chance" (48).

Huckleberry's costume, in this first description, suggests splendid deviance, the witty appropriation and distortion of respectable maturity: "Huckleberry was always dressed in the cast-off clothes of full-grown men, and they were in perennial bloom and fluttering with rags. His hat was a vast ruin with a wide crescent lopped out of its brim; his coat, when he wore one, hung nearly to his heels and had the rearward buttons far down the back; but one suspender supported his trousers; the seat of the trousers bagged low and contained nothing; the fringed legs dragged in the dirt when not rolled up" (48). This costume is at once clownish and shabby-genteel in ways that recall the Artful Dodger and anticipate tramps from Chaplin to Beckett.

Twain then animates this clothes horse:

> Huckleberry came and went, at his own free will. He slept on doorsteps in fine weather and in empty hogsheads in wet; he did not have to go to school or to church, or call any being master or obey anybody; he could go fishing or swimming when and where he chose, and stay as long as it suited him; nobody forbade him to fight; he could sit up as late as he pleased; he was always the first boy that went barefoot in the spring and the last to resume leather in the fall; he never had to wash, nor put on clean clothes; he could swear wonderfully. In a word, everything that goes to make life precious, that boy had. So thought every harassed, hampered, respectable boy in St. Petersburg.
>
> (48)

And so, the cumulative rhythms and syntax suggest, does the narrator himself.

Having prepared the way with such increasingly extravagant description, the narrator then propels us into dialogue and scene. Here Huck acquires a grand new label; he is not simply "son of the town drunkard" anymore:

> Tom hailed the romantic outcast:
> "Hello, Huckleberry!"
> "Hello yourself, and see how you like it."
> "What's that you got?"
> "Dead cat."
>
> (49)

As we've noted above, the cat is Huckleberry's totemic animal, useful for folkloric magic rites (removing warts), clutched like a toddler's transitional object, and serving in its grotesque but powerful magic to alert us to the Gothic graveyard and drunken criminal world that Huck can negotiate and eventually master (as Tom will later master the cave). It is through meowing, of course, that the boys signal to each other and begin their adventures.

Some limits on Huckleberry are worth noting, however: Tom "did not care to have Huck's company in public places" (195). Huck is a solitary animal, unfit for town life. Indeed, his only friend seems to be Tom. The narrator also explicitly declares Huck has a "slow mind" (248). He's illiterate, ignorant, and intimidated by Tom's cultural expertise: he is "filled with admiration of Tom's facility in writing, and the sublimity of his language" (80). He may be comic, earthy, Sancho Panza–esque in his physicality and low dialect, but he must be contained by Tom's larger quixotic vision of history, civilization, playful idealistic robbery, and occasional playful deviance. Despite his identification as the "romantic outcast," Huck has no connection to the world of romance, neither chivalry nor courtly love (as Tom has with Becky Thatcher), and this in *Tom Sawyer* is implicitly a limitation. To be without culture is to be less human.

The town and the countryside are portrayed as a sunny, summer, pastoral paradise or (occasionally in thunderstorms) a thrilling romantic spectacle. Tom frequently attempts to impose garbled cultural or literary conventions (or rules of magic) on the boys' ostensibly natural life. Much of the comedy of *Tom Sawyer* arises from misapplied, misunderstood literary conventions about colorful social deviants: pirates and thieves. School may be a useless confining social ritual, but much of Tom's play involves emulating social and cultural rituals as well. At one point Tom imagines various roles and identities that he thinks might provide perpetual freedom (clown, soldier, Indian, pirate, robber), but by the end of the novel he recommends robbers for quite snobbish reasons: robbers are "more high-toned than what a pirate is—as a general thing. In most countries they're awful high up in the nobility—dukes and such" (258). (There are dukes and kings of a different sort in *Huckleberry Finn.*) To be a robber—Robin Hood—is to be a civilized deviant, more dependent on European literary conventions than those provincial American ones. Tom's emotional life is also tied to conventional society. He may run off to the wilderness of Jackson's Island, but he soon becomes homesick for Aunt Polly and sneaks back into town and is also drawn to romance with Becky Thatcher.

Twain's portrait of Huck in the concluding chapter of *Tom Sawyer* proves to be a simpler version of the ending of *Huckleberry Finn*:

> Huck Finn's wealth and the fact that he was now under the widow Douglas's protection, introduced him into society—no, dragged him into it, hurled him into it—and his sufferings were almost more than he could bear. The widow's servants kept him clean and neat, combed and brushed, and they bedded him nightly in unsympathetic sheets that had not one little spot or stain which he could press to his heart and know for a friend. He had to eat with a knife and fork; he had to use napkin, cup and plate; he had to learn his book, he had to go to church; he had to talk so properly that speech was become insipid in his mouth; whithersoever he turned, the bars and shackles of civilization shut him in and bound him hand and foot.
>
> (255)

The imagery is both Rousseau's ("Man is born free, and everywhere he is in chains") and Wordsworth's ("shades of the prison-house").

Huck escapes and people drag the river for his body (as had happened before and will happen again in the second novel), but "Tom Sawyer wisely went poking among some old empty hogsheads down behind the abandoned slaughter-house, and in one of them he found the refugee. Huck had slept there; he had just breakfasted upon some stolen odds and ends of food, and was lying off, now, in comfort with his pipe. He was unkempt, uncombed, and clad in the same old ruin of rags that had made him picturesque in the days when he was free and happy" (256). The conventionality and condescension of "picturesque" seriously limits how much of a noble savage Huck really is, of course. He has become no more than a bit of local color.

Discovered by Tom, Huck embarks upon a justificatory soliloquy:

> "It's awful to be tied up so. . . . No, Tom, I won't be rich, and I won't live in them cussed smothery houses. I like the woods, and the river, and hogsheads, and I'll stick to 'em, too. Blame it all! just as we'd got guns, and a cave, and all just fixed to rob, here this dern foolishness has got to come up and spile it all!"
>
> Tom saw his opportunity—
>
> "Lookyhere, Huck, being rich ain't going to keep me back from turning robber."
>
> (257–58)

So, in no time flat, in this final dialogue between them, the rhetorician of the whitewashed fence persuades Huck to go back to the Widow

Douglas in order to be permitted to join Tom Sawyer's Gang. Huck rejects the life of solitary tramp for the countercultural community of Tom's literary playing at robber gangs. And, of course, they risk nothing in their now make-believe rebellion, for they're living off the interest of $12,000 of buried treasure invested, we've learned, at 6 percent. They've become fine examples of radical chic *avant la lettre*, compromised, theatricalized romantics with trust funds to fall back upon.

This harsh judgment on these characters at their very last appearance in *Tom Sawyer* is stimulated, in part, by the overt theatricality of Huck's soliloquy—it's all stage effects, quite different in diction and rhythm from the tighter, sharper colloquialism of most of Huck's words earlier in the novel. The odd diction in these final pages even extends to Tom calling Huck "old chap" and Huck expostulating "that's gay—that's mighty gay, Tom, I tell you" (259). They sound like English schoolboys. A very bad sign indeed.

So the novel that began with a boy defying an old maid ends with another, much more rebellious boy eagerly returning to the care of an old widow: "I'll stick to the widder till I rot, Tom; and if I git to be a reglar ripper of a robber, and everybody talking 'bout it, I reckon she'll be proud she snaked me in out of the wet" (259). The emphasis falls upon the widow's approval and the community's gossip and upon Huck's fear of a solitary life unsheltered from the rain or the river that threatens to drown him. Better to be "snaked in" from the natural world than to be a dead cat, after all. Tom and Huck have capitulated to small-town norms; their compromises are portrayed as necessary maturity, socialization. These embodiments of American freedom must shrink to preserve the remnants of boyish glee. Shades of the prison house are to be accepted as unavoidable conditions of life. How different things will be at the end of the second novel where Huck announces that he'll "light out for the Territory" to escape "sivilization" and its discontents.

HUCKLEBERRY FINN'S OWN STORY

While containing a Satanic half-breed (a murderous minotaur in his cave) and reestablishing small-town order is the essential, defining, heroic task for Tom Sawyer in the first novel, the liberation of a beneficent, sometimes fatherly black slave is the essential task for Huck Finn in the second. But Huck's task is compromised when the more socially and educationally dominant Tom intervenes and insists that it conform to European literary precedents. The human reality of the slave's existence—his physical, emotional, and social misery—is subordinated to a cultural charade that serves nothing but Tom's narcissism. The process of freeing the slave is no more than a pretext for a declaration of cultural dependence. As ever, the slave is a useful object.

The relationship among Huck, Tom, and Jim is defined early in the novel and foreshadows what is to come. In Huck's preamble to the narrative, he emphasizes that, at the end of the previous book, Tom was the agent of his return to Widow Douglas's repressive realm and that the most disturbing aspect of his newly respectable life is not the absurdities of etiquette, spelling drills, or Bible lessons (his reference to the story of "Moses and the Bulrushers" [14] anticipates many themes, of course) but feeling "lonesome" (16) (a key word throughout the novel) and a superstitious, melodramatic fear of death. What delivers Huck from lonesomeness and fear is Tom's meowing through the window—Tom awaits him in the realm of night to lead him to adventures. But Tom's assistance in Huck's escape out the window (which echoes Tom's escape from Aunt Polly in the opening pages of *Tom Sawyer*) is predicated on Tom's own conception of what adventures are, and the first adventure turns out to be the manipulation of a black slave, "Miss Watson's big nigger, named Jim" (18).

As the boys sneak across the yard in the dark, Jim hears Huck trip over a root and calls out, "Who dah?" He then elaborates: "Say—who is you? Whar is you?" (18) and in effect demands that our heroes define and declare themselves, as they will in their relationship to him throughout the novel. Here they are silent, hiding. Jim then falls asleep and they crawl away, but "Tom whispered to me and wanted to tie Jim to the tree for fun; but I said no; he might wake and make a disturbance, and then they'd find out I warn't in. . . . I was in a sweat to get away; but nothing would do Tom but he must crawl to where Jim was, on his hands and knees, and play something on him. I waited, and it seemed a good while; everything was so still and lonesome" (19).

This is remarkably skillful. We see Tom's eagerness to have "fun" by tying the slave to a tree (he'll have even more fun with the escape at the end of the novel); we see Huck's objection to this not on grounds of morality but from a more realistic grasp of the practical consequences than Tom has; and we see that, despite Tom's now problematic companionship, Huck is still "lonesome." Finally, to emphasize further the contrast between the boys, Twain has Tom go back and slip "Jim's hat off his head and [hang] it on a limb right over him" (19). This is followed by a long divertissement describing how Jim later attributes this to witches and spins a huge, magical narrative that turns him into a celebrity: "Niggers would come miles to hear Jim tell about it, and he was more looked up to than any nigger in that country. . . . Jim was most ruined, for a servant, because he got so stuck up on account of having seen the devil and been rode by witches" (19).

So, at first blush, despite the egregiously racist comedy about dumb "niggers," their colorful lingo, and their ignorant superstitious ways, Tom has inadvertently empowered Jim, turned him into a teller of magical tales, even made him, in his new self-esteem, "ruined for a servant." But, in fact, the comic emphasis and the verb "ruined" (which is not unambiguously ironic in this context) convey that Tom has miscalculated the social consequences of his fun. And we cannot overlook the image of Jim's hat hanging on a limb right over him. It conveys a threat that he may be lynched, after all (if not crucified). This suggests that the boys, and especially Tom, are prepared to turn Jim into a martyr for their own amusement and self-esteem, which, of course, they will do at the end of the book.

BETRAYALS

Few passages in American literature have occasioned more admiring, even adulatory comment than Huck's crisis of conscience in chapter 31 when he proclaims that rather than betray Jim, "All right, then, I'll *go* to hell" (223). But before we consider this, it's necessary to examine the two earlier instances where Huck does indeed betray Jim. The boy hero of American freedom turns out to be anxiously ambivalent toward the fatherly slave, after all.

The first of these betrayals, when Jim is bitten by a rattlesnake in chapter 10, is very complexly motivated. On one level it springs from Huck's established fear of his father, Pap, and Huck's mixed feelings about Jim's fatherly and ostensibly prophetic powers. In chapter 4, where Jim appears in the book for the second time, Huck consults him and his all-knowing magic hairball to find out what Huck's father is planning to do and especially whether he is going to stay in the vicinity. Jim speaks in the voice of the hairball and declares that while it's impossible to say what Pap will do, Huck should "keep 'way fum de water as much as you kin, en don't run no resk, 'kase it's down in de bills [written like an invoice in the book of fate] dat you's gwyne to git hung" (30). The next sentence reports that Pap is waiting for Huck in his room that very night. Jim cannot protect Huck from Pap, after all.

Jim's warning about water also seems mistaken. After several chapters Huck escapes from Pap and the town by faking his own death and floating down the river to take refuge on Jackson's Island. After three days alone, he discovers that Jim, too, has escaped by water to the island, "I was ever so glad to see Jim. I warn't lonesome, now" (53). When the river rises and floods the island, they paddle about in a miniature ark in a peaceable kingdom of tamed animals—all of which suggests further deliverance, not death by water. They discover a dead man in a frame house that floats down the river (Jim tells Huck "Come in . . . but doan' look at his face—it's too gashly") and retrieve from it a hoard of useful tools for survival, somewhat on the model of Robinson Crusoe and his wrecked ship. As they row away from the house of death (as it's come to be called), Huck is careful to have Jim lie "down in the canoe and cover up with the quilt, because if he set up, people could tell he was a nigger a good ways off." The image doubles the dead body they just found and echoes Huck's earlier virtuoso fabrication of his own death by drowning. The chapter ends with a major declaration of their close, collaborative, indeed, familial relationship: "We got home all safe" (62)

But the next morning Huck is troubled by thoughts of the dead man and by Jim's refusal to discuss it. In his frustration he tells Jim that his prophesies of coming bad luck are false. Huck had touched a snakeskin "day before yesterday" (before the discovery of the house) and yet "we've raked in all this truck and eight dollars besides. I wish we could have some bad luck like this every day, Jim." To which Jim, at his most paternal, replies "Never you mind, honey, never you mind. Don't you git too peart. It's a-comin'. Mind I tell you, it's a-comin." And the next line runs, "It did come, too." Three days later Huck kills a rattlesnake and "curled him up on the foot of Jim's blanket, ever so natural, thinking there'd be some fun when Jim found him there" (63). We immediately remember it was Tom who wanted to have some "fun" with Jim by tying him to a tree or hanging his hat on a limb. Here Huck wants to escape his sense of dependency, to seize control or at least threaten and humiliate Jim (by mocking Jim's fear of death), but Huck has forgotten that a dead snake's mate "always comes there and curls around it" and the rattlesnake bites

Jim on the heel. Jim suffers for "four days and nights" (drinking whisky and going "out of his head" like Huck's Pap [64]). Huck never confesses what he's done, and Jim recovers and says "he reckoned I would believe him next time" and that "handling a snake-skin was such awful bad luck that maybe we hadn't got to the end of it yet" (64). True enough.

Huck's denial of his affectionate intimacy with Jim and his dependency on his fellow fugitive has nearly fatal results (at the very least, Jim is temporarily similar to drunken, bestial Pap). The snake's mate is more naturally loyal than Huck, who calls himself a "fool" to forget this. But Huck's deception turns out—at the end of the novel—to be less than Jim's, for the dead man in the floating house is Huck's father. Jim keeps this news to himself until "Chapter the Last" (the forty-third) in order to bind Huck to him—if Huck knew his father were dead he would not have to assist Jim's escape but be free to resume his life in town with full use of the dollar a day interest on his $6,000 hero's reward. This is the only instance of Jim's deceit, but (like so many crucial elements at the end of the novel) it is barely mentioned. And we never learn Huck's response to this world-altering retrospective revelation; no whiff of judgment is passed on Jim, either.

So here in the rattlesnake scene in chapter 10 Huck almost kills Jim in a self-comforting attempt to have "some fun." And Jim turns out to have fatherly powers of survival (more than Pap) and of prophecy, though as the novel proceeds, of course, the water of the river is as much an agent of deliverance as doom.

Although Huck never acknowledges remorse in this first instance of bad faith toward Jim, in the much more elaborately orchestrated second instance, in chapter 15, Huck's admission of guilt and his request for forgiveness are the climactic actions. Separated from Jim and the raft by a thick fog, Huck is terrified and "lonesome" once again. When he fortuitously rejoins the raft hours later and discovers Jim asleep, Huck immediately compensates for his hours of fear and sorrow and urgent dependency by declaring he never left the raft, that Jim was either drunk (as with the snake) or dreaming (as with the hat). Jim allows himself to be persuaded, attempts to interpret the dream (using his prophetic powers once more), but is abruptly mocked by Huck, who points to the evidence of their violent separation and his return ("leaves and rubbish on the raft, and the smashed oar"), and asks Jim, "What does *these* things stand for?" (95).

Jim's reply is overwhelmingly authoritative, emotionally, morally, and cognitively (a true interpretation, after all). His speech is among the most theatrically eloquent in the book, and Huck's reaction is crucial preparation for the celebrated crisis of conscience ("I'll *go* to hell") in chapter 31. Here in chapter 15 on the wooden stage of the raft, Twain carefully constructs a theatrical ceremony:

> Jim looked at the trash, and then looked at me, and back at the trash again . . . he looked at me steady, without ever smiling, and says:
>
> "What do dey stan' for? I's gwyne to tell you. When I got all wore out wid work, en wid de callin' for you, en went to sleep, my heart wuz mos' broke bekase you wuz los', en I didn' k'yer no mo' what become er me en de raf'. En when I wake up en fine you back agin, all safe en soun', de tears come en I could a got down on my knees en kiss' yo' foot I's so thankful. En all you wuz thinkin 'bout wuz how you could make a fool uv ole Jim wid a lie. Dat truck dah is *trash*; en trash is what people is dat puts dirt on de head er dey fren's en makes 'em ashamed."
>
> Then he got up slow, and walked to the wigwam, and went in there, without saying anything but that. But that was enough. It made me feel so mean I could almost kissed *his* foot to get him to take it back.
>
> It was fifteen minutes before I could work myself up to go and humble myself to a nigger—but I done it, and I warn't ever sorry for it afterwards, neither. I didn't do him no more mean tricks, and I wouldn't done that one if I'd a knowed it would make him feel that way.

(95)

The trash that confirms their separation in the fog and Huck's mockery of their relationship is both natural (leaves) and cultural (the oar that guides the vehicle of their survival and deliverance). The trash becomes a metaphor for Huck's moral identity—with a clear allusion to Huck as "white trash." Jim's solemn withdrawal into the wigwam situates him in the habitation he built for them both and suggests the action of a regal sachem, a father indeed. But the double reference to kissing feet alludes to loyalty, slavery, and biblical texts. In Luke, chapter 7, Jesus forgives a sinful woman who washes his feet with tears, wipes them with her hair, kisses them, and anoints them with oil. Jesus rebukes the disapproving Pharisee Simon with the words, "Her sins, which are many, are forgiven; for she loved much: but to whom little is forgiven, the same loveth little. And he said unto her, Thy sins are forgiven . . . thy faith has saved thee; go in peace" (Luke 7:47–50). The grandeur of these allusions makes Huck's phrase "mean tricks" deliberately inadequate to the moral and personal offence. Nevertheless, Huck has now gained enlarging and maturing knowledge, and his sins are forgiven by the prophetic Jim. The crucially limiting aspect of this is that we never see the actual scene or hear the dialogue of humbling and forgiveness. Huck veils himself from the full gaze of the reader, or Twain cannot construct the shameful exchange between races and generations in which a black father absolves a white son.

In any case, after humbling himself, Huck again starts to pull away from Jim almost immediately. As Jim becomes "all over trembly and feverish to be so close to freedom," Huck is "scorched" by his conscience, "so miserable I most wished I was dead" as he realizes he's complicit in Jim's escape. And when Jim tells him he plans to work to buy his wife and buy or steal his two children, Huck "most froze. . . . Here was this nigger which I had as good as helped to run away, coming right out flat-footed and saying he would steal his children—children that belonged to a man I didn't even know; a man that hadn't ever done me no harm. I was sorry to hear Jim say that, it was such a lowering of him." Huck resolves to betray him. As he paddles away from the raft ostensibly to determine if they're close to Cairo and freedom, Jim calls out his warmest moral praise: "I's a free man, en I couldn't ever ben free ef it hadn't ben for Huck; Huck done it. Jim won't ever forgit you, Huck; you's de bes' fren' Jim's ever had; en you's de *only* fren' ole Jim's got now. . . . Dah you goes, de ole true Huck; de on'y white genlman dat ever kep' his promise to old Jim." In response, Huck "just felt sick." He tries to tell two slave catchers he encounters about Jim, but "I warn't man enough—hadn't the spunk of a rabbit. I see I was weakening; so I just give up trying" (110–11). When he reflects on this later, Huck acknowledges that if he'd "done right and give Jim up" he'd feel no better than he does now that he's done wrong, and since "the wages [of sin] is just the same . . . I reckoned I wouldn't bother no more about it, but after this always do whichever come handiest at the time" (113).

What we see here is a more actively plotted and less psychologically elaborate crisis of conscience than the celebrated one to come in chapter 31. But here in chapter 16 the conflict is essentially the same: between the official public morality that supports slavery (internalized as "conscience") and the private feelings and promptings of personal loyalty, between unjust law and "naturally" moral spirit. The satire of Huck's disapproval of Jim's "lowering himself" to obey the presumptively natural law of aiding his wife and children condemns official morality for the reader but not for Huck. He can only seek emotional comfort and resolves to abandon any moral reasoning in the future and do whatever is expedient. He retreats into the realm of private feeling; the issue becomes personal not political; it's all a matter of self-interest, "whatever come handiest at the time."

The theme of loyalty is soon complicated. Huck and Jim are separated after a steamboat crashes into the raft, and we follow Huck into the grim world of the Grangerford and Shepherdson feud. These wealthy and respectable representatives of the civilization of the Mississippi shore grotesquely murder one another (even their children) in the name of family honor. Twain contrasts them to the secret community of slaves who reunite Huck and Jim and enable them to escape the deadly world of the town and shore to the vital world of the raft and the river: "I was powerful glad to get away from the feuds, and so was Jim to get away from the swamp [where he had hidden]. We said there warn't no home like a raft, after all. Other places do seem so cramped up and smothery, but a raft don't. You feel mighty free and easy and comfortable on a raft" (134).

This kind of declaration has become an American anthem, of course. But it presupposes a harmonious society of two and an entirely beneficent natural force supporting them, which, as Twain repeatedly emphasizes, the river is not. This is not to minimize the extraordinary beauty of the Mississippi sunrise scene that follows. In the course of two pages the harmony of the river (and its human traffic and shoreline activities, too) can even encompass "lonesomeness" (136). This is paradise regained: Huck and Jim here are what Lionel Trilling enthusiastically called "a family, a primitive community—and it is a community of saints."[6] Others have understandably described them as noble savages, and Leslie Fiedler famously identified them as the archetypically American loving duo of black man and white boy.[7] And yet this paradise is quickly lost. In just one more page, the King and the Duke will invade the scene and dominate much of the action for the next hundred pages until they're tarred and feathered and run out of town—and the book—in chapter 33.

FATHER FIGURES

Though Huck quickly recognizes that the King and the Duke are nothing but "liars . . . low-down humbugs and frauds," he keeps this to himself to "keep peace in the family." He never shares this with Jim; he just declares "it warn't no use to tell Jim, so I didn't tell him." Huck justifies this passivity toward the King and Duke and his new deceit of Jim by invoking the example of his father: "If I never learnt nothing else out of Pap, I learnt that the best way to get along with his kind of people is to let them have their own way" (142).

There are indeed many similarities between the con men and Pap—marginality, manipulative theatricality, amoral greed, drunkenness, and violence. Huck in his silence becomes complicit with them in part because Pap is also capable of extravagant, fraudulent self-presentation, as when he pretends to be a reformed drunk to the sentimental judge who takes him into his home as a repentant sinner. Pap can also deliver virtuoso drunken denunciations, as of the government and the "prowling, thieving, infernal, white-shirted free nigger" (40). And we must also remember that the very first instance in the book of the natural paradise achieved by two renegade men is the two months Huck and Pap share in the woods back in chapter 6: "It was kind of lazy and jolly, laying off comfortable all day, smoking and fishing, and no books nor study. . . . It was pretty good times up in the woods there, take it all around" (36–37). Of course, this breaks down as Pap beats him, locks him in the cabin for three days, suffers delirium tremens, and tries to kill him, which precipitates Huck's escape. But these patterns suggest that Huck's time with Jim has touched some relatively positive memories of Pap that are then intensified by the appearance of the King and the Duke. Drawn to them, however slightly, Huck pulls away from his surrogate father, Jim.

These echoes or memories of Pap also lie behind Huck's curious historical disquisition in chapter 23, when he tells Jim, "All kings is mostly rapscallions, as fur as I can make out. . . . You read about them once—you'll see" (168). What follows is a comically garbled English history lesson that suggests Huck needs to reaffirm his superiority, to distance himself from Jim at exactly the moment Jim has announced that he's suspicious of the King and Duke. Huck seems determined not only to establish his identity as a white man but also to mimic a bookish learning he has never before pretended to have. Indeed, Huck here becomes as close as he can to Tom Sawyer, with his historical obsessions and sense of "style."

This distancing from Jim and regressive identification with Pap and other fraudulent white men makes the conclusion of chapter 23 even more remarkable, for in it Huck must re-acknowledge Jim's humanity, which is epitomized by his love for his children: "I do believe he cared just as much for his people as white folks does for theirn. It don't seem natural, but I reckon it's so. He was often moaning and mourning, that way, nights, when he judged I was asleep. . . . He was a mighty good nigger, Jim was" (170). The last paragraph of the chapter is composed of Jim's set-piece narrative of loss and guilt that he'd once mistakenly punished his daughter for apparent disobedience that was the result of her being "deef en dumb" (170). Jim is torn by regret that he did not perceive his daughter's physical condition and, indeed, had beaten her for it—just as Jim is abused for a physical condition, his color, though he's as human as "white folks" and, unlike any other man in the book, a loving father, pointedly different from the physically and emotionally abusive Pap. These associated narratives suggest that Huck's affirmed racial prejudices are, in part, the result of his relationship with his father. And once again Jim's narrative function is to place Huck's moral, historical, and racial misconceptions in larger human context.

This is developed in the next chapter, which begins with Jim complaining that "it got mighty heavy and tiresome to him when he had to lay all day in the wigwam tied with the rope," so he wouldn't appear to be a fugitive. To remain free he must appear bound. The Duke then

> dressed Jim up in King Leer's outfit—it was a long curtain-calico gown, and a white horse-hair wig and whiskers; and then he took his theatre-paint and painted Jim's face and hands and ears and neck all over a dead dull solid blue, like a man that's been drownded nine days. Blamed if he wan't the horriblest looking outrage I ever see. Then the duke took and wrote out a sign on a shingle, so—*Sick Arab—but harmless when not out of his head*. And he nailed that shingle to a lath, and stood the lath up four or five foot in front of the wigwam. Jim was satisfied . . . the duke told him to make himself free and easy

but to jump around and howl like a wild beast if anyone comes by (171).

This comedy, too, is uncommonly rich in associations: At first Jim must be tied up to appear to be the fugitive slave he is, but he finds this disguise too "heavy and tiresome," which echoes Tom's wanting to tie him up in the first chapter and foreshadows the "evasion" in the last part of the book. The second disguise refers not only to the most tragic neglectful father in literature, King Lear (we've just heard of Jim's abuse of and guilt toward his daughter), but also to the recurrent threat of death by drowning (or the simulacrum of it, as in Huck's case). The second disguise also identifies Jim with the animalistic and obscene blue-painted king in the Royal Nonesuch scam. The Duke's instructions that Jim must jump around and howl recall Pap in the throes of his delirium tremens. And the final twist is that this black slave is labeled a dangerous demented Arab—protected by relabeling him as a member of a race not as conspicuously subject to slave laws. Jim is transformed into a grotesque object, a parody of fatherhood and a safely classified social and racial deviant. "Why, he didn't only look like he was dead," says Huck, "he looked considerable more than that"—like a demon (171). Later, when Huck finally gets back to the raft to be reunited with Jim after escaping from town, he is so frightened by the sight of Jim looking like "old King Leer and a drownded A-rab all in one" that he falls "overboard backwards" and Jim (in so many ways and once again) "fished me out" of the river (214–15).

But the King and Duke catch up to them, and in the "shabby village" of Pikesville, the King turns Jim in as a runaway slave "for forty dirty dollars" (219, 221). This separation and betrayal precipitates Huck's famous crisis in chapter 31.

HUCK'S CRISIS OF CONSCIENCE

"After all this long journey," it begins, . . . here was it all come to nothing, everything all busted up and ruined, because they could have the heart to serve Jim such a trick as that, and make him a slave again all his life, and among strangers, too" (221). Huck's separation from Jim prompts his identification with Jim's separation from his family and home. Huck reflects that it would be "a thousand times better for Jim to be a slave at home where his family was, as long as he'd *got* to be a slave." He will write to Tom Sawyer "and tell him to tell Miss Watson." The sentence structure emphasizes Huck's remove from direct action. He needs Tom's superior social and rhetorical skills but also wishes to hide behind him, and he wants to maintain his own freedom since he is presumably dead. But Huck immediately realizes this won't work. Miss Watson would be "mad and disgusted at [Jim's] rascality and ungratefulness for leaving her, and so she'd sell him straight down the river again." Or even "if she didn't, everybody naturally [thematically crucial word, of course] despises an ungrateful nigger," so Jim would soon "feel ornery and disgraced" (221).

The thought of Jim's shame prompts Huck's next thought: "And then think of *me!* It would get all around, that Huck Finn helped a nigger to get his freedom; and if I was ever to see anybody from that town again, I'd be ready to get down and lick his boots for shame" (222). This brilliantly alludes to Huck's wanting earlier to kiss Jim's foot in shame for deceiving him about their separation in the fog. Here his "conscience went to grinding me," and he feels "ornery," like Jim. But this fleeting identification with Jim in disgrace pushes Huck into the less vulnerable rhetoric of moral denunciation: "I was stealing a poor old woman's nigger that hadn't ever done me no harm" (222). The apparently ungrammatical reference of "that"—ostensibly to Miss Watson but in fact to Jim—enacts Huck's conflict: Miss Watson is anything but a "poor old woman" who never harmed Huck, and Jim certainly "hadn't ever done [Huck] no harm."

Moving further away from vulnerable feelings and memories of Jim, Huck begins to speak (as Jonathan Arac has shown) in the voices of a Sunday schoolteacher, a camp-meeting preacher, and a born-again revivalist witness.[8] He worries about "everlasting fire," tries to pray and "to quit being the kind of boy I was," but discovers "you can't pray a lie." So he writes a letter betraying Jim to Miss Watson, and "I felt good and all washed clean of sin for the first time I had ever felt so in my life." This is a false, social baptism unlike the natural one of the river, which he immediately begins to remember. The repetitions convey the process of thought and feeling: he "went on thinking. And got to thinking over our trip down the river; and I see Jim before me, all the time, in the day, and in the night-time, sometimes moonlight, sometimes storms, and we [the plural pronoun is the emotional and moral goal of the passage] a floating along, talking, and singing, and laughing." His memories become more specific; he recalls Jim's love and goodness and remembers the last time he almost betrayed him to the slave catchers near Cairo as Jim called out "I was the best friend old Jim ever had in the world, and the *only* one he's got now" (222–23).

Jim's words in Huck's mouth switch Huck back into the present predicament:

> And then I happened to look around, and see that paper. It was a close place. I took it up, and held it in my hand. I was trembling, because I'd got to decide, forever, betwixt two things, and I knowed it. I studied a minute, sort of holding my breath, and then says to myself: 'All right, then, I'll *go* to hell'—and tore it up. It was awful thoughts, and awful words, but they was said. And

I let them stay said; and never thought no more about reforming. I shoved the whole thing out of my head; and said I would take up wickedness again, which was in my line, being brung up to it, and the other warn't. And for a starter, I would go to work and steal Jim out of slavery again.

(223)

This is perhaps the most celebrated passage in American literature. Lionel Trilling in 1948 famously praised Huck's heroism here and attributed prophylactic powers—intellectual, moral, psychological, political, and cultural—to this scene: "No one who reads thoughtfully the dialectic of Huck's great moral crisis will ever again be wholly able to accept without some question and some irony the assumptions of the respectable morality by which he lives, nor will ever again be certain that what he considers the clear dictates of moral reason are not merely the engrained customary beliefs of his time and place."[9] Arac cites the historian and public intellectual Arthur Schlesinger Jr., who wrote in the *New York Times Book Review* that this is "the finest scene of the greatest of American novels" and said of "all right, then, I'll *go* to hell," "that, if I may say so, is what America is all about."[10] For Toni Morrison this is "Huck's ultimate act of love, in which he accepts the endangerment of his soul."[11]

But not all readers have agreed with this. For W. H. Auden, "what Huck does [here] is a pure act of moral improvisation. What he decides tells him nothing about what he should do on other occasions, or what other people should do on other occasions. . . . [There is no] sudden realization . . . that slavery [is] wrong."[12] The cultural historian Perry Miller was caustic: in 1885 "all could rejoice in this triumph of instinctive benevolence over the ancient formalities of a crude society and a crude theology—and congratulate themselves upon their sophistication."[13] Such diverse figures as Leo Marx, Jane Smiley, and Stuart Hutchinson also demurred. And Arac notes that as early as the first chapter Huck has declared his readiness to go to hell: Miss Watson "told me all about the bad place, and I said I wished I was there. . . . I couldn't see no advantage in going where she was going so I made up my mind I wouldn't try for it" (15–16).[14] Arac emphasizes how narrow the rhetorical and thematic focus of the passage in chapter 31 is: rather than drawing upon the discourse of abolitionist ministers and newspaper editors, of legal and political debate, of Fourth of July orations in praise of the Declaration of Independence and the equality of man, of Christian love and the Sermon on the

Mount, Twain confines Huck's soliloquy to a satire of religious cant and a private personal adjustment of feeling, emotional comfort.[15]

Twain himself acknowledged the centrality of this scene. In a notebook entry ten years later, he declared *Huckleberry Finn* to be "a book of mine where a sound heart & a deformed conscience come into collision & conscience suffers defeat."[16] Of course, no comment by an author can ever delimit the meaning of a text, particularly one as rich as this, but it is worth noticing how sentimental Twain's opposition is: The morally and socially "deformed conscience" is defeated by a familiar romantic and Victorian power: the "sound heart." Natural healthy human goodness can overcome the twisted internalized moralistic structure of a corrupt society. It's Dickens and water.

In fact, the passage is much more subtle. Huck identifies with Jim but then retreats from feelings of vulnerability by taking refuge in clichés and generalizations until a river of specific memories pours in and carries Huck to safety—not to any new ideas or opinions about slavery in general or Missouri slave society in particular but to enough emotional stability to defiantly identify himself with his Pap ("I would take up wickedness again, which was in my line, being brung up to it") and declare "I would go to work and steal Jim out of slavery again" (223).

TOM RETURNS

The only trouble is that Huck is almost immediately mistaken for Tom Sawyer by the Phelpses and, even worse, that Tom Sawyer himself appears and imposes himself on the book. In this famously problematic and vexing final section—from the middle of chapter 31 (Huck's crisis) to chapter 43, some seventy pages or one-quarter of the book—Twain uses the boys to explore the limits of American independence by deliberately frustrating comedy. For Toni Morrison, "in its structure, in the hell it puts its readers through at the end, the frontal debate it forces, it simulates and describes the parasitical nature of white freedom," which is not freedom at all.[17] By the end of the novel, Twain has constructed a valedictory to American freedom, black and white. There is no escape—not even for the boys and the runaway slave whose freedom they play around with. The novel becomes a tragicomic threnody to the American pursuit of happiness and liberty and justice for all. The concluding section examines through grotesque and often ostentatiously literary comedy how "shades of the prison-house" enclose the boys, not least because they carry the prison within them psychologically, morally, culturally. Even the ending ("lighting out for the Territory" to get away from "sivilization") perpetuates their bondage and seals their doom. And whether readers laugh or wince with aesthetic or moral or political frustration at the protracted comedy of the aptly named "evasion," all these reactions propel them to consider how ready they might be to use the slave and his predicament for their own pleasure or self-satisfaction, just as the boys are doing.

The final section begins as Huck hides the raft and the canoe, surveys the Phelpses' sawmill, and walks to town. But the first person he meets is the Duke (a criminal, as Huck is becoming), who tries to divert him from his search for Jim. Huck doubles back to the Phelpses'— the plantation is elaborately described with such thematically freighted terms as "lonesome and like everybody's dead and gone" (228). "Trusting to Providence to put the right words in my mouth" (229) (so much for going to hell!), Huck is greeted like a lost child, a member of the family, "cousin Tom." In one of the most notorious passages in the book, he attributes his delay to the steamboat "blow[ing] out a cylinder-head" and establishes his cultural bona fides by replying to Aunt Sally's "anybody hurt?" with "No'm. Killed a nigger." "Well, it's lucky," she replies, "because sometime people do get hurt" (230). There is not the slightest signal that Huck notes the racism of this exchange: it's impossible to tell if he is manipulating Sally by putting distance between him and any concern for "niggers," particularly runaway ones, or if he is just speaking reflexively (with nary a thought about Jim) to buy a little time to figure out "who I was" (231). It's entirely possible that Huck's cognitive dissonance about "niggers"—which we'll see much more of soon—is part of Twain's satirical point and a way of preparing us, though perhaps too ambiguously, for Huck's complicity in Tom's having "fun" with Jim's liberation.

But Twain's clear purpose in the Phelpses' misidentification of Huck as Tom Sawyer is to conflate the boy's identities. Huck experiences this assimilation into a respectable white family as a "joyful" event: "it was like being born again, I was so glad to find out who I was" (232). This rebaptism as Tom is the culmination of a narrative and thematic process that began in isolation (the crisis and solitary preparation of the raft and canoe), continued through confrontation with an all-too-familiar rogue who wants to gain by Jim's betrayal (the Duke here represents the road not taken), and now culminates in a reentry into conventional civilization and family structure. The only way in is to become Tom Sawyer, a "respectable" boy from a proper home. What we'll soon discover is that Huck is in fact more like Tom than he thinks—and eager to become even more so, submitting to Tom's personal and social domination, even to the extent of modifying and imperiling the mission to free Jim. For Huck, "being Tom Sawyer was easy and comfortable" (233).

Tom reappears after thirty chapters, some two hundred pages. When Huck intercepts Tom coming down the road, Tom's first words to Huck (whom he thought dead) are, "I hain't ever done you no harm" (234). Huck had used "harm" most recently in the midst of his crisis of conscience in reference to his obligations to both Miss Watson and Jim. Here Tom immediately becomes the third locus of moral duty and human possibility: not repressive convention or criminal rebellion but boyish "play." To establish his physical reality, Huck emphasizes "I hain't come back [as a ghost]—I hain't been *gone*." In order to convince Tom "I warn't ever murdered at all—I played it on them," Huck tells him, "You come in here and feel of me if you don't believe me," and this biblical echo assuages doubting Thomas. Huck calls his account of his escape from Pap "a grand adventure, and mysterious, and so it hit [Tom] where he lived." Having risen from the dead, Huck then declares his mission: "There's a nigger here that I'm trying to steal out of slavery—and his name is *Jim*—old Miss Watson's Jim." Tom replies, "'What? Why Jim is—' He stopped, and went to studying" (234–35). What we learn at the end of the book is that Tom is here deciding to withhold the information that Jim has already been freed by Miss Watson's will; he is concealing information as crucial to the plot as Jim's concealed knowledge that Pap is dead and thus no threat to Huck.

Huck perceives Tom's silence at this moment as disapproval: "'You'll say it's dirty, low-down business; but what if it is?—I'm low-down; and I'm agoing to steal him, and I want you to keep mum and not let on. Will you?' His eyes lit up, and he says: 'I'll *help* you steal him!' Well, I let go all holts, then, like I was shot [Tom will be shot later in the evasion]. It was the most astonishing speech I ever heard—and I'm bound to say Tom Sawyer fell, considerable, in my estimation. Only I couldn't believe it. Tom Sawyer a *nigger stealer!*" (235).

This establishes Huck's sense of Tom's superiority and respectability, however "lowered." Note how the rhythms and tone of Huck's voice take on the manner of a disapproving, genteel schoolmarm ("I'm bound to say Tom Sawyer fell, considerable, in my estimation"). It's also worth noting that Huck is right to be astonished because Tom—for all the make-believe he's about to perpetrate—is not, in fact, a "nigger stealer." He knows Jim is free. So Huck gets Tom right, after all: he's respectable, law-abiding, middle-class. He'd never steal a slave. Huck's eager affirmation here of Tom's position in the conventional social and moral hierarchy prepares us for Huck's passivity, complacency, and domination by Tom and his games. The boys' identities do begin to merge, but Tom will always be dominant.

Tom immediately perpetrates a double scam on the Phelpses. He claims to be a stranger and then abruptly "kisse[s] Aunt Sally right on the mouth" (237), and then justifies it by claiming to be his brother Sid Sawyer. Tom is here the trickster, even sexually, much older emotionally and socially than Huck. His trickery is altogether more sophisticated and apparently respectable (and boyish, presumably benign) than that of the King and Duke, who, for narrative convenience, are tarred and feathered and run out of town in a cameo reappearance. Just as the spectacle of Injun Joe in defeat aroused the narrator's pity, so the defeat of the "Royal Nonesuch rapscallions" stimulates Huck's: "they was all over tar and feathers, and didn't look like nothing in the world that was human—just looked like a couple of monstrous big soldier-plumes [this foreshadows the loony European theatricality of the coming evasion]. Well, it just made me sick to see it; and I was sorry for them poor pitiful rascals, it seemed like I couldn't ever feel any hardness against them any more in the world. It was a dreadful thing to see. Human beings *can* be awful cruel to one another" (239). Huck feels "ornery, and humble, and to blame, somehow—though *I* hadn't done nothing." He mistakes his sympathetic identification with the victims for the workings of the "yaller dog" of conscience. The chapter ends with Huck taking refuge from his perplexed feelings with the abrupt statement "Tom Sawyer he says the same"—to invoke Tom's authoritative closing of any debate about the nature of that social object called a "conscience" (240).

THE EVASION

Tom takes charge immediately, and the evasion itself will run some fifty pages, a fifth of the book. Throughout, it is Tom's rococo imagination that especially arouses Huck's admiration: "What a head for just a boy to have! If I had Tom Sawyer's head, I wouldn't trade it off to be a duke [but dukes are "rapscallions"] nor mate of a steamboat [one maliciously ran over the raft], nor clown in a circus [only this third profession has positive value, that of a genuine artist in the scheme of the book], nor nothing I can think of" (241). Tom objects to Huck's pragmatic plan of escape as "too blame' simple" so it "wouldn't make . . . talk" (242). Huck praises Tom's grotesquely encumbered plan as "worth fifteen of mine, for style, and would make Jim just as free a man as mine would, and maybe get us all killed, besides. So I was satisfied, and said we would waltz in on it" (242). The criteria are aesthetic and social, not practical. But the tone wobbles: "maybe get us all killed, besides" is not Huck's irony so much as Twain's intrusive gesture mocking Huck and anticipating the end of the evasion. Huck says he should be Tom's "true friend," prevent the evasion, and make him "save himself" (242) (an ironically contrasting reference to Huck and Jim's relationship, of course). But Tom cuts off the conversation. Of course, Tom actually has nothing to lose.

Huck does briefly establish a strong connection between himself and Jim by suggesting the boys set Jim free by "saw[ing] him out, the way I done before I was murdered, that time" (243). Tom approves this because "it's real mysterious, and troublesome, and good"—or "romantical" as Huck puts it later as he picks up Tom's vocabulary (243–44). Huck's recurrent racism—despite his recent crisis—is abundantly clear from a reference to one of the Phelpses' slaves: "this nigger had a good-natured chuckle-headed face. . . . The nigger kind of smiled around gradualy over his face like when you heave a brickbat in a mud puddle" (244)—an extremely violent image indeed. And white domination is reasserted when Tom convinces a slave that what he just saw and heard never took place but was the result of witches (echoes of Huck convincing Jim their separation in the fog was just a dream). The clear point is that white power crushes the blacks' perception of reality.

The thirty-fourth chapter ends by opposing white to black, white reason to black superstition, and, in ways that will become progressively muted, Tom's romanticism to Huck's pragmatism. "Honor" lies in inventing difficulties to conform to "the custom in Europe" (247). Tom tells Huck, "You don't ever seem to want to do anything that's regular: you want to be starting something fresh all the time" (247–48). This is as close as Twain gets to overtly suggesting that Huck is essentially American in ways Tom is not. For Tom, sawing off Jim's leg or using his blood to write messages or stealing a sheet (despite the risk of discovery) or pretending to take thirty-seven years to set him free are all legitimate in winning honor for the rescuers (more important than freeing the victim). "It don't make no difference how foolish it is; it's the *right* way—and it's the regular way. And there ain't no *other* way, that ever I heard of; and I've read all the books that gives any information about these things" (251). Huck's suggestions are "unregular and irreligious" (252) but always respond to the human consequences and especially the attendant risks. His eyes, unlike Tom's, are always on the prize, not the social acclaim: "I don't give a dead rat what the authorities thinks about it, nuther" (254). But Huck submits to Tom, and so does Jim.

It's a telling sign of Twain's anxiety about narrative plausibility that he omits any direct presentation of the crucial scene in which the boys are reunited with Jim and Tom explains how "unregular" it would be to escape immediately. We hear that Jim "called us honey, and all the pet names he could think of" (255), but the scene is done through summary and indirect discourse in order to contain any possibly disruptive emotions at the preposterous task Tom is imposing. "Jim he couldn't see no sense in the most of it, but he allowed we was white folks and knowed better than him; so he was satisfied and said he would do it all just as Tom said" (256). Tom announces "it was the best fun [as in chapter 2 with Jim] he ever had in his life, and the most intellectural; and said if he only could see his way to it we would keep it up all the rest of our lives and leave Jim to our children to get out." Jim will "come to like it better and better the more he got used to it," and the escape could be strung out for eighty years and "be the best time on record" and "make us all celebrated" (256). Tom's culture distorts reality and perpetuates slavery. Huck and Jim submit.

To help the boys, Jim is even explicitly self-enslaving: he "raised up his bed and slid the chain off the bed-leg, and wrapt it round his neck, and we crawled out" and dragged a grindstone back to the shack for the illiterate Jim to scratch his inscriptions on (266). Tom insists that vermin be brought into the shack, though Jim is terrified of rattlesnakes (the reference is clearly to Huck's nearly fatal trick with the rattlesnake back on the island). To furnish supplies for their game, the boys despoil the Phelpses' house of shirts, candles, sheets, and spoons (in contrast to Huck and Jim's earlier collection of useful supplies from the wrecked house drifting down the Mississippi) and infest the house with spiders, bugs, frogs, and snakes "dripping from the rafters" (270). Even food is distorted: Jim breaks his teeth on "rope-pie," and they all get sick from eating sawdust produced by needlessly cutting through the logs at the base of the shack. Tom even insists that Jim have a coat of arms because "all the nobility does" (265).

After three weeks and four chapters (some twenty-five pages), Tom composes a "nonnamous" letter warning the Phelpses of the impending escape, which to his delight ("*Ain't* it bully!" [277]) produces fifteen armed men who storm the shack and pursue the three, who manage to make it back to the raft moored off an island in the river. "And when we stepped on the raft [home free], I says: '*Now*, old Jim, you're a free man *again*, and I bet you won't ever be a slave no more.' 'En a mighty good job it wuz, too, Huck. It 'uz planned beautiful, en it uz *done* beautiful; en dey ain't *nobody* kin git up a plan dat's mo mixed-up en splendid den what dat one wuz.' We was all as glad as we could be, but Tom was the gladdest of all because he had a bullet in the calf of his leg" (279). Self-deluded, self-destructive chivalry, indeed.

But true chivalry immediately appears: As Tom, in pain and bleeding, starts to rave, Jim refuses to abandon him: "I doan' budge a step out'n dis place, 'dout a *doctor*, not ef it's forty year!" (279) (his capture was worth forty dollars). In one of the book's most disturbing moments, this declaration of genuine, self-sacrificing loyalty produces one of Huck's most notoriously racist affirmations: "I knowed he was white inside" (279). So much for any fundamental moral or political development! As Tom had instructed them earlier, in one of Twain's most adroitly ironic ambiguities, "When a prisoner of style escapes, it's called an evasion" (273). The escape is indeed an evasion of both reality and moral action, and Tom, Huck, and Jim are all prisoners of style.

After an extremely awkward chapter filled with dialect humor from farmers' wives and ending with an emphatically sentimental tableau of Aunt Sally asleep by Huck's bedside, chapter 42 opens as the doctor brings in wounded Tom and Jim in a "calico dress, with his hands tied behind him" (287). The dress unmans him, of course, and also recalls his earlier costume as "King Leer" and the mad drowned Arab. The towns-people want to hang him but decide it's not worth paying his owner for "their satisfaction," and settle on cursing him, giving him "a cuff or two, side the head, once in a while" (288), dress him in his own clothes, chain him back in the shack, and post a full-time guard in the night and a bulldog throughout the day. The "kind" doctor says, "Don't be no rougher on him than you're obleeged to, because he ain't a bad nigger" (288) and relates how Jim had come out of hiding and helped him treat wounded, violently raving Tom. "I never see a nigger that was a better nuss or faith-fuller, and yet he was risking his freedom to do it . . . a nigger like that is worth a thousand dollars," not forty. The townspeople agree not to "cuss him no more. Then they came out and locked him up." Huck regrets all this, but "I reckoned it warn't best for me to mix in" (289).

TWISTS

There follow some of the least accomplished scenes in the entire novel. Tom rises up from his sick bed and boasts of his achievement to Aunt Sally: "We set the runaway nigger free . . . you can't think *half* the fun it was . . . and *wasn't* it bully, aunty?" (290). Her reply levels a strong moral judgment on Tom and Huck as "little rapscallions," like the King and the Duke (290). Whereupon Tom, learning that Jim is "in that cabin again, on bread and water, and loaded down with chains, till he's claimed or sold," cries out "turn him loose! he ain't no slave, he's as free as any cretur that walks this earth! . . . Old Miss Watson died two months ago, and she was ashamed she ever was going to sell him down the river, and *said* so; and she set him free in her will" (291).

This abrupt twist is not only narratively maladroit but also fatal to the moral themes of the book. As Leo Marx has observed, "The satis-factory outcome of Jim's quest for freedom must be attributed to the benevolence of the very people whose inhumanity first made it neces-sary."[18] The problems this revelation immediately causes are enormous and inescapable. In the next line, Aunt Sally asks, "Then why on earth did *you* want to set him free for, seeing he was already free?" And Tom replies, "Well that *is* a question, I must say; and *just* like women! Why, I wanted the *adventure* of it; and I'd a waded neck-deep in blood to— goodness alive, AUNT POLLY" (291–92). This preposterous appearance of a deus ex machina rescues Twain as much as Tom, of course. Aunt Polly may look "as sweet and contented as an angel half-full of pie" (292) but, though she's a woman (and Twain's attitude toward Tom's misogyny is supportive), she's brought the novel, indeed both this and its predeces-sor, full circle. *The Adventures of Tom Sawyer* began with her voice and her attempt to control Tom. Huck's only reaction to Tom's revelation is that it confirms that Tom "with his bringing-up" could never have really "help[ed] a body set a nigger free" (292). No thought about Jim, here, and no thought that Tom has deceived Huck too.

When Huck does question him, Tom tells him (in indirect discourse, as before whenever plausibility is strained) "what he had planned in his head, from the start, if we got Jim out, all safe, was for us to run him down the river, on the raft, and have adventures plumb to the mouth of the river, and then tell him about his being free, and take him back up home on a steamboat, in style, and pay him for his lost time, and write word ahead, and get out all the niggers around, and have them waltz him into town with a torchlight procession, and a brass band, and then he would be a hero, and so would we." Huck's reaction is only, "I reckoned it was about as well the way it was" (294).

In a chilling detail, Tom gives Jim forty dollars (once again the same as the King got for turning him in as a runaway) and then produces another plan: "Le's all three slide out of here, one of these nights, and get an outfit, and go for howling adventures amongst the Injuns, over in the Territory, for a couple of weeks or two" (295). This plan infantilizes Jim, of course; none of them has a thought that he might want to go home to his wife and children rather than join the boys for more fun and games among a population even more remote from civilization than those along the shore or drifting down the river.

In a final abrupt twist, Jim then reveals to Huck and the reader that Pap is dead—it was his corpse that Jim saw in the floating house of death. There is absolutely not one word of reaction to this; Twain goes right to "Tom's most well, now" (295). I can't recall another first-person narrative written in an essentially realistic mode in which the death of a father does not elicit some acknowledgment. Given the novel's prevailing modus operandi, a reader might expect that Huck would feel relief that he's no longer threatened by his father (not to mention some regret, since there were moments when they were "lazy and jolly"), or comfort that he has the use of his $6,000 again, or anger toward Jim for Jim's betrayal. But there's nothing. And it cannot be plausibly argued that the silence speaks volumes: Twain has often made rich use of Huck's "unreliability" as a narrator, but he's never permitted himself so jarring an elision. (Compare his expert use of Huck's reluctance to say much about the sight of the murdered Grangerford boy.)

THE END

The last two sentences of the book are among the most famous in American literature. They have almost always been taken as Huck's ultimate declaration of independence, his ever-westward, on-the-road proclamation, his final denunciation of conventional American society and its feminized "sivilization." But read in the context of Tom's plan for the three to "go for howling adventures amongst the Injuns," these famous phrases are not quite so unqualified as they appear: "But I reckon I got to light out for the Territory ahead of the rest [i.e., Tom and Jim], because aunt Sally she's going to adopt me and sivilize me and I can't stand it. I been there before" (296). Huck may denounce "sivilization," but he plans to meet Tom and Jim for more adventures, presumably like the evasion. They're all just playing—even Jim, whom Huck had earlier portrayed as a loving father and disturbingly loyal friend. So Twain's novel ends even more darkly than is often perceived. For there is no freedom in the Territory, just cruel, deluded, childish "fun" and games. Even our presumptive hero is still in thrall to "respectable" Tom. There's no way out. There is no possibility of liberty and justice, and the pursuit of happiness is just a boys' game.

The only enacted freedom in the book is the language in all its virtuoso energy and variety. But such aesthetic or more narrowly "stylistic" gestures are also problematic. The larger narrative structure of the book is flawed (few readers now would agree with Lionel Trilling that "in form and style [it] is an almost perfect work"),[19] and it often violates the traditional imperatives of its ostensible genre. As many have noted, this is a picaresque novel in which the young hero does not come to a greater, disillusioned perception of the ways of the world (Huck was never innocent) and an autobiographical novel without the hero's growth, education, and development. This leads some to argue—not unreasonably—that the book in fact provides aid and comfort to irresponsible moral and political denial, to indulge in nostalgia and childish fun and verbal games or in a virulent abundance of demeaning racist stereotypes and terms ("nigger" occurs 213 times).[20] Jonathan Arac calls it a "wonderful book" but laments that it has become "a talisman of self-flattering American virtue," "a defensive alibi for our own failures," and protests that it is "currently being read and publicly used in support of complacency."[21]

Ernest Hemingway famously praised it as the source of "all modern American literature" but called the evasion "cheating."[22] He was clearly contrasting the style and the narrative structure. Ralph Ellison responded that Hemingway "missed completely the structural, symbolic and moral necessity for that part of the plot in which the boys rescue Jim. Yet it is precisely this part which gives the novel its significance. Without it, except as a boy's tale, the novel is meaningless."[23] For Ellison, Huck's crisis of conscience is a triumphant affirmation of humanity, much as Twain's notebook entry asserts. Ellison is eloquent in his understanding of the potential of this theme, but he never comments on the ephemerality of Huck's resolution or the betrayal of Jim by the evasion. More recently, Toni Morrison has registered her alarm, admiration, and rage at "this amazing, troubling book."

Perhaps these most celebrated readings could be encompassed by recalling Nabokov's account of the inspiration he felt when he came upon an (apocryphal) news story about scientists who discovered "the first drawing ever charcoaled by an animal"—an ape's sketch of the bars of his cage.[24] Like Humbert Humbert, Huck is drawing the bars of his prison house. That Twain tries too often, too vainly, too maladroitly, too lazily, too ignorantly, too fearfully to spring Huck—by comedy, virtuoso digressions, facile satire, word games—should not detract from the success he so often achieves elsewhere in the novel. The book is filled with justly celebrated, unequivocally successful elements: the escape from Pap, the feud, the murder of Boggs, the circus, the aubade on the raft at the beginning of chapter 19, the protean "performing selves" of the con men, and the large thematic oppositions of raft and town, river and shore.

But perhaps Twain's greatest effect is also his most problematic. He's used the children as representatives of American freedom, but ultimately the novel is dramatizing the crushing defeat of American liberty and humanity. Even the children are doomed. All men are slaves. This from the man Howells called "the Lincoln of our literature."[25]

HENRY JAMES'S DEMONIC LAMBS

Miles and Flora in *The Turn of the Screw*

THE TURN OF THE SCREW is Henry James's most famous and infamously provoking work of fictional art. Since 1898 when it was published to great acclaim (and some revulsion: "sickening," "repulsive," "very cruel and untrue"),[1] it has elicited more than 500 works of literary criticism and stimulated such adaptations as a notable (if crucially transformed) opera by Benjamin Britten in 1954; a dismal play, *The Innocents*, by William Archibald (1950); at least eleven maladroit movies (including a Hollywood version of *The Innocents* with Deborah Kerr in 1961 and efforts by such otherwise plausible actors as Ingrid Bergman in 1959, Marlon Brando in 1972, and Lauren Bacall and Harvey Keitel in 1999); a Gothic prose variation by Joyce Carol Oates, "Accursed Inhabitants of the House of Bly," in 1992; and a ballet by William Tuckett, the 1999 Royal Ballet premiere of which included a transvestite ghost. Every one of these adaptations proceeds by destroying the story's most original and enduring aesthetic effect—its essential narrative uncertainty. Only Britten's opera attempts to construct an equivalent if necessarily different effect and thereby begins to approach the distinction of the original.

Although the majority of readers have always been happy to take this most famous ghost story in the English language at face value, as early as 1907, then in 1921, 1924, and, most conspicuously, in 1934 with Edmund Wilson's "The Ambiguity of Henry James"—which occasioned more than twenty years of learned dispute—the unnamed governess who narrates the central story has been subjected to ferocious scrutiny:

Is she sane or mad? Are the ghosts she sees real or imaginary? Are the children she is caring for innocent or corrupt? The critical reception of the story encapsulates a century of literary criticism from the belletristic expatiations of the 1890s through the New Critical and Freudian labors of midcentury to the increasingly intricate displays of technocratic criticism—deconstructivist, neo-Marxist, feminist, postcolonial—that characterize our own recent fin de siècle. Today many critics of the story tend first to grant the intrinsic indeterminacy of the text but then drive some hermeneutic plow right over its living bones. Peter Brooks and Millicent Bell are notably inspiriting exceptions, and both Tzvetan Todorov and Shoshana Felman have responded to the text in highly perceptive and unreductive ways. For our purposes, *The Turn of the Screw* is crucial for understanding the different ways children have been depicted—or deployed—over the past two hundred years.

FORCING KNOWLEDGE

As many have observed, *The Turn of the Screw* is, in part, a critique of the governess's—and our—desire for absolute moral and cognitive clarity. Children often provoke Manichaean absolutes in our responses to them—we are quick to say they are divine or demonic. Adults—caretakers and readers alike—may impose such violent absolutes on children in ways that empower adults and destroy children. In such efforts what's at stake is not merely adult responsibility for the next generation but the adult construction of reality itself.

One of the earliest and most influential creators of romantic childhood recognized this problem as early as 1798. In Wordsworth's poem "Anecdote for Fathers: How the Art of Lying May Be Taught," the narrator repeatedly demands that the five-year-old boy with whom he's taking a country walk not only state a preference for one place or another but also justify that preference. The narrator holds on to the boy until he answers the five times repeated "Why . . . tell me why" do you prefer this place to that? This bullying provokes the child to lie—he says it's because one place has a weather cock (an instrument of orientation)—and the narrator ends the poem with guilt and self-reprobation. For Wordsworth the anecdote is an instance of the fatal mutilation of the natural goodness and intrinsic otherness of a child, who is a different sort of being, though no less human than the adult. Conventional notions of cause and effect ("what makes you prefer this to that?") and this particular adult's neurotic insistence that articulate reason must confirm or solidify a pleasurable intimate moment between an adult and a child have morally damaged the boy. To placate an adult, he is taught to lie. The same abuse of adult authority in the name of "forming" children's souls and social and intellectual behavior, thereby confirming the adult's construction of reality, even sanity, and justifying the adult's power and moral virtue, are all dramatized in *The Turn of the Screw*.

"What do the children know?" is an obsessive question throughout the story, and the idea of the children's forbidden knowledge of some primal or edenic scene haunts the governess and the housekeeper. It's important to recall that in the sequence of James's works *The Turn of the Screw* comes between two other novels of a girl's or a woman's heroic response to cognitive defloration: *What Maisie Knew* (1897) and *The Awkward Age* (1898–99). What sets it apart from these—and ensures its perpetual life—is its first-person narrative, which is cunningly constructed to dramatize and interrogate cognitive defloration in such a way that it's intrinsically uncertain exactly who is losing innocence or gaining fatal knowledge—the children, the governess, or the reader.

So for more than one hundred years readers have felt pleasure at confronting and mastering horror but have also felt urgent discomfort at the persistent possibility that the horror is entirely created by the narrator, who may be not only mad but, acting out of that madness, fatally cruel, performing the very act she believes she is attempting to prevent: possession of a child's autonomous soul. The story's so far inexhaustible provocations are enhanced by the climactic image of the dead boy in the governess's arms, an image that arouses both horror and pleasure. The image is that of a (possibly) corrupted, abused, and murdered but always angelically beautiful child who may or may not, in fact, be a demon. Is the governess a motherly guardian or a witch? Is she, like an Oedipal detective, the criminal she seeks and fears? And insofar as the reader is inside her mind, surrounded by her voice, does this not make him an accomplice? To focus on the governess is to neglect the children, but the children can only be approached through the words of the governess.

THE GOVERNESS

The tale takes added power from its stimulation of the reader's own vestigial longing and mistrust of maternal authority. This particular mother figure is especially vulnerable: a country parson's inexperienced twenty-year-old daughter has been given absolute authority over the lives of two children by their London uncle, a seductive Gothic *deus abscondus*, the absent god of late Victorian culture, who is always referred to simply as "the Master." The governess's romantic fantasies about him and the strict prohibition of her ever taking steps to fulfill them (a prohibition not merely against class and sexual transgressions but even against ever contacting him again) are abundantly clear.

Every time a ghost appears it reflects the governess's own immediate psychological situation. They mirror her soul. As she fantasizes about the Master, she fears that she will become like the dead valet and governess, Quint and Jessel—violating class and moral boundaries, entering into a forbidden liaison that leads to disgrace and death. She describes Jessel as a "terrible miserable woman" of "woe" (57) who has succumbed to the seductions of the Master's own man, Quint, a "base menial" (34) who appropriates the Master's clothes and authority at Bly and is full of "vices" and altogether "too free" with everyone (27, 25).

The governess first sees Quint while fantasizing about the Master paying an unannounced visit and bestowing his approval on her. She imagines him appearing suddenly at a "turn" in the garden (15). Instead, it is Quint whom she sees watching her from a tower on the roof of the house. At the next visitation, she feels Quint breaking into her realm when she sees him at the window; but she then (in one of James's masterstrokes of composition) runs outside and takes his place at the window, as if she were the intruder, and thereby scares the housekeeper, Mrs. Grose. This is the same window where she will see Quint in the final scene. After seeing her dead predecessor, Jessel, by the lake and then on the staircase, she sees her sitting in a schoolroom seat as if writing to a lover. This apparition occurs just after the governess has returned from her graveyard interview with the boy, Miles, in which he has declared his desire for freedom and his determination to get it from his uncle (even if it means disgracing the governess to do so). The governess speaks to the ghosts only twice—to express pity for Jessel ("you terrible miserable woman" [57]) and to taunt Quint at the end. Every other exchange is a glance. There is ample reason to fantasize.

But we must also acknowledge the governess's courage and strength. She is determined to rise to any challenge. She is herself "young, untried, nervous" (5), "a fluttered anxious girl" (4) whose previous experience is "narrow." She refers to her "small smothered life" (14), to "disturbing letters from home, where things were not going well" (19). It is notable that it is only in the full-length mirrors in her room at Bly that this girl first sees herself "from head to foot" (7). She is anxious about losing her job for not telling the Master about Miles's expulsion from school. And her anxiety is quite firmly and realistically grounded in her social and professional circumstances. Millicent Bell has found herself responding to her with increasing sympathy over many years of rereading: "More than ever . . . [the governess] seems to me a significant and moving figure, both exquisite and degraded."[2] Of course, the governess is also a self-dramatizing figure—"magnificent," "wonderful," "at the helm," "grand" (39, 13, 9, 78), surprised and pleased at her own spirit, ready to sacrifice herself to serve the Master and save the children.

She acknowledges she is "lifted aloft on a great wave of infatuation and pity" (14) for the children, in a "passion of tenderness" (13). They are "beatific, angelic, radiant," with "the deep sweet serenity of one of Raphael's holy infants" (7, 8). "As my little conductress, with her hair of gold and her frock of blue, danced before me round corners and pattered down passages, I had the view of a castle of romance inhabited by a rosy sprite" (9). She suggests she herself is a child and her life at Bly "a story-book over which I had fallen a-doze and a-dream" (9). Miles, "incredibly beautiful," particularly emits "the positive fragrance of purity" (13). He's a "little gentleman" (8) and a "cherub," an "angel" (19). "I was dazzled by their loveliness" (19). "We lived in a cloud of music and affection and success and private theatricals" (38).

What is driving much of this is indeed a fantasy: she is attracted to Miles because he has "something divine . . . his indescribable little air of knowing nothing in the world but love" (13). He looks as if "he had never for a second suffered," unlike her (19). But this fantasy completely denies the actual reality of his life, his family history of death and neglect—the deaths of his parents and grandparents and of Jessel and Quint; the many separations and displacements; the relocations from India to London to Bly; the changes of caretakers; and the neglect of their guardian uncle. This angelic fantasy is soon succeeded by its demonic twin. The governess thinks they're "wretches"; she "hates" them (51, 52).

All of which suggests, as some argue, that the ghosts have come not for the children, as she imagines, but for the governess. They possess her as their revenge for their own loss and displacement. Jessel's sexual infatuation is hers; Quint's intrusive possessing gaze is hers. The "psychoanalytic argument" suggests the governess kills Miles out of her own rage for possession, triumph, guilt. The "moral argument" proposes that the ghosts do exist—in her—and that they triumph. More recent interpretations suggest that we have made them real. Her manuscript, which is the transcript we hold and try to grasp, is her ghost since she is, after all, long dead.[3]

Recent social and historical interpretations emphasize the realities of class and gender in the 1840s, when the action presumably takes place and when an entire genre of governess novels flourished. Millicent Bell also reminds us that governesses were reported to be the most populous female group in Victorian mental asylums,[4] and Bell's own sympathy for the governess character has grown, as I noted, in view of the real difficulties a governess had to confront, which included "status incongruity" as a "lady" but also a servant,[5] as well as celibacy, economic dependence, isolation, and the "really great loneliness" that James emphasizes in the frame narrative (5).

THE FIRST AND LAST LINES

If one compares the first and last lines of the text, the fundamental theme of holding and possessing is sounded with the architectonic solidity and metamorphic potential of a Wagnerian motif. The opening frame narrative begins with an adroit confusion of reference: "The story" (but not this one) "had held us, round the fire, sufficiently breathless, but except the obvious remark that it was gruesome, as on Christmas Eve in an old house a strange tale should essentially be, I remember no comment uttered until somebody happened to note it as the only case he had met in which such a visitation had fallen on a child" (1). The last two sentences of the tale read: "I caught him, yes, I held him—it may be imagined with what a passion; but at the end of a minute I began to feel what it truly was that I held. We were alone with the quiet day, and his little heart, dispossessed, had stopped" (85).

In the opening, "the story" holds its auditors "breathless" round the Christmas fire—as the author holds the reader's attention and the reader holds the book in his hand. The reference to the tradition of ghost stories on Christmas Eve conjures a Christian community that takes aesthetic pleasure in thinking of death within the comforting ritual reassurance of the birth of eternal life and salvation. We are also witnessing a community engaged in critical comment, interpretation, contextualization. The Christian context is clear, but the immediate use of the word "case" refers us to the medical and scientific endeavors of late-nineteenth-century spiritualism. James explicitly rejects these in his preface—he is not concerned with the ghosts who come under contemporary investigation but with those of "pure romance" (like Hawthorne's): "goblins, elves, imps, demons as loosely constructed as those of the old trials for witchcraft; if not, more pleasingly, fairies of the legendary order, wooing their victims forth to see them dance under the moon" (127). So in the opening sentence the words "gruesome" and "strange tale" are played off against the sanitizing topical reference to a "case." And we note at the end of that first sentence that the "visitation" (which could be either demonic or angelic, after all) is seen as having "fallen," a somewhat overdetermined reference to the original sin that is present even in apparently innocent babes.

At the book's other extreme, the narrator holds a dead child whose heart is "dispossessed." By what, though, is unresolved: by the child's own soul, or that of Peter Quint, the (presumptive) Erlkönig-like demon or ghost who has been seductively stalking him, or by the passionate governess herself, the surrogate mother who has crushed him in her "grasp" (there's been much play with the double meaning of grasp [to hold, to understand] throughout the closing pages, too). The "story" holds its auditors (and readers) as the narrator (of the story within the story) holds the "angelic" body of ten-year-old Miles (the little "soldier"), whom she may have killed in her passion to possess him.

So masterful is James's composition that we can trace throughout the text (as Shoshana Felman has done so well) references to hands and to holding, grasping, and possessing. For example, the Master holds the governess's hand in persuading her to serve him, and she focuses on Quint's hand as he moves around the tower. When she is sitting on Miles's bed, he holds her hand, and "I would have given . . . all I possessed on earth really to be the nurse or the sister of charity who might have helped to cure him" so she "seize[s] once more the chance of possessing him" (61, 62). The children themselves, we learned in the prologue, are "in possession" of Bly (5). She tells Mrs. Grose that Miss Jessel wants to "get hold" of Flora (31). After Flora is alarmed that the governess has left their room (to look for ghosts), the governess narrates, "when she had got into bed, I had, a long time, by almost sitting on her for the retention of her hand, to prove that I recognized the pertinence of my return" (41). At the end with Miles she holds him turned away from the window where Quint appears and "my hands—but it was for pure tenderness—shook him" (83).

The story ends abruptly, asymmetrically. There is no return to the frame narrative, no return to the real world of the Christmas host Douglas and the narrator who made a transcript of the governess's manuscript, which Douglas had sent him before Douglas himself died (doubling the effect). We never come back to the opening scene with its community of storytellers and auditors. There's no security of closure. We're left holding a dead child.

THE TALE FROM THE CHILDREN'S POINT OF VIEW

Much has been made about the fact that the ghosts can only be seen by the governess. But likewise the children can only be glimpsed through the governess's self-justifying and self-dramatizing narration. What follows here is not a précis but a retrospective reconstruction of the story in which the children's experience, not the governess's, is described. What we see most clearly are the children's attempts to achieve conventional childhoods. Miles is "scarcely ten" as the narrative begins; Flora is eight. Their history is certainly traumatic: They were born in India, orphaned, and taken under the care of their grandparents, who died. The children were then brought to England by their uncle and were briefly cared for in his country house, which he rarely visited, by a governess who was compelled to leave when she presumably became pregnant by the Master's socially ambitious valet, who also served as quondam tutor and companion to the boy. The governess dies—in childbirth or by her own hand—and the valet is found dead on the road from a blow to the head, possibly murdered or else the victim of a drunken accident. The children are briefly cared for by a nursemaid and then separated from each other for the first time in their lives when the boy is sent off to school. The girl is kept under the supervision of the illiterate housekeeper, Mrs. Grose, who had been the Master's mother's maid. At school the boy misbehaves in ways that cause him to be prohibited from returning after the summer vacation (critics speculate that he may have lied or used foul language learned from the valet or engaged in homosexual acts, but James never specifies).

Despite this series of deaths, dislocations, and abandonments, the uncle does not return to the house and take charge of their lives. Instead, he sends a totally inexperienced governess—the twenty-year-old youngest daughter of a "poor country parson," "untried, nervous," "a fluttered anxious girl out of a Hampshire vicarage," as noted above—to whom he gives no less than "supreme authority" over the children and also prohibits from communicating with him for any reason (4, 5). The children themselves write letters to him, but the governess tells them they are no more than "charming literary exercises" never to be sent: "They were too beautiful to be posted," she tells the reader, "I kept them myself; I have them all to this hour" (52).

The situation becomes even more acute when the boy realizes at the end of the summer that he's not being sent to off to (another) school but is to be kept at home with his sister (none of the adults has told him he's been expelled or asked him about his experiences at school). He responds by leaving his room at midnight and wandering the grounds in an act of declared autonomy, which he calls his capacity to be "bad." He has arranged this demonstration with his sister, and he candidly announces to the governess that his purpose was to show he could be other than she imagines him—to exceed her definition of him. His calm pride that he has accomplished his goals also suggests his need to feel some degree of influence over his adult caretakers, to provoke their concerned action.

His sister soon imitates this by leaving the house one afternoon and rowing a boat across a small lake, hiding it, and then waiting to be pursued and discovered playing in a remote field. Her brother violated spatial and temporal rules by leaving his bed at night; she violates spatial rules by going even farther away from the house during daylight. Her use of the boat is an indication of the strength of her urge to imitate his rebellion and likewise to declare her independence and attract adult care. (One also notes that earlier Flora had made a toy boat with a screwed-in mast [to the delight of legions of early psychoanalytic critics] and that the governess refers to herself as being at the "helm" of the "great drifting ship" of Bly [9]).

It's altogether understandable, then, that when the governess and housekeeper do find her, the little girl is alarmed by their evident disarray (they are "undressed" she says) and immediately asks where Miles is. The governess replies, "I'll tell you if you'll tell *me*. . . . Where, my pet, is Miss Jessel?" (68). Since the answer can only be "dead and in her grave"—and since the child has never heard the governess so much as mention her predecessor's name before this—the first implication of this violent question must be that Miles is dead. The second is that the little girl's acts of rebellion (leaving the house and rowing across the lake) deserve death. The child responds with a "quick smitten glare," and when the governess then screams "she's there, she's there!" and points to what she says is the ghost of Miss Jessel standing on the opposite bank, the child looks at the governess with "an expression of hard still gravity, an expression absolutely new and unprecedented and that appeared to read and accuse and judge me. . . . [It] somehow converted the little girl herself into a figure portentous" who "showed me . . . a countenance of deeper and deeper, of indeed quite suddenly fixed reprobation" (68–69).

The governess reacts to this weighty moral and personal rejection by thinking "her incomparable childish beauty had suddenly failed, had quite vanished . . . she was literally, she was hideously hard; she had turned common and almost ugly" (70). And there follows one of the few moments in the text when we get a direct quotation of the little girl's words, a glimpse of Flora speaking for herself: "I don't know what you mean. I see nobody. I see nothing. I never *have*. I think you're cruel. I don't like you!" We could not be further from the silken net of the governess's syntax. She calls this blunt childish speech "that of a vulgarly pert little girl in the street." Flora "buries" her "dreadful little face" in the housekeeper's skirts. "In this [regressive] position she launched [cf. the boat] an almost furious wail. 'Take me away, take me away— oh take me away from *her!*' 'From *me?*' I panted [like the threatening "beast" that she's referred to before]. 'From you—from you!' she cried [like a child]" (70).

An act of adventurous autonomy, leaving the confines of home in imitation of her older brother—an act designed to stimulate a declaration of love and a happy return—instead results in the spectacle of her governess's outburst of accusation, rage, and hallucination. The loving motherly guardian has become a witch. No wonder the child wants to be taken away from so violent a judge, a judge, moreover, who sees dead people and accuses Flora of seeing them, too. No wonder the child is immediately removed from the governess's room, runs a high fever, and is taken away to London in the housekeeper's care—and separated from her home and her brother.

The boy is even clearer in his attempts to engineer a return to normal childhood, and his efforts, of course, prove fatal. The "last act of [the] dreadful drama" begins with the governess's acknowledgment that she is "like a gaoler with an eye to possible surprises and escapes." Miles's "revolution," as she calls it, begins in a graveyard on the way to church. "'Look here, my dear, you know,' he charmingly said, 'when in the world, please, am I going back to school? . . . You know, my dear, that for a fellow to be with a lady *always* . . . Ah of course she's a jolly "perfect" lady; but after all I'm a fellow, don't you see, who's—well, getting on. . . . And you can't say I've not been awfully good, can you?'" He concedes his one disobedience of running out on the lawn at night but declares it was "just to show you I could" and then reiterates, "passing his hand [n.b.] into my arm. 'Then when *am* I going back?'" He is not unhappy and not dissatisfied with her tutelage, though he doesn't know "half" of what he wants to know (53–54).

But what he most wants is what every heroic figure in James's fiction most passionately desires: "I want to see more life"—not just "of life" but "life" itself. At Bly with her there's insufficient "life" for a "fellow": "I want my own sort!" He doesn't want to be confined to the measure of his younger sister. And then, having cajoled the governess in as seductively masculine a way as he can, he threatens her: Does his uncle know "the way I'm going on?" To which the governess replies by accusing the uncle—her employer—of willful neglect: "I don't think your uncle much cares." The implication is that only she does, to which the boy responds, "Don't you think he can be made to [care] . . . by his coming down" to Bly? She challenges him with, "Who'll get him to come down?" "*I* will!' the boy [says] with extraordinary brightness and emphasis . . . and then marched off alone into church'" (54–55).

She is terrified of this freedom. He will expose her refusal to confront the fact of his expulsion and to arrange to send him off to another school. He will expose her holding him in a "life that's so unnatural for a boy," as she herself puts it. Unable to join the others at church (self-excommunicated), she decides to "bolt" (sure professional suicide) but is stopped back at the house by the apparition in the schoolroom of her predecessor in all her "haggard beauty and unutterable woe." Jessel is nowhere more clearly her mirror image, and she addresses the phantom as "you terrible miserable woman!" (56–57).

The next step in Miles's "revolution" occurs when the governess goes to his room late at night and sits on his bed, holding his hand. He tells her he doesn't sleep but thinks of her and "of this queer business of ours . . . the way you bring me up. And all the rest," which could imply not ghosts but her seductive intimacy. She accuses him of withholding information about school from her and appeals to his loyalty by saying,

"I thought you wanted to go on as you are" with her at Bly. Whereupon he "languidly" (as if ill) replies "I don't—I don't. I want to get away. . . . Oh *you* know what a boy wants!" She dodges this; he catches her and declares, "My uncle must come down and you must completely settle things." What he wants, he says, is to be taken away, "that's exactly what I'm working for. . . . You'll have to *tell* him—about the way you let it all drop: you'll have to tell him a tremendous lot! . . . I don't want to go back! . . . I want a new field." She "throws" herself upon him and kisses him. "Well, old lady?" he responds, flirtatiously, like his uncle, but also putting a distance of generations between them. And then he explicitly, if gently, declares that what he wants is for her "to let me alone" (60–62).

At this, the governess comments, "There was even a strange little dignity in it, something that made me release him. . . . God knows *I* never wished to harass him, but I felt that merely, at this, to turn my back on him was to abandon or, to put it more truly, lose him." But she cannot relent and is soon dropping on her knees beside the bed to "seize once more the chance of possessing him. . . . 'I'd rather die than hurt a hair of you. Dear little Miles'—oh I brought it out now even if I *should* go too far—'I just want you to help me to save you!'" (62–63), whereupon there's "an extraordinary blast and chill," and the boy gives "a loud high shriek . . . of either jubilation or terror" and (he says) blows out the candle, plunging them in darkness (63). He's effectively startled her off the bed and away from him. This scene of coercive intimacy and escape is immediately followed by Flora's disastrous revolt, attempted escape, and breakdown.

That night Miles joins the governess at the fire, but—despite Flora's crisis—she maintains a silence that can only be repressive. His sister is feverish, raving, and has been removed from the governess's room and care. But the governess makes no effort to comfort him or explain. She is intent on coercion. As she proclaims the next morning, "I'll get it [what happened at school, what happened and is happening still at Bly] out of him. . . . He'll confess. If he confesses he's saved" (76), and so would she be saved (from dismissal and the fear of madness). Feeling very "grand" (76), she has dinner with Miles (as if they are an adult couple and she the mistress of the house) in the main hall where she had seen Quint at the window. She "whimsically" compares herself and Miles to "some young couple who, on their wedding journey, at the inn, feel shy in the presence of the waiter" (78). But she never lets up. As they "circle about with terrors and scruples, fighters not daring to close," she feels "horror of what I was doing . . . an act of violence . . . the obtrusion of the idea of grossness and guilt on a small helpless creature who had been for me a revelation of the possibilities of beautiful intercourse. Was n't it base" (81). She is using the very word used earlier about Quint, the "base menial," who was "too free" with everyone, particularly Miss Jessel. But the governess perseveres and accuses Miles of theft.

This plunges us into the final chapter of the story, with its play on "grasp" and "hold" as she "springs" at the boy and now (in a reversal) prevents him from seeing what she sees, the ghost of Quint (81). She utters "a moan of joy" (82) when Miles admits taking a letter she wrote, and she quickly intensifies her interrogation. "My sternness . . . made him avert himself again, and that movement made *me*, with a single bound and an irrepressible cry, spring [again] straight upon him. . . . 'No more, no more, no more!' I shrieked to my visitant [Quint's ghost] as I tried to press [Miles] against me" (84). The boy imagines the governess is seeing the ghost of Jessel again, as she had with Flora. He goes at her "in a white rage" (to the governess, Quint's ghost is "the white face of damnation"), and he searches in vain for what she sees. She, however, to get her "proof" of his knowledge of the ghosts (which could, in fact, be proof only that he knows she thinks she sees ghosts), forces him to say that if it's not Miss Jessel it must be "'Peter Quint—you devil!'" The punctuation is famously ambiguous, but everything suggests Miles is calling the governess a devil (85).

His last word is a child's interrogative: "His face gave again, round the room, its convulsed supplication. '*Where?*'" (85). She feels triumph at his "surrender" and says, "'I have you . . . but he has lost you for ever!' Then for the demonstration of my work, 'There, *there!*,' I said to Miles. But he had already jerked straight round, stared, glared again, and seen but the quiet day" (85). Her ability here to deduce that Miles sees only the natural world is a masterly reaffirmation of her residual grasp of the boy's independent existence and some context of objective reality. But she soon plunges on: "With the stroke of the loss I was so proud of [that Quint is not there] he uttered the cry of a creature hurled over an abyss, and the grasp [n.b.] with which I recovered him might have been that of catching him in his fall." We recall not only the obvious Christian fall of the "natural man," but also the opening of the story, where she wrote, "I remember the whole beginning as a succession of flights and drops" (6). But here at the end, "I caught him, yes, I held [n.b.] him—it may be imagined with what a passion; but at the end of a minute I began to feel what it truly was that I held. We were alone with the quiet day, and his little heart, dispossessed, had stopped" (85). The governess's repetition of "the quiet day" restores reality. Miles has suffered a fatal stroke or heart attack induced by her passionate possession.

Perhaps. There are twenty-five other interpretations provided in Peter Beidler's critical casebook and plenty more to forage in. The one incontrovertible point is that the death of this child is the consequence of adult violence. The Oedipal pieta or vampiric sacrifice we see at the end is composed for both maximum provocation and maximum resistance to reductive interpretation. For us, however, the key significance is that it is a child who is the vehicle for James's indubitably classic interrogation of the reader's capacity for response. It is a child whose thrilling end accomplishes what Walter Benjamin said every reader of a novel always desires: "What draws the reader to [a] novel is the hope of warming his shivering life with a death he reads about."[6] The reader is being asked to see that he is all-too-humanly ready to sacrifice the life of a child in the name of saving it, delivering it from evil. The twist is that the evil is our own desire to crush the child's beautiful, arousing, terrifying independence—its essential cognitive and emotional autonomy—on the wheel of our need for certainty and moral and emotional comfort.

THE PREFACE

In his 1908 preface to the New York edition of *The Turn of the Screw*, James cunningly prepares the reader to encounter what he calls a "perfect" work (124)—a perfect example of a work constructed to defeat the reader's effort to resolve its intrinsic indeterminacy, its perpetually unanswered question, its evasion of all comforting interpretation. The story is a beautiful trap for the morally and aesthetically—and intellectually—vain. It is very much of the 1890s in its ostentatious play with moral and aesthetic categories, and no less a virtuoso of such fin-de-siècle games than Oscar Wilde (whom James loathed) was caught by its magic: "A most wonderful, lurid, poisonous little tale, like an Elizabethan tragedy. I am greatly impressed by it."[7]

The climax of the preface is James's description of his most masterly technical feat: "What, in the last analysis, had I to give the sense of? Of their being, the haunting pair, capable, as the phrase is, of everything—that is of exerting, in respect to the children, the very worst action small victims so conditioned might be conceived as subject to." But there is no eligible *absolute* of the wrong; it remains relative to fifty other elements . . . quite exactly in the light of the spectator's, the critic's, the reader's experience. Only make the reader's general vision of evil intense enough, I said to myself—and that already is a charming job—and his own experience, his own imagination, his own sympathy (with the children) and horror (of their false friends) will supply him quite sufficiently with all the particulars. Make him *think* the evil, make him think it for himself, and you are released from weak specifications.

(128)

"Make him *think* the evil, make him think it for himself"—it is James's success at this that assures the classic status of *The Turn of the Screw*. For in it James has spun a magic web to catch the reader collaborating in the creation (out of the reader's own experience and imagination) of absolute evil toward children. The horror and delight, the outrage and the self-congratulation that so many readers of such different times, places, and powers have experienced, for so long now, are the results of a work of genius that we participate in. Our aesthetic response to imagined evil occasions the ultimate turn of the screw: our awareness of our capacity for sadistic delight in the name of moral and spiritual salvation (both ours and our children's) and of our penchant for fatal (moral, intellectual, spiritual) absolutism. Not that James would ever suggest that relativism (postmodern or not) is to be preferred. For him, truth—as his brother William's philosophy of pragmatism teaches—is an infinite, socially constructed pursuit, an evolutionary process, not a product.

So James employs the literary device of the limited point of view—we have only the governess's words to go by—as a means of exploring the problematic ways we construct objective reality. James's narrative technique—anything but traditionally and securely omniscient—alerts the reader to the intrinsic human condition of partial knowledge and provides the reader with a demonstration of one of the ways to remedy (but never finally resolve) that condition, for the truth—as in pragmatism—must be endlessly revised and refined. The children are used to symbolize and to be sacrificed in affirmation of the endlessly evolutionary, elusive nature of any human truth.

James most famously believed that the novel was an incomparable cognitive device, a means for comprehending and enlarging human experience: "It is art that *makes* life, makes interest, makes importance . . . and I know of no substitute whatever for the force and beauty of its process," he wrote.[8] "The success of a work of art, to my mind, may be measured by the degree to which it produces a certain illusion; that illusion makes it appear to us for the time that we have lived another life— that we have had a miraculous enlargement of experience."[9] *The Turn of the Screw* is a deliberately terrifying, devilish challenge to the reader's capacity for such enlargement.

4

J. M. BARRIE'S ETERNAL NARCISSIST

Peter Pan

IN THE LAST DECADE of the nineteenth century and the early years of the twentieth, J. M. Barrie seemed destined for literary immortality. Mark Twain called *Peter Pan* "a great and refining and uplifting benefaction to this sordid and money-mad age."[1] Robert Louis Stevenson and Max Beerbohm proclaimed Barrie "a man of genius,"[2] and the word crops up again and again in contemporary accounts. William Archer, the translator of Ibsen, called Barrie "a humourist of original and delightful genius who happens to have an extraordinary knack of expressing himself in dramatic form."[3]

Barrie was also uncommonly successful. A recent biographer asserts that he "made more money from writing than any other writer on record," and another speaks of his "stupendous wealth."[4] From its first performance two days after Christmas in 1904, *Peter Pan* was an unending source of income (it brought him half a million pounds in his lifetime), with commercial spin-offs, clothes, toys, souvenirs, and theatrical and fictional adaptations. The play was produced in London every Christmas from 1904 to 1939 and was continually revived after the war both in England and in the States. In its first fifty years it was produced some 10,000 times. There have also been silent and sound movie productions of all sorts from 1927 through the utterly anodyne 1952 Disney cartoon, the legendary Mary Martin musical in 1954 (repeatedly shown on early television), and Steven Spielberg's maladroit *Hook* in 1993.

But *Peter Pan* was only part of Barrie's celebrity. He was exceptionally prolific in a wide range of literary forms including a series of best-selling stories, sketches, essays, and novels on quaint Scottish small-town life; two half-disguised but surprisingly autobiographical novels about the childhood, marriage, and career of a best-selling novelist; and a series of enormously successful plays, including *Quality Street, The Admirable Crichton, What Every Woman Knows,* and *Dear Brutus.* This seventh of eight children of a Scottish loom weaver and a stonemason's daughter turned himself into a rich international celebrity: a baronet, the rector of Saint Andrews, the chancellor of Edinburgh University, a recipient of the Order of Merit, the man Charlie Chaplin most wanted to visit in London, and a friend of Stevenson, Hardy, Meredith, Conan Doyle, and the royal family itself (he told stories to young Princess Margaret).

Yet by the time of his death at seventy-seven in 1937, Barrie was considered an outdated Edwardian, a relic who had somehow happened to create the immortal Peter Pan but had little lasting literary importance himself. As a highly intelligent and nuanced obituary article in the *TLS* put it: "Europe has taken little notice of him. He has influenced none of his contemporaries except, vaguely, Mr. Milne. . . . It is probable that an influential part of modern criticism will dismiss him as a pot-boiler for the bourgeoisie and no more. . . . Of his skill as a man of the theatre there is no question. [He had] genius for the stage . . . ease of dialogue and, above all, . . . power to tell a story." He was "brilliant . . . but he seemed continually to be diverted from the substance of his plays by his delight in the manner of them . . . avoiding, because he feared, the full implications of his own theme. . . . No one can deeply consider the play [*Peter Pan*] without perceiving that it is a spiritual autobiography and that Peter himself, neither boy nor man nor fairy and yet a male being always to be represented by a girl, is a projection of a tragically divided mind." For all the "tormented negativism" of Peter Pan's rejection of Wendy's love, the play "continually gives the impression that the Barrie who conceived it failed to recognize the tragic essence of his own idea and was comfortably hoodwinked by the prettiness of his treatment." Yet, the article concludes, one can't ignore the "continued vitality of the play during a quarter of a century . . . the thing before [the audience's] eyes has the quality of a legend that they are making up for themselves." In *Peter Pan* Barrie "was able not merely to instruct or entertain but to impregnate the collective mind of his audience. And if he did, indeed, possess this power, which is precisely the power of the great fairy-tales, criticism may as well throw its pen away, for then he is immortal by election and there is no more to be said about it."[5]

Easier said than done. The great midcentury theater critic Kenneth Tynan loathed *Peter Pan*'s "unctuous sentimentality."[6] The literary scholar David Daiches attacked its "real cruelty," "revenge . . . on life for daring to pose adult problems involving real human relationships," and "disturbing cunning"—which last phrase, of course, suggests a critic all too responsive to this "sexless sentimentalist."[7] Even a more perceptive midcentury critic, Peter Coveney, calls *Peter Pan* "a regressive escape into the emotional prison of self-limiting nostalgia." For Coveney the play epitomizes the late-nineteenth-century "cult of the child," which "serves not to integrate childhood and adult experience, but to create a barrier of nostalgia and regret between childhood and the potential responses of adult life. The child indeed becomes a means of escape from the pressures of adult adjustment, a means of regression toward the irresponsibility of youth, childhood, infancy."[8]

More recently, however, one of Barrie's most accomplished academic critics, R. D. S. Jack, argues he is no less than "a daring forerunner of deconstructionist art."[9] The highly perceptive Jacqueline Rose maintains that Barrie's art deliberately "undoes itself."[10] Ann Yeoman calls it a critique of Edwardian childhood, an "explicit devaluing and questioning of cozy domesticity."[11] (Barrie himself remarked that the statue of Peter Pan put up in Kensington Gardens "doesn't show the Devil in Peter.")[12] And Humphrey Carpenter argues that "Barrie wants to show us the appalling depths to which our sentimentality towards children can lead us. One part of him is being horribly sentimental; the other part is standing back and mocking it."[13]

I have come to believe that the greatness of Peter Pan—the mythic character whose tale Barrie told in ten different literary forms from 1896 to 1928—is inextricable from his power to provoke intensely conflicting and conflicted responses. Peter Pan exhibits a complex interaction of advance and retreat, exposure and disguise, sentimental evasion and unblinking ironic expression, nostalgia and rage, charm and ferocity.

The sheer multiplicity of the forms Peter Pan has taken suggest, indeed, that his story is something of a myth for a postreligious or, more accurately, post-Christian age. It's notable that the novel *Peter and Wendy* is neither a nursery or adult classic and is not widely read while the play *Peter Pan; or, the Boy Who Would Not Grow Up* is among the most secure and enduring classics of the English-speaking stage. Why the play? Because it is a ritual enacting a myth of eternal, recurrent youth. The novel can be read alone or read to a child, but the play is a public event, performed at a special time of year (the winter solstice) in a special kind of building designed for magic spectacle, group celebration, witness, affirmation.

The essential elements of the play are familiar: first, the flying children—with the power of birds, fairies, and angels; second, the four main characters (of more than fifty)—Peter, the eternally youthful demigod; Wendy, his priestess, mother, and chaste would-be bride; Tinker Bell, her diminutive but dangerous and sexy fairy rival; and Captain Hook, Peter's great antagonist and double, a glamorous, mutilated, dark angel fallen prey to time (the crocodile who swallowed a clock), a Lucifer bedecked in history, rhetoric, literature, and social class; and, finally, two complementary worlds: the cozy, domestic, bedtime nursery and Neverland, the island of lost boys, fairies, mermaids, redskins, pirates, wild beasts: all the ingredients of both girls' and boys' fantasy adventures.

And what are the most famous lines of the play? "Second to the right and then straight on till morning"; "to die will be an awfully big adventure"; "do you believe in fairies?"[14] All three refer to death: as an exultant flight to a heavenly home, as a courageous rite of passage, as a condition that can be overcome by willpower, an affirmation of counterfactual belief, sheer good will, and hope (clapping hands). The power of these lines is remarkable: when Barrie's great theatrical producer, Charles Frohman, found himself on the sinking *Lusitania* in 1915, his widely reported last words referred to the "adventure" of death.[15] These three most famous lines enforce the sense that the play is about a bittersweet attempt to overcome death, an attempt that fails. The play affirms that the only thing that is eternal is the demigod's recurrent but brief appearance to generation after generation of children. Every year, at the winter solstice when the Christmas season gets underway, he can be seen in theaters throughout the world, crowing in the promise of spring. This pagan ritual of Peter Pan has flourished even while the traditional Christian Nativity has been nearly buried in the potlatch of commercial Santa Claus.

The genius of *Peter Pan* lies in its ability to accommodate ambiguities, its constant traffic between extremes; it encompasses and takes its recurrent energy from the polarities it moves between. The most obvious oppositions are between death (Peter's costumes of skeleton leaves and cobwebs and his captaincy of dead boys) and life (his cock-a-doodle-doo), between past and eternal present, and between time lost and time recovered. Peter is youth and joy, but he is also forgetful, cruel, heartless.

He is hopelessly narcissistic and ignorant of sex and romantic love but also freely, innocently, and transiently affectionate, utterly pregenital. He is both hostile to mothers and longing for a mother, both excluded and abandoned by mother and yet always escaping and free of her confinement. He is hostile to evil father Hook but replicates his Napoleonic tyrannies and theatrical language (doubled by father Darling's domestic rants). He defiantly declares he will never grow up and is, in fact, forever young. The play welcomes nostalgic adults and exultant children who live in the moment. It is sentimental and sardonic, lyric and satiric, tender and violent, willfully silly and regressive and adroitly tough-minded, and—through its chameleon changes of tone and time and pronoun reference and verb tense and mood—it even becomes psychologically and morally complex. But it never comes to a thematic conclusion; it just recommences.

Barrie has fashioned a god out of Greek and Roman myths, Blake's babies and Wordsworth's boys, Victorian and Edwardian pieties and disputes about women and children, British imperial fantasies, Treasure Island, and fairytales. All this, he realized, could be accommodated by employing the figure of a boy of six or seven. How useful children are. How grand.

FIRST HINTS

The best way to understand the essential power of *Peter Pan* is by tracing its development in the course of Barrie's life and art. There is no single text for *Peter Pan*. It grew and changed and was revised and reimagined over three decades. Barrie couldn't let it go. The first hint of it comes in Barrie's often excruciating analysis of his unhappy marriage, the novel *Tommy and Grizel* (1896), where the narrator is describing his novelist-hero's book *The Wandering Child*:

> I wonder whether any of you read it now. Your fathers and mothers thought a great deal of that slim volume, but it would make little stir in an age in which all the authors are trying who can say Damn loudest. It is but a reverie about a little boy who was lost. His parents find him in a wood singing joyfully to himself because he thinks he can now be a boy for ever; and he fears that if they catch him they will compel him to grow into a man, so he runs farther from them into the wood and is running still, singing to himself because he is always to be a boy.[16]

After this came entries in Barrie's notebook on "Peter a demon boy (villain of story)," and on "The Boy Who Hated Mothers," and on "The happy Boy: boy who couldn't grow up—runs away from pain and death—is caught *wild*—(and escapes)."[17] The play first produced in 1904 was called *Peter Pan; or, The Boy Who Wouldn't Grow Up.* (It has been noted that Maurice Hewlitt's 1898 play *Pan and the Young Shepard* contained the lines, "Boy, boy, wilt thou be a boy forever?")[18]

The central issue throughout these notes and possible titles, as his biographers and critics observe, is whether the boy "won't" or "wouldn't" or "can't" or "couldn't" grow up. Is it choice or "curse?" We can watch the permutations of all this running throughout *Tommy and Grizel*: "'Oh, that we were boys and girls all our lives!' Poor Tommy! He was still a boy, he was ever a boy, trying sometimes, as now, to be a man, and always when he looked round he ran back to his boyhood as if he saw it holding out its arms to him and inviting him to come back and play. He was so fond of being a boy that he could not grow up."[19] Barrie's most recent biographer, Lisa Chaney, cites a line that Barrie cut from the last page of the manuscript of the novel: "What God will find hardest to forgive in him, I think, is that Grizel never had a child."[20] And in his notebooks there appears, "Perhaps the curse of his life [was] that he never 'had' a woman."[21]

CHANGES AND PROLIFERATIONS

Even the authorship of *Peter Pan* is unstable: In the original 1904 program of the play, the author is listed as Miss Ela Q. May, the actress who played the Darling's maid. In the complex 1928 dedication to the published play, Barrie says he doesn't remember writing it, then claims it was created by rubbing some boys together from which spark it was born, then suggests it was written by a stagehand. The script of the play never stayed still. It began as three acts and after the first year was both cut and enlarged to five acts. There are more than twenty variant endings. And Barrie never stopped revising the text of the play and delayed publication of the official script until 1928.

So what began in *Tommy and Grizel* as a fictional novelist's book called *The Wandering Child* soon spawned nine other kinds of literary treatment of Peter Pan.[22] Moreover, even though *Peter Pan* began as the work of one man, within a year of the play's first performance many other people started writing and producing versions, too. There were many different kinds of adaptations—as many as thirty—by other hands in formats ranging from nursery versions to illustrated pop-ups to school readers. Not to mention the clothes, toys, golf clubs, bus lines, crackers, posters, stained-glass windows, and even a 5,000-ton car ferry.[23]

This vast accumulation suggests the kind of collective cultural fantasy associated with the creation of a myth. In a secular age Peter Pan arouses the love and longing of a divine archetype: the eternal boy. He has flourished through the long twilight of the empire, two world wars, decades of totalitarian politics, the rise of American empire, and the hegemony of its popular culture and counterculture. And Peter Pan still flourishes over one hundred years since he first appeared. (A recent sequel sold 350,000 copies in the United States, and another sequel was published with an international marketing campaign in the fall of 2006.)[24]

To come to grips with all this, we should concentrate on four basic texts. The first is Barrie's memoir of his mother, *Margaret Ogilvy*, published in the same year as *Tommy and Grizel* (1896) and containing what I believe is the true literary and biographical origin of Peter Pan. The second is the extremely complex novel *The Little White Bird* of 1902, which includes six chapters about Peter Pan later published separately with Arthur Rackham illustrations as *Peter Pan in Kensington Gardens* in 1906. The third is the novel *Peter and Wendy* published in 1911. And the fourth is the published text of the play, *Peter Pan; or, The Boy Who Would Not Grow Up*, which Barrie finally issued with extensive stage directions and revisions in 1928, twenty-four years after the original version was produced.

MARGARET OGILVY AND MOTHERHOOD

In 1896, the year after his mother died at seventy-six in the family home in Kirriemuir, Angus, Scotland, and the year that, after four years of work, he produced his dark anatomy of his art, character, and marriage in the novel *Tommy and Grizel*, Barrie published another book that also moves between biography and autobiography, private and public, past and present. It was called *Margaret Ogilvy by her Son, J. M. Barrie*, and at first glance appeared to be a biography and memoir of his mother. But in fact even the title is misleading: his mother proudly used her married name, Barrie, not her maiden name, Ogilvy, despite old Scottish custom, so the title effectively separates her from her husband (who is barely mentioned in the book) and suggests that J. M. Barrie, the celebrated author, was the creator of this literary character, his mother, "Margaret Ogilvy."

The book was highly successful: 40,000 copies were quickly sold, and reviewers praised it as a loving memoir: "It stands unmatched in literature as an idyll of the divinest of human feelings—a mother's love. . . . This is Mr. Barrie's finest and noblest book."[25] Some did feel it "suffered from indelicacy,"[26] altogether too intimate and confessional, and Barrie's oldest brother strongly objected to what he saw as its unreliable mixture of fact and fiction and its distortion of his mother's life. What strikes a reader today is how complex and even tricky the intimate confessional narrator is as he unwinds long, self-modifying sentences that move among past, present, praise, blame, longing, and exultation, between her life and his both as a boy and as a successful London author describing his work habits and current needs—not the least of which was to comfort and support his demanding, manipulative, seductive, infantilizing, jealous, sarcastic, self-dramatizing, and finally demented mother still living in the family home in rural Scotland (the locus of that series of novels and stories that had brought him his first great success).

From the first sentence of *Margaret Ogilvy* we're embroiled in a tangle of objects, people, hearsay, memory, narrative, fact, and fantasy that serves to dramatize (and question and finally overcome) how unimportant our narrator's birth was to this striving family. Throughout the book, for all its suave fluency and ostensible "whimsy," Barrie's style reclaims, recovers, and triumphantly restores the past—not just to celebrate it but also often to attack and master it and convert neglect into obsessive mutual dependency, what we'd call Oedipal victory.

Again and again in *Margaret Ogilvy*, we return to what was the central trauma and creative inspiration of Barrie's life. When he was six his thirteen-year-old brother, David, died in a skating accident. His mother never recovered from the loss of her favorite son; even on her death bed she was calling for David (as Barrie informs us): "Is that you, David? . . . Wha's bairn's dead? Is a bairn of mine dead?"[27] The font and origin of Barrie's entire creative and emotional life lies in the oft-quoted scene of his going up to his mourning mother when he was six:

> My mother lay in bed with the christening robe beside her, and I peeped in many times at the door and then went to the stair and sat on it and sobbed. I know not if it was that first day, or many days afterwards, that [my sister] told me to go ben [up] to my mother and say to her that she still had another boy. I went ben excitedly, but the room was dark, and when I heard the door shut and no sound come from the bed I was afraid, and I stood still. I sup-

pose I was breathing hard, or perhaps I was crying, for after a time I heard a listless voice that had never been listless before say, 'Is that you?' I think the tone hurt me, for I made no answer, and then the voice said more anxiously 'Is that you?' again. I thought it was the dead boy she was speaking to, and I said in a little lonely voice, 'No, it's no him, it's just me.' Then I heard a cry, and my mother turned in bed, and though it was dark I knew that she was holding out her arms.

(11–13)

If the passage had ended there, we would clearly be in the land of David Copperfield, a future literary celebrity being embraced and comforted by his loving mother. But Barrie goes on to show how this one embrace provoked the boy to desperate efforts to make his mother think of something other than dead David and to distract her from her tears with comic stories, reenactments, dramatic performances, and plays:

After that I sat a great deal in her bed trying to make her forget him, which was my crafty way of playing physician, and if I saw any one out of doors do something that made the others laugh I immediately hastened to that dark room and did it before her. I suppose I was an odd little figure; I have been told that my anxiety to brighten her gave my face a strained look and put a tremor into the joke (I would stand on my head in the bed, my feet against the wall, and then cry excitedly, 'Are you laughing, mother?')—and perhaps what made her laugh was something I was unconscious of, but she did laugh suddenly now and then, whereupon I screamed exultantly to that dear sister, who was ever in waiting, to come and see the sight, but by the time she came the soft face was wet again. Thus I was deprived of some of my glory, and I remember once only making her laugh before witnesses. I kept a record of her laughs on a piece of paper, a stroke for each, and it was my custom to show this proudly to the doctor every morning.

(13–14)

This wildly anxious young artist is screaming, standing on his head, striving for glory, keeping a "record of her laughs on a piece of paper . . . to show this proudly to the doctor every morning." But there's one more step to come:

At first, they say, I was often jealous [of David], stopping her fond memories with the cry, 'Do you mind nothing about me?' but that did not last; its place was taken by an intense desire . . . to become so like him that even my mother should not see the difference, and many and artful were the questions I put to that end. Then I practiced in secret, but after a whole week had passed I was still rather like myself. He had such a cheery way of whistling, she had told me, it had always brightened her at her work to hear him whistling, and when he whistled he stood with his legs apart, and his hands in the pockets of his knickerbockers. I decided to trust to this, so one day after I had learned his whistle (every boy of enterprise invents a whistle of his own) from boys who had been his comrades, I secretly put on a suit of his clothes, dark grey they were, with little spots, and they fitted me many years afterwards, and thus disguised I slipped, unknown to the others, into my mother's room. Quaking, I doubt not, yet so pleased, I stood still until she saw me, and then—how it must have hurt her! 'Listen!' I cried in a glow of triumph, and I stretched my legs wide apart and plunged my hands into the pockets of my knickerbockers, and began to whistle.

(16–17)

Thus was Peter Pan born: not simply in the vivid, horrifying resurrection—the reenactment, complete with costume and studied art—of a dead boy but also in Barrie's knowledge that the virtuoso performance of this make-believe eternal boy is ultimately a failure: "But I had not made her forget the bit of her that was dead; in those nine-and-twenty years he was not removed one day farther from her" (18–19). Out of both Barrie's exultation in this theatrical virtuosity and his knowledge of its limits ("heartless" immaturity and grotesque necrophilia) comes the full, labile power of the myth of Peter Pan, forever young and flying and apparently free, but barred, locked out of mother's nursery, eternally recurrent and utterly, narcissistically forgetful. To be out of time is to be out of one's mind. Barrie's literary art captures all this. He creates a narrator who is moving, sentimental, unreliable (and hence ironically portrayed) because he's so self-comforting and nostalgic, still yearning to merge with mother.

THE LITTLE WHITE BIRD AND FATHERHOOD

But Barrie is seldom able to sustain this kind of complexity. He lacks the structural and tonal control. He ducks and runs for cover into whimsy, charm, self-pity. Still, what are we to make of the wild instability—the ostentatious obscurity—of much of the first text where Peter Pan overtly appears, Barrie's 1902 novel, *The Little White Bird*?

It was hardly obscure information for the readers of this bizarrely swerving text that the celebrated J. M. Barrie's wife was the actress Mary Ansell and that they had no children, much to their regret. What we also know now is that in 1900 Barrie had met the Llewellyn Davies family and been utterly smitten by five-year-old George, three-year-old Jack, and even the baby, Peter. For two years before publishing *The Little White Bird* he had been playing with them almost daily in Kensington Gardens and spending endless hours doting on their mother, insinuating himself into their family life, and (with the boys' highly active collaboration) creating the two fantasies—of fairies and pirates—that would be combined with a narrative of domestic comedy to create the fully developed Peter Pan in the play of 1904 and the novel of 1911.

The Little White Bird is about a struggle for the love of a six-year-old boy named David(!) between a young London mother and her "good fairy" (as she calls him), the gruff, hostile, misogynistic, emotionally defended Captain W, the narrator, a childless, lonely middle-aged bachelor who spies on other people's family lives and sometimes benevolently interferes with them, like a grouchy god. He affects to believe that he is David's true father because without his help David's parents would never have married and had him. And the narrator goes even further when he asserts that he knew David long before he was born, when he was still a bird, a thrush playing in the water in Kensington Gardens. What the narrator most passionately desires is to "take [David] utterly from her and make him mine."[28] At one mad moment in the narrative the Captain even absconds with the baby David and runs away with him to Kensington Gardens. But the narrator's most successful appropriation of the boy is their joint creation of the six central chapters of the novel—the chapters that would be republished four years later as an independent book with illustrations by Arthur Rackham: *Peter Pan in Kensington Gardens.*

These six central chapters of *The Little White Bird* begin with David and the Captain taking us readers on "a Grand Tour of Kensington Gardens," the "pleasantest club in London."[29] Judging from the nursery tone and private references to garden landmarks (Coco Hewlett's Tree, the Big Penny, the Baby Walk), we must be well-to-do London children between the ages of three and seven who know "all the people who are worth knowing" (*Peter Pan in Kensington Gardens*, 4), quite unlike the "common people [who] press quite hard against the glass, and that is why their noses are mostly snubby" (32). At the far end of the Garden the Serpentine lake "passes beneath a bridge to far away where the island is on which all the birds are born that become baby boys and girls. No one who is human, except Peter Pan (and he is only half-human), can land on the island" (10).

We are at the first incarnation of what will later be called Neverland, though in this book the island is a place of birds about to become babies and the Gardens at night are the realm of the fairies. Peter Pan himself is not a boy so much as a baby (Rackham portrays him mostly as an eighteen-month-old toddler in a nightgown) who "escaped from being human when he was seven days old; he escaped by the window and flew back to the Kensington Gardens. If you think he was the only baby who ever wanted to escape, it shows how completely you have forgotten your own young days" (12). We learn, however, that "every fairy he met fled from him," that "every living thing was shunning him," and that he is a "poor little half-and-half," a "Betwixt-and-Between" (15, 17) who longs to play as children do and keeps trying to get from the island to the Gardens and finally makes it after many attempts. Like his classical namesake, Pan, he plays reed pipes and sometime rides on a goat, but most of his time is spent frolicking about in a nursery sort of way, sailing his thrush-nest boat in the Serpentine and wandering through the Gardens after "Lock-out Time," when the gates are closed for the night.

But if Peter Pan's adventures began with an escape from being human, he now and forever finds himself trapped in the inhuman world of fairies and birds. He had thought "Mother always keeps [the nursery window] open in the hope that I may fly back" (36), but when he finally did make an attempt to return,

> the window was closed, and there were iron bars on it, and peering inside he saw his mother sleeping peacefully with her arms around another little boy. Peter called, 'Mother! mother!' but she heard him not; in vain he beat his little limbs against the iron bars. He had to fly back, sobbing, to the Gardens, and he never saw his dear again. What a glorious boy he had meant to be to her! Ah, Peter! We who have made the great mistake, how differently we should all act at the second chance. But . . . there is no second chance, not for most of us. When we reach the window it is Lock-out Time. The iron bars are up for life.

(40)

What matters most here is Peter's violent ambivalence; he wants to escape "being human" but then wants to escape being "half-human." He gleefully flies out the nursery window but then discovers to his desperate sorrow that he's been locked out. The polarity is the key to the power of the myth, and it is Barrie's great gift to explore both poles, however slyly or coyly he disguises his efforts. At this particular point, all the emphasis is on maternal separation, displacement by another boy, lamentation. But even in this first rudimentary version of Peter, Barrie is also careful to emphasize the death that surrounds this eternal boy. At night, we learn, he prowls the Gardens looking for "lost ones" (64), children who may have been left behind or fallen out of their carriages.

> You may perish of cold and dark before Peter Pan comes round. He has been too late several times . . . he digs a grave for the child and erects a little tombstone, and carves the poor thing's initials on it. . . .
>
> David sometimes places white flowers on these . . . innocent graves.
>
> But how strange for parents, when they hurry into the Gardens at the opening of the gates looking for their lost one, to find the sweetest little tombstone instead. I do hope Peter is not too ready with his spade. It is all rather sad.
>
> (65)

This dying fall, this creepy necrophiliac echo of the mythic Pan's father, Hermes, the messenger god who leads mortals to the land of the dead, comes as the last words of *Peter Pan in Kensington Gardens*.

One of Barrie's most impressive effects throughout these six chapters is to convey Peter's mythic timelessness by moving with extreme fluidity among past, present, and future, among what the omniscient narrator knows, what he tells, what David knows and did and does and says, and what Peter did in the past and is doing right now in the present moment, when the narrator is telling his story with extreme informal spontaneity to the presumably child reader/auditor and his parents. For example, Peter's early attempts to sail in a thrush's nest from the bird island to the Gardens of children and fairies are described in a lengthy literary parody of Elizabethan travel writing (hardly the stuff of nursery tales). Barrie concludes this stylistic oddity by flaunting the narrator's creative freedom with time: "Such was [Peter's] first voyage to the Gardens, and you may gather from the antiquity of the language that it took place a long time ago. But Peter never grows any older, and if we could be watching for him under the bridge tonight (but, of course, we can't), I dare say we should see him hoisting his nightgown and sailing or paddling towards us in the Thrush's Nest. When he sails, he sits down, but he stands up when he paddles. I shall tell you presently how he got his paddle" (27). The narrator is also constantly stressing the presence of David as his collaborator: the tale is proof of their intimacy. As he describes it, the story is composed of "bald narrative," "moral reflections," and David's "reminiscences" and so mixes three kinds of knowledge and expression: fiction, philosophy, and memoir.

In the last two chapters, Barrie shifts his narrative focus and introduces another character, Maimie Mannering, a bold four-year-old girl who deliberately stays in the Garden after Lock-out Time one night to see the fairies. She meets a brownie (elf), witnesses a grand romantic fairy ball, and takes refuge from the cold in a wooden house the fairies build to keep her safe. But it quickly shrinks and vanishes: "Maimie stamped her foot naughtily, and was putting her fingers to her eyes, when she heard a kind voice say, 'Don't cry, pretty human, don't cry,' and then she turned round and saw a beautiful little naked boy regarding her wistfully. She knew at once that he must be Peter Pan" (56).

So Peter first appears to her as a consolation for her loss of the fairy house. He comforts her and instructs her in the ways of his world, and she tells him how real children play. But when he tells her his story of maternal separation, she is so alarmed she feels she must return. This serves to intensify Peter's need and anger: He was "in quaking fear of losing her. He was so fond of her, he felt he could not live without her. 'She will forget her mother in time, and be happy with me,' he kept saying to himself, and he hurried her on, giving her thimbles [kisses] by the way." She leaves, of course, and, despite her promises, never comes back, and Peter—now "the tragic boy"—goes on with his rounds eternally (60–61, 62).

This first incarnation of Wendy as Maimie makes her the more active one who abandons Peter. She is not at all the storytelling older sister and bustling little mother with a vain hope of marrying him one day. But Peter—in this first version—is just a magic baby boy. He has yet to become the seductive captain of Neverland. There is no developed domestic frame narrative of the Darling family household. There are no Lost Boys (just their dead precursors whom Peter buries), and there is no Captain Hook. Instead, these six chapters are mostly fairy business, and they can get excruciatingly sweet: "When the first baby laughed for the first time, his laugh broke into a million pieces, and they all went skipping about. That was the beginning of fairies" (32). Even the dark and morbid burial in the ending verges on coy self-pity, Barrie's least attractive (and most dated) disguise.

THE LITTLE WHITE BIRD AND PEDOPHILIA

After these six chapters, *The Little White Bird* immediately continues with what has become one of the most notorious things Barrie ever wrote. Following the narrative of Maimie's overnight with Peter, the next chapter begins: "David and I had a tremendous adventure. It was this, he passed the night with me. We had often talked of it as a possible thing, and at last [his mother] consented to our having it."[30] The narrator's tone is all atremble: "With an indescribable emotion, I produced a night-light from my pocket and planted it in a saucer on the wash-stand. . . . I took [his boots] off with all the coolness of an old hand, and then I placed him on my knee and removed his blouse. This was a delightful experience, but I think I remained wonderfully calm until I came somewhat too suddenly to his little braces [suspenders], which agitated me profoundly. I cannot proceed in public with the disrobing of David" (*The Little White Bird*, 130). When the boy wakes up in the middle of the night the narrator asks if he is frightened:

> I knew his hand was groping in the darkness, so I put out mine and he held on tightly to one finger.
> "I am not frightened now," he whispered.
> "And there is nothing else you want?"
> "Is there not?" he again asked politely. "Are you sure there's not?" he added.
> "What can it be, David?"
> "I don't take up very much room," the far-away voice said.
> "Why, David," said I, sitting up, "do you want to come into my bed?"
> "Mother said I wasn't to want it unless you wanted it first," he squeaked.
> "It is what I have been wanting all the time," said I, and then without more ado the little white figure rose and flung itself at me. For the rest of the night he lay on me and across me, and sometimes his feet were at the bottom of the bed and sometimes on the pillow, but he always retained possession of my finger, and occasionally he woke me to say that he was sleeping with me. I had not a good night. I lay thinking.

Of this little boy, who, in the midst of his play while I undressed him, had suddenly buried his head on my knees. . . .

Of David's dripping little form in the bath, and how when I essayed to catch him he had slipped from my arms like a trout.

Of how I had stood by the open door listening to his sweet breathing, had stood so long that I forgot his name and called him Timothy.

(132–33)

I expect it's almost impossible for us today to read this calmly. The narrator sounds at times like Humbert Humbert. The postmodernist twist at the end, which is the end of the chapter—"I forgot his name and called him Timothy"—plunges the whole episode into fiction: Timothy was the name of the narrator's imaginary dead son. It ups the ante, for it invites us to consider that the conflict between David's mother and the narrator is not merely about the boy but also about the relative creative power of women and men, mothers and novelists, flesh and spirit, fact and fancy, conventional realism and Barrie's hybrid species of imaginative literature. This war between the sexes about boys and books will take center stage in the novel's last chapter.[31] But what on earth are we today to make of the (to us) flagrant pedophilia of this overnight scene?

To begin with, it didn't strike Barrie's contemporaries as either odd or perverse. "One of the most charming books ever written," declared the London *Times*. "If a book exists which contains more knowledge and more love of children, we do no know it."[32] And we have the testimony, late in life, of Nico, the youngest of the five Llewellyn Davies boys, who wrote to Andrew Birkin, "All I can say for certain is that I . . . never heard one word or saw one glimmer of anything approaching homosexuality or paedophilia: had he had either of these leanings in however slight a symptom I would have been aware. He was innocent—which is why he could write *Peter Pan*."[33] It's also worth noting that Barrie's recent biographers, Andrew Birkin and Lisa Chaney, who were certainly writing in our time of heightened sensitivity to pedophilia expressed and repressed, do not dispute this characterization of the man as asexual (or so psychologically or hormonally deficient as to appear such). As for the text itself, it seems impossible to ignore the trembling, but we mustn't ignore the final twist either: the narrator is violently longing for a son—and to be a son himself.

But the sad biographical irony is that Barrie's own marriage was (apparently) unconsummated and that Barrie's wife would leave him for another man. He would then turn even more to the Llewellyn Davieses, but both the husband and wife soon died. Barrie adopted their five boys himself, and they grew up and pulled away. One was killed in trench warfare in France in 1915. Another drowned in 1921 in his last year at Oxford, an apparent suicide in the embrace of another boy. A third, Peter, was to commit suicide in middle age, years after Barrie had died.

WENDY, PETER, AND THE DARLINGS

The most immediately striking difference between the 1911 novel, *Peter and Wendy*, and its predecessor, *Peter Pan in Kensington Gardens*, is the omnipotent, omniscient narrator who exhibits an utterly secure command of his vast fictional empire. He effortlessly negotiates time past, present, and future, changing verb tense and mood with virtuoso aplomb, and moves between real and imagined space—from a London townhouse to the magical island of Neverland, which is located both in children's sleeping minds and their waking imaginations and somewhere out the nursery window, "second [star] to the right . . . then straight on till morning" (which famous phrase itself conflates space and time, of course).[34]

This supremely confident narrator easily drops first- and second-person remarks, directly addressing his audience of both children ("you") and adults ("we"). He coolly talks to his characters in mid-action and tosses a coin to determine what episode he's going to give us next. He gives us firm instructions: "Now, reader, time what happened by your watch" (196). He feels utterly free to tell us he "despises" one character (then changes his mind) and admires another who is "quixotic" but "magnificent" (*Peter and Wendy*, 208, 209) He can flawlessly evoke the purling sentimentality of Edwardian child worship and then skewer it. And he can portray imperial military heroism as the feckless child's play of a narcissistic boy who is happy to change sides at a whim and who seems to forget any promise he may have made, and to be "heartlessly" indifferent to the feelings of anyone who needs or cares for him. ("Children are ever ready, when novelty knocks, to desert their dearest ones" [170]).

The narrator is also a consummate master of an abundant cast of characters, from a fumbling City accountant with a need to be admired and a "passion for being exactly like his neighbors" to an "audacious" fairy in a negligee, from a "cadaverous and blackavised" pirate captain to a "prim" Newfoundland dog who is "a treasure of a nurse," from a pretty girlish housewife who "loved to have everything just so" to her "tidy" daughter who wants both to play the sock-darning, storytelling mother to little lost boys and to fly away and marry an enchanting demigod named Peter Pan, who is not an eighteen-month-old baby in a night-gown but an eight-to-ten-year-old flying adventurer in a sort of Robin Hood outfit (115).

This change of costume is crucial to the larger and more subversive meaning of Peter Pan, for in fact he's "clad in skeleton leaves and the juices that ooze out of trees" in the novel and in "autumn leaves and cobwebs" in the play. This eternal boy may "crow" like a cock in the later novel, "I'm youth, I'm joy,"[35] but from his first appearance he's also an agent of death. Peter's mythic namesake (best known from Ovid's *Meta-morphoses*) is obviously the cloven-footed son of Hermes and a nymph, the demigod who rides a goat and plays reed pipes that are all that re-main from his doomed love for the fleeing nymph Syrinx. Peter shares the tricky mercurial powers of Hermes, silver-tongued thief, liar, and messenger of the gods who leads the souls of the dead to Hades, but Pan's rampant sexuality has been watered down to the unaging charms of a lissome fin-de-siècle youth—though it must be said that the visible homoerotic touches are nothing to bring a blush to the cheek of a young person.

The first paragraph of *Peter and Wendy* is explicitly about the knowl-edge of time, change, and death. It begins, most famously, "All children, except one, grow up. They soon know that they will grow up, and the way Wendy knew was this" (69). The first story will be of the birth of knowl-edge of time and change: "One day when she was two years old she was playing in a garden [an Eden], and she plucked another[!] flower and ran with it to her mother. I suppose she must have looked rather delightful," he continues—the casual Edwardian tone here perfectly catches the nar-rator's courteously disguised omniscience lest he seem too intimidating at first—"for Mrs. Darling [a lightly comic allegorical name] put her hand to her heart and cried, 'Oh, why can't you remain like this forever!'" The very slight mockery of her melodrama here is emphasized by the narrator's change to an arch and slightly pedantic tone: "This was all that passed between them on the subject, but henceforth Wendy knew that she must grow up." And then the narrator turns to us directly and things get darker: "You always know after you are two. Two is the beginning of the end" (69). The comic disguise of the concluding epigram characteristically sugarcoats the pill.

The narrator very quickly takes refuge in chatty social narrative: "Of course they lived at 14, and until Wendy came her mother was the chief. . . . She was a lovely lady, with a romantic mind and such a sweet mocking mouth. Her romantic mind was like the tiny boxes, one within the other, that come from the puzzling East" (69). The image of the mind as a series of boxes is brilliantly brought back and elaborated in just a few pages: "Mrs. Darling first heard of Peter when she was tidying up her children's minds." The whimsical tone does not entirely obscure the narrative and psychological point that such motherly control is doomed and dangerous. "It is the nightly custom of every good mother after her children are asleep to rummage in their minds and put things straight for next morning, repacking into their proper places the many articles that have wandered during the day" (72–73).

This satire of repressive propriety is immediately strengthened by direct address to the audience of children: "If you could keep awake (but of course you can't) you would see your own mother doing this, and you would find it very interesting to watch her. It is quite like tidying up drawers [note the nasty pun]. You would see her on her knees, I expect, lingering humourously over some of your contents"—not of your mind but of you. The coy roundelay continues (she makes "discoveries sweet and not so sweet, pressing this to her cheek as if it were as nice as a kitten, and hurriedly stowing that out of sight"), and the paragraph concludes: "When you wake in the morning, the naughtiness and evil passions with which you went to bed have been folded up small and placed at the bottom of your mind; and on the top, beautifully aired, are spread out your prettier thoughts, ready for you to put on" (73). Mother puts "evil passions" at the bottom and "prettier thoughts" on top like cute clothes for socially acceptable use. The tone perfectly captures the sentimentally benign dictatorship of mother in the nursery, and the utter defeat of this rule will be the action of the story. It is no accident that this tidying-up paragraph was introduced by the grand narrative gesture: "There never was a simpler, happier family until the coming of Peter Pan" (72).

This undermining of Edwardian nursery certainties becomes particularly effective a bit further on as the Darlings say goodnight to the children. The comic melodramatic hyperbole is both witty and true:

"A nameless fear clutched at her heart and made her cry 'Oh, how I wish I wasn't going to a party tonight!' Even Michael [the youngest], already half-asleep, knew that she was perturbed, and he asked, 'Can anything harm us, mother, after the night-lights are lit?' 'Nothing, precious,' she said; 'they are the eyes a mother leaves behind her to guard her children.'" (86). The cloying and transparently regressive and self-comforting sententiousness of this is precisely what Peter is about to "break through" and rend as he flies in from Neverland.

But long before Peter arrives we have already encountered the most immediately palpable difference between *Peter and Wendy* and its fairy predecessor, *Peter Pan in Kensington Gardens*: the fully dramatized domestic comedy of the Darlings' family life. There were plenty of cozy class signals in the earlier version, but nothing resembling the vivid characters of father and mother, three children, dog nurse, and housemaid. Moreover, Barrie's comedy makes its instantly clear that Edwardian family life is filled with delusion and make-believe. G. K. Chesterton, writing in 1920, found this unsettling: "It seemed to me to be inartistic, strictly speaking, that the domestic foreground should be almost as fantastic as the fairy background."[36] But Barrie's art here anticipates both modernism and, in its constant playful authorial self-reflexivity, postmodernism. In the play, the first action the audience sees is the dog Nana turning down the children's beds. In the novel, the fantasy begins with whimsical metaphors and a faux-naïve characterization of Mr. Darling: "He was one of those deep ones who know about stocks and shares. Of course, no one really knows, but he quite seemed to know, and he often said stocks were up and shares were down in a way that would have made any woman respect him" (*Peter and Wendy*, 70). In no time he's anxiously and goofily totting up the household budget to see whether they can afford to keep a newborn infant, and this leads us right to "as they were poor, owing to the amount of milk the children drank, [their] nurse was a prim Newfoundland dog, called Nana, who had belonged to no one in particular until the Darlings engaged her. . . . She proved to be quite a treasure of a nurse" (71).

Mr. Darling is a fatuous ass, a hysterical, self-pitying domestic tyrant who desperately needs his wife's assistance and everyone's bottomless admiration, even the dog's: "I refuse to allow that dog to lord it in my nursery for an hour longer" (85). In what would become a century of popular comic fathers whose authority is utterly specious, he is by far the biggest baby in the family and mothered by all. He won't take his medicine, and the children try to shame him into it: "'Father, I am waiting,' said Michael coldly" (84). He can't tie his tie: "'I warn you of this, mother, that unless this tie is round my neck we don't go out to dinner tonight, and if I don't go out to dinner tonight, I never go to the office again, and if I don't go to the office again, you and I starve, and our children will be flung into the streets.' Even then Mrs. Darling was placid. 'Let me try, dear,' she said . . . while the children stood around to see their fate decided" (81). So much for the Edwardian *pater familias*. Mother knows best. But the point of the book is that she doesn't, of course. Barrie knows best.

Peter's appearance in this third chapter—entitled "Come Away, Come Away," a phrase that carries echoes from the Elizabethans to Yeats—has been prepared, thanks to the narrator's omniscience, with an extremely complex pattern of reminiscences and past, present, and future actions. Mrs. Darling has a faint memory of Peter, as we've seen; she spots traces of him in the minds of her sleeping children. She talks to Wendy about him, and Wendy tells her that Peter visits her to play songs on his pipe while she's sleeping. They discover leaves (momenti mori) in front of the nursery window. A few days later Mrs. Darling, half-asleep, looks up to find Peter in the room; Nana barks and attacks. Peter escapes, but they "slam" the window and "snap off" and trap his shadow, which Barrie describes as an "ordinary one," like an article of clothing. Rather than hanging it out the window and "lower[ing] the whole tone of the house," they roll it up and put it in a drawer (like the children's thoughts before) (78). We then flash forward to the parents discussing with great regret ("Ah me!" interjects the narrator) the events of "that never-to-be-forgotten Friday" (79), and after the comedy of Mr. Darling's rant and the parents' anxious departure, we finally make it into continuous action as Peter sails in the window looking for his shadow (that part of himself that leaves a passing trace behind: part of his self-image, his identity).

It's important to note that when Peter had first come to the Darlings' house he'd heard Mrs. Darling telling nursery stories and that his wish to hear the ending of "Cinderella" brings him back. Peter craves stories ("how he would like to rip the stories out of her" in the play's stage directions [*Peter Pan and Other Plays*, 102]) because he knows none. He lives in a world of an extremely narrow present, without time or seasonal change or more than the most rudimentary memory of people and their actions. Without time there is no morality, no emotional reciprocity, and there are no stories.

Peter is surrounded by a glamorous aura of nostalgia, but he is trapped in the present tense—though his narcissistic self-absorption also makes him "cocky." No sooner does he enter the nursery than he's shut Tinker Bell—the fairy who has accompanied him and finds the shadow he's searching for—in a jar and forgotten her. After Wendy sews his shadow back on he jumps about "in the wildest glee. Alas, he had already forgotten that he owed his bliss to Wendy. He thought he had attached the shadow himself. 'How clever I am,' he crowed rapturously, 'oh, the cleverness of me.' . . . To put it with brutal frankness, there never was a cockier boy" (*Peter and Wendy*, 91). In the next chapter, when he flies with the children to Neverland, he forgets to teach them how to stop flying or sleep in mid-air and even seems to forget them whenever he comes back from some in-flight adventure. He lets Michael drop until he almost falls into the sea and then rescues him at "the very last moment, and you felt it was his cleverness that interested him and not the saving of human life. Also he was fond of variety . . . so there was always the possibility that the next time you fell he would let you go" (103). (Note how seductively the narrator's easy direct address makes the audience a part of the action here.)

In dramatic contrast to Peter's self-absorption is Wendy's matronly solicitude. On first meeting him she "courteously" asks, "'Why are you crying?'" (89). She delights in her motherly skills, cleaning and darning and putting children to bed. Peter plays upon this, luring her to Neverland by saying she can be mother to the Lost Boys and tell them stories. But Wendy wants not only to play mother but also to fly and to play with mermaids (who turn out to be nasty—one mermaid will try to drown her in the lagoon).

So—most counter-stereotypically—Peter wants to sit still and hear a mother's tales about time. He wants to enter the world of the nursery, even though he says he has no mother and finds mothers "very overrated persons" (90). And also counter-stereotypically, Wendy wants to escape from the nursery, to fly, to pursue physical action, and to grow up enough to marry Peter. He, most famously, declares "with passion," "'I don't want ever to be a man. . . . I want always to be a little boy and to have fun'" (92). But his haunting the London nursery suggests he'd like to be a baby even more. (Wendy immediately understands how needy he is for a mother and "felt at once she was in the presence of a tragedy" [90], which arouses her sympathetic powers.)

Their ensuing mutual seduction is tinged with sexuality: "There can be no denying that it was she who first tempted him"—like Eve. "Greedy," he "grips her" and "begins to draw her toward the window." "Let me go," she "orders," but he says he'll teach her to fly. "Oh, how lovely to fly." "I'll teach you how to jump on the wind's back, and then away we go." "'Oo!,' she exclaimed rapturously." Soon she is "wriggling her body in distress . . . as if she were trying to remain on the nursery floor. But he had no pity for her." This "frightfully cunning . . . sly one" will teach her to fly, and she can tuck the boys into bed and sew pockets for them. "How could she resist?" asks the narrator. We understand that Peter is offering her the physical, emotional, and moral delights of adult femininity. "Wake up," she cries to her brothers, "Peter Pan has come and he is to teach us to fly" (97). And in no time at all, as their parents and Nana rush up the stairs, "the birds were flown" (101). This echo of the bird and fairy stories of *Peter Pan in Kensington Gardens* (where he no longer lives) suggests their escape is a regressive rebellion that has put their lives at risk.

The island of Neverland is first described as a "fearsome" place (*Peter and Wendy*, 106), a predatory circle of Darwinian violence: "The pirates were out looking for the lost boys, the redskins were out looking for the pirates, and the beasts were out looking for the redskins" (112). And as Peter, Tinker Bell, and the Darling children fly in, it turns out that they, too, are less than harmoniously allied. In a jealous rage, Tinker Bell plots to lure Wendy to her doom, and Peter is revealed to be a grim reaper of his troop of lost boys: "The boys on the island vary, of course, in numbers, according as they get killed and so on; and when they seem to be growing up, which is against the rules, Peter thins them out" (112). It's entirely characteristic of Barrie's sly tactics that his candid, casual tone obscures the violence and betrayal of this pruning; it is only through slow reading or in retrospect that we overcome Peter's charm and our own rosy nostalgia. Barrie quickly sweeps us into a highly colorful parade or pageant of the six lost boys and ten pirates of whom the captain (same rank and function as Peter, of course) is "Jas. Hook" (Barrie often employs this most unromantic, snobbish, upper-middle-class suburban moniker) who "lay at his ease in a rough chariot drawn and propelled by his men" like a god (114).

HOOK

Like Milton's Lucifer, Hook glamorously inhabits the very pinnacle of literary evil:

> In person he was cadaverous and blackavised and his hair was dressed in long curls, which at a little distance looked like black candles [Gothic dandy and blasphemer], and gave a singularly threatening expression to his handsome countenance. His eyes were the blue of the forget-me-not, and of a profound melancholy, save when he was plunging his hook into you[!], at which time two red spots appeared in them and lit them up horribly. [These are malign lights, unlike fairy lights or night lights.] In manner, something of the grand seigneur still clung to him, so that he even ripped you up with an air, and I have been told that he was a *raconteur* of repute [like the narrator]. He was never more sinister than when he was most polite, which is probably the truest test of breeding [an eighteenth-century or regency aristocrat]; and the elegance of his diction, even when he was swearing, no less than the distinction of his demeanor, showed him one of a different caste from his crew. [In fact Hook's class anxiety is tremendous; much is made of his trembling preoccupation with matters of Etonian good form.] A man of indomitable courage, it wtas said of him that the only thing he shied at was the sight of his own blood, which was thick and of an unusual color [a monster]. In dress he somewhat aped the attire associated with the name of Charles II. . . . But undoubtedly the grimmest part of him was his iron claw.
>
> (*Peter and Wendy*, 115)

Restoration rake, Augustan gentleman, Byronic hero, vampiric spirit, Hook is Peter's mirror image and double and, on stage, is often played by the same actor who plays Mr. Darling. (Thus in *Peter Pan's* Oedipal dynamic, the father is seen as both comic domestic tyrant and melodramatic killer.) Barrie's comic genius here is to summarize in Hook some three hundred years of literary villainy and then with insouciant aplomb chop off his hand and turn him into a castrated Fisher King. The narrator's Wildean comic pasticherie, the pagan mythic echoes, and Hook's fear of ever-approaching time (the clock within the crocodile that swallowed the hand that Peter struck off, the beast that stalks Hook till the very end) all combine to mute the evil, to be sure, but for the children who saw the play in its earliest performances, Hook was terribly frightening.

Daphne du Maurier describes how her actor father played the first Hook in a way quite different from the

> grotesque figure whom the modern child finds a little comic. He was a tragic and rather ghastly creation who knew no peace, and whose soul was in torment; a dark shadow; a sinister dream; a bogey of fear who lives perpetually in the grey recesses of every small boy's mind. All boys had their Hooks, as Barrie knew; he was the phantom who came by night and stole his way into their murky dreams. . . . When Hook first paced his quarter-deck in the year of 1904, children were carried screaming from the stalls. . . . How he was hated, with his flourish, his poses, his dreaded diabolical smile! That ashen face, those blood-red lips, the long, dank, greasy curls; the sardonic laugh, the maniacal scream, the appalling courtesy of his gestures.[37]

Barrie tinkered with his descriptions of Hook for years. In the novel we read, "The man was not wholly evil; he loved flowers (I have been told) and sweet music (he was himself no mean performer on the harpsichord); and let it be frankly admitted, the idyllic nature of the scene stirred him profoundly" (*Peter and Wendy*, 181). In the play we read in a stage direction: "The man is not wholly evil: he has a *Thesaurus* in his cabin, and is no mean performer on the flute" (*Peter Pan and Other Plays*, 136). He is "frightfully distingué." The final published text of the play contains one of the great comic soliloquies in English theatrical history:

> Split my infinitives, but 'tis my hour of triumph! . . . And yet some disky spirit compels me now to make my dying speech, lest when dying there may be no time for it. All mortals envy me, yet better perhaps for Hook to have had less ambition! O fame, fame, thou glittering bauble. . . . No little children love me. I am told they play at Peter Pan, and that the strongest always chooses Peter. They would rather be a Twin than Hook; they force the baby to be Hook. The baby! that is where the canker gnaws. . . . No, bi-carbonate of Soda, no . . .
>
> (*Peter Pan and Other Plays*, 139)

The strut and self-pity, the grandiose third person, the giddy anachronisms and the splendid leap in time and space right out of the present action of the play itself in "I am told they play at Peter Pan": all contribute to the exceptional expressive energy of this soliloquy.

Barrie exuberantly employs Hook to both evoke and mock the theatrical certainties of melodramatic good and evil: "Silence all," cries the captain, "for a mother's last words to her children" (to which Wendy obliges him with: "We hope our sons will die like English gentlemen" [*Peter and Wendy*, 192]). "'Proud and insolent youth,' said Hook, prepare to meet thy doom.' 'Dark and sinister man,' Peter answered, 'have at thee.'" When Hook drops his sword, Peter hands it back to him: "'Pan, who and what art thou?' he cried huskily. 'I'm youth, I'm joy,' Peter answered at a venture. 'I'm a little bird that has broken out of the egg'" (203). To this the narrator comments, "This, of course, was nonsense, but it was proof to the unhappy Hook that Peter did not know in the least who or what he was, which is the very pinnacle of good form" (203). Hook's anxious snobbery and fear about keeping up "good form" as an old Etonian gets full comic treatment: His last words in the play are the school motto "Floreat Etona" (*Peter Pan and Other Plays*, 146). The narrator bows him out of the novel with "James Hook, thou not wholly unheroic figure, farewell" (*Peter and Wendy*, 204).

Barrie repeatedly emphasizes the similarities between Hook and Peter. The extended episode in the mermaid's lagoon is conspicuous for Peter's imitation of Hook's voice. In the 1928 play, Barrie uses a stage direction to comment: "Peter can imitate the captain's voice so perfectly that even the author has a dizzy feeling that at times he was really Hook" (*Peter Pan and Other Plays*, 120). Their doubling is never more emphasized than when Hook hears that the "spirit that haunts this dark lagoon tonight" is James Hook and asks, "'If you are Hook . . . come, tell me, who am I?' . . . 'A codfish,' replied the voice, 'only a codfish.' . . . Hook felt his ego slipping from him" (*Peter and Wendy*, 147). At the climax of their duel, they meet on top of a slippery ball of rock (like the globe) until their faces are almost touching—two halves of the same person. After Hook is finally killed and Peter takes over the pirate ship, he gets Wendy to create a suit for him out of Hook's "wickedest garments," and "it was afterwards whispered among them that on the first night he wore this suit he sat long in the cabin with Hook's cigar-holder in his mouth and one hand clenched, all but the forefinger, which he bent and held threateningly aloft like a hook" (207). In the play, in a brief silent tableau that Barrie refused to cut, "the curtain rises to show Peter the very Napoleon of his ship" (*Peter Pan and Other Plays*, 146). Hook is as close as Barrie comes to portraying the infantile rage at maternal deprivation and neglect that lies at the center of Peter Pan.

RACE, SEX, AND GENDER

If Hook and the pirates tap into the long literary history of the devil, the redskins are pure eighteenth- and nineteenth-century racism by way of Fenimore Cooper and Mayne Reid: They

> carry tomahawks and knives, and their naked bodies gleam with paint and oil. Strung around them are scalps, of boys as well as pirates, for these are the Piccaninny tribe, and not to be confused with the softer-hearted Delawares or Hurons. In the van, on all fours, is Great Big Little Panther, a brave of so many scalps that in his present position they somewhat impede his progress. Bringing up the rear, the place of greatest danger, comes Tiger Lily, proudly erect, a princess in her own right. She is the most beautiful of dusky Dianas and the belle of the Piccannines, coquettish, cold and amourous by turns . . . she staves off the altar with a hatchet.
>
> (*Peter and Wendy*, 116)

In addition to the exotic sexism, the racism is compounded later when Tiger Lily actually speaks after Peter has saved her life: "Me Tiger Lily. . . . Peter Pan save me, me his velly nice friend. Me no let pirates hurt him" (157)—an imperial stew of Native American, black, and Chinese.

In the early versions of the play, the sexual rivalry of Tinker Bell, Tiger Lily, and Wendy was much more extensively developed, but Hook's part got larger and theirs shrank. But three varieties of female identity are still to be seen—the savage, "dusky" Amazonian belle; the seductive, "common" fairy flirt, who was "slightly inclined to *embonpoint*" (plumpness), as our catty narrator puts it (88); and, of course, Wendy, neither savage "squaw" nor vulgar seductress but the ideal mother who tells the boys stories, puts them to bed, and darns their socks. (These skills are much prized on the island, of course: Hook promises the pirates that by defeating Peter he will make Wendy their mother.)

It's a running joke in both the novel and the play that Wendy has eyes for Peter and that he never understands: "'Peter,' she asked, trying to speak firmly, 'What are your exact feelings for me?' 'Those of a devoted son, Wendy'" (*Peter and Wendy*, 162). Peter's unwavering incomprehension of any relation between the sexes other than that of child and mother—defined as housekeeper, nanny, and storyteller—is the last expression of Tommy and Grizel's asexual marriage. For most of *Peter Pan* this asexuality appears as a recurrent comic instance of charmingly "boyish" prepubescent innocence, but by the end it is clearly sterile and "heartless." For most of the time, however, the comedy veils incapacity and flatters adult notions of proper childhood.

In Peter's realm, sex can certainly kill you. Tinker Bell's sexual jealousy of Wendy can prove fatal: When Wendy first approaches the island, Tinker Bell incites the boys to shoot her. The arrow strikes the "thimble" (it's actually an acorn nut) that Peter has given her and that she wears like a necklace or amulet around her throat. In a conspicuous recurring joke, he calls this thimble a kiss, and so he can boast, "The kiss I gave her . . . saved her life" (126). The comic confusion of thimble and kiss expresses the difference between maternal and romantic love: to be a mother rather than a lover will save your life.

It's also noteworthy that Peter and Wendy play with the clichéd gender roles of Edwardian family life: "'Ah, old lady,' Peter said aside to Wendy, warming himself by the fire and looking down at her as she sat turning a heel, 'there is nothing more pleasant of an evening for you and me when the day's toil is over than to rest by the fire with the little ones near by'" (161). Wendy concludes her bedtime story by saying:

> "'Ah, now we are rewarded for our sublime faith in a mother's love.' So up they flew to their mummy and daddy; and pen cannot describe the happy scene, over which we draw a veil." That was the story, and they were as pleased with it as the fair narrator herself. Everything just as it should be, you see. Off we skip like the most heartless things in the world, which is what children are, but so attractive; and we have an entirely selfish time; and then when we have need of special attention we nobly return for it, confident that we shall be embraced instead of smacked.
>
> (166)

THE NARRATOR GROWS NASTY AND GRAND

The narrator has permitted himself a conspicuously sardonic comment here. His hostility arises from his envious knowledge as an adult that children's "heartless" beauty exempts them from moral order. They are beyond good and evil. By the penultimate chapter, "The Return Home," Barrie intensifies this anti-sentimental tone. The narrator becomes a freely sarcastic adult who is hurt and offended by the children and feels quite free to jeer:

We are no more than servants. Why on earth should their beds be properly aired, seeing that they left them in such a thankless hurry? Would it not serve them jolly well right if they came back and found that their parents were spending the weekend in the country? It would be the moral lesson they have been in need of ever since we met them . . . [Mrs. Darling] has no proper spirit. I had meant to say extraordinarily nice things about her; but I despise her, and not one of them will I say now. . . . For all the use we are to her, we might go back to the ship. However, as we are here we may as well stay and look on. That is all we are, lookers-on. Nobody really wants us. So let us watch and say jaggy things, in the hope that some of them will hurt.

(207–8)

This petulant self-pity resembles Mr. Darling's, of course, and suggests the narrator is feeling excluded from Mrs. Darling's affections. But soon enough he's admitting,

Now that we look at her closely and remember the gaiety of her in the old days, all gone now just because she has lost her babes, I find I won't be able to say nasty things about her after all. If she was too fond of her rubbishy children she couldn't help it. Look at her in the chair, where she has fallen asleep. The corner of her mouth, where one looks first, is almost withered up. Her hand moves restlessly on her breast as if she had a pain there. Some like Peter best and some like Wendy best, but I like her best. Suppose, to make her happy, we whisper to her in her sleep that the brats are coming back. . . . Let's. It is a pity we did it, for she has started up, calling their names.

(210)

What we're following here is the narrator's transformation from a jealous child to a loving god once again taking up his divine powers. And the cause of this transformation is his pity, which arises from his perception of Mrs. Darling's aging, her "withered mouth," her coming death (the echoes of *Margaret Ogilvy* are clear). Though time undoes us, it also empowers us emotionally, morally, aesthetically (as storytellers).

Such technical facility makes it all the more curious that Barrie rushes and stumbles when he comes to the double reversal at the end of this chapter devoted to the children's return. Feigning surprise at the events he's relating, the narrator neatly flies Peter and Tinker Bell into the nursery before the children arrive and has Peter bar the window so that Wendy will feel as rejected by her mother as Peter had felt before.

But Peter then observes grieving Mrs. Darling, weeping at the piano (and playing "Home Sweet Home," for pathos, not irony here, alas), and he all too quickly undergoes a change of heart and unbars the window. He "skipped about and made funny faces"—like six-year-old Barrie before his mother in *Margaret Ogilvy*—"but when he stopped it was just as if she were inside him, knocking" (212). The last image suggests both that he's imprisoned Mrs. Darling, barred her up inside himself, and that heartfelt conscience always will out. The peripeteia comes much too abruptly in the next sentence: "'Oh, all right,' he said at last, and gulped. Then he unbarred the window. 'Come on, Tink,' he cried, with a frightful sneer at the laws of nature; 'we don't want any silly mothers'; and he flew away" (212). Barrie is rushing this and quite carelessly invokes the transcendental "laws of nature," which must have wandered in from his Darwinian play, *The Admirable Crichton*.

Clearly, to show the dawn of Peter's empathetic moral conscience is utterly beyond the narrator's powers. It would require a psychological inwardness at odds with Peter's characterization everywhere else. So Barrie rushes over it. Nevertheless, the large thematic point is strongly made: Peter's selfishness is so huge that now he, not the mother, is the agent of exclusion. He has become his enemy. And the final well-dramatized irony is that Peter himself is barred anew from family life: "There could not have been a lovelier sight; but there was none to see it except a strange boy [nice alienation here] who was staring in at the window. He had ecstasies innumerable that other children can never know; but he was looking through the window at the one joy from which he must be forever barred" (214).

But Barrie clearly felt he couldn't end with this unambiguous image of the eternal boy successfully excluded from the family world where we began. In the play Barrie clearly wanted a more emphatic (and explicitly repetitive) conclusion, so he adds a scene that views the house from the outside: we see Mr. Darling "romping in at the door" (*Peter Pan and Other Plays*, 150) with the newly adopted lost boys; there is an exchange between the diminutive housemaid and the smallest lost boy in which she comforts him by declaring that she is his mother; and then Wendy flies down to talk to Peter, who has been "hovering in the air and knocking off tall hats" of the passersby in the street below (151). She invites him to speak to her parents about the "very sweet subject" of his feelings for her, but he brushes her off. Mrs. Darling leans down from the window

and offers to adopt him, but he "passionately" rejects this, too, in a famous declaration: "I don't want to go to school and learn solemn things.
No one is going to catch me, lady, and make me a man. I want always
to be a little boy and to have fun" (151). He attempts to lure Wendy back
to Neverland with talk of fairies and Tink, but Mrs. Darling "gripping
[Wendy] for ever," declares, "I have got you home again, and I mean
to keep you." But she "magnanimously" agrees to let Wendy visit Peter
"once a year for a week to do your Spring Cleaning" (152). At this Peter
flies off, and Mrs. Darling bars the window.

This conspicuous allusion to the Greco-Roman myth of Ceres per-
mitting her daughter Proserpina to visit Pluto in the underworld once a
year would certainly offer grand closure, a comforting reconciliation with
the cycle of the seasons, but Barrie wants pathos and glamour. So he
provides a quick scene a year later between Wendy (more grown up and
carrying a broomstick to help her fly) and an unchanged, self-absorbed,
forgetful Peter who doesn't remember the lost boys or Hook or Tinker
Bell and only "gloats" for stories about himself. The last spoken word
of the play, spoken "astride her broomstick," is Wendy's command—
"Home!" (153). And the last thing the audience sees is a final tableau of
Peter "gay . . . with rapturous face" playing his pipes to his "admirers,"
the clustering birds and fairies on the roof of the little house he'd built
for mother Wendy when she first arrived. He is in his eternal, inhuman,
glamorous realm. And in the last words of the script, "He plays on and
on till we wake up" (154): a dream of longing.

THE PLAY'S "AFTERTHOUGHT" AND THE NOVEL'S LAST CHAPTER

That is certainly the most familiar ending, but it's entirely characteristic
of Barrie's incessant revisionism (which enacts a never-ending process
of mythic repetition and dissemination) that four years after the first
performance he produced another version that was only staged once, on
February 8, 1908, and never published as a script in his lifetime. This ad-
dendum, "When Wendy Grew Up: An Afterthought," was inserted between the end of the nursery scene when Mrs. Darling bars the window
and the final tableau of Peter playing his pipes.

The "Afterthought" begins with grown-up Wendy (with "an exces-
sively matronly manner" [*Peter Pan and Other Plays*, 157]) telling a bed-

time story of Peter Pan to her daughter, Jane. The first lines we hear are Jane's "won't go to bed, Mommy, won't go to bed" (157), which echo Michael's at the beginning the play, of course. The bed-time tale of Peter Pan becomes a collaborative affair with Jane both asking for elaborations and correcting her mother's account, which recapitulates Wendy's sorrow that Peter forgot to come get her and concludes as Jane falls asleep to the narrative of her own birth. Whereupon "Peter's crow is heard—Wendy starts up breathless—then the window opens and Peter flies into the room. He is not a day altered. He is gay. Wendy gasps, sinks back in chair" (160).

The ensuing exchange is expertly managed. Peter has no memory of Captain Hook. In a crucial line, he casually remarks, "I forget them after I kill them." "Oh, Peter," exclaims Wendy, "you forget everything!" "Everything except mother Wendy," he insouciantly replies. Wendy slowly demonstrates that she has aged and cannot fly, that she has a daughter now, "I'm grown up—I couldn't help it!" (161–62). Peter is enraged that the little girl calls Wendy "mother" and as Wendy "rushes in agony from the room," he collapses sobbing

on the same spot as when crying about his Shadow in Act I. Presently his sobbing
  wakes Jane. She sits up.)
JANE: Boy, why are you crying?
(Peter rises—they bow as in Act I)
JANE: What is your name?
PETER: Peter Pan.
JANE: I just thought it would be you.
PETER: I came for my mother to take her to the Never Never Land to do my
  Spring Cleaning.
JANE: Yes, I know. I've been waiting for you.
PETER: Will you be my mother?
JANE: Oh, yes. (Simply)
(She gets out of bed and stands beside him, arms round him in a child's conception of a
  mother—Peter very happy . . .)

(162–63)

Repetition both intensifies and refutes our sense of time. Here the repetitions and childish solemnity of this ceremony of succession take it beyond sentimentality to an ironic enactment of eternal recurrence. They fly off and Wendy kneels down and addresses Nana:

Don't be anxious, Nana. This is how I planned it if he ever came back. Every Spring Cleaning, except when he forgets, I'll let Jane fly away with him to the darling Never Never Land, and when she grows up I will hope *she* will have a little daughter, who will fly away with him in turn—and in this way may I go on for ever and ever, dear Nana, so long as children are young and innocent.
(Gradual darkness—then two little lights seen moving slowly through heavens)
CURTAIN.

(163)

Wendy's final speech in this "Afterthought" much too transparently expresses Barrie's wish that he (though childless) might achieve literary immortality through successive generations attending his mythic play: "in this way may I go on for ever and ever . . . so long as children are young and innocent." But the profound urgency of this "afterthought" is confirmed by the fact that its one performance was also the only time in his entire career that Barrie himself appeared as author on stage; he stood in a black cape, for a curtain call.

The script of the 1908 "Afterthought" was not published until 1956, nineteen years after Barrie's death. But, in fact, he did adapt much of it in the extremely complex and ambitious last chapter of the novel *Peter and Wendy* in 1911. Entitled "When Wendy Grew Up," this chapter immediately follows the description of Peter outside the barred window of the nursery and looking in at the world of the reunited Darling family, "the one joy from which he must be for ever barred."

In fact, the novel works much better than the theatrical "Afterthought." The narrator is right there: "The years came and went without bringing the careless boy; and when they met again Wendy was a married woman, and Peter was no more to her than a little dust in the box in which she had kept her toys" (220). The dust is both literal and an allusion to the fairy dust that helps children fly and also, of course, to "ashes to ashes, dust to dust." The narrator's tone can become quite anti-sentimental: "All the boys were grown up and done for by this time; so it is scarcely worth saying anything more about them" (220). Wendy's daughter, Jane, "loved to hear of Peter, and Wendy told her all she could remember in the very nursery from which the famous flight had taken place. It was Jane's nursery now, for her father had bought it at the three per cents from Wendy's father, who was no longer fond of stairs. Mrs. Darling was now dead and forgotten" (221). The extreme time compression, incorporation of adult terms and references ("three per cents"), and brutal dismissal of Mrs. Darling reemphasize how powerful the narrator can be: he can kill off his "favorite" character and report that she was simply "forgotten." So Peter is not the only forgetful one.

Wendy and Jane then retell the story of Peter Pan in a bed-time ritual that reprises many crucial lines and themes ("Boy, why are you crying?") and repeats no less than four times the key notion that children can fly because they are "gay and innocent and heartless" (222). Barrie then moves to the novel's last fully presented scene with the unfortunately sentimental, "And then one night came the tragedy." Peter appears and Wendy "huddle[s] by the fire not daring to move, helpless and guilty, a big woman" (223). To show Peter how changed she now is, Wendy offers to turn up the light and "for almost the only time in his life that I know of, Peter was afraid. 'Don't turn up the light,' he cried. She let her hands play in the hair of the tragic boy. She was not a little girl heart-broken about him; she was a grown woman smiling at it all, but they were wet smiles" (224). The label "tragic" and the sentimentality of "wet smiles" suggest a retreat into adult rhetorical clichés. Far better is Peter's sobbing and Jane's asking, "Boy, why are you crying?" (225). The scene in the novel is a bit quicker and lacks the ceremonial effect of the play (though it follows the dialogue), but it does permit the narrator to say, "When Wendy returned diffidently she found Peter sitting on the bedpost crowing gloriously, while Jane in her nighty was flying round the room in solemn ecstasy" (225). Wendy is "forlorn"; Jane is "shameless" that she can fly. It is now Jane, not Peter, who bluntly tells Wendy that she can't come too because she can't fly.

The last two paragraphs of the novel shift from narrative past to present to future, enacting the narrator's godly powers. "Of course in the end Wendy let them fly off together. Our last glimpse of her shows her at the window watching them receding into the sky until they were small as stars" (225–26). This adapts the final tableau of the "Afterthought," of course, but the narrator is also completing the arc begun in the novel's first chapter. There two-year-old Wendy picks "another flower" and runs forward toward her mother and the reader. Here our "last glimpse" of her shows the matronly Wendy seen from the back, framed in a window, looking at her child receding into the heavens, the realm of death and mythic immortality.

Barrie develops this brilliantly in a coda that rushes us into the future. There's no need for this to be done as it was on stage in the "Afterthought" by Wendy in a speech to the dog. Here the narrator can do it himself:

> As you look at Wendy you may see her hair becoming white, and her figure little again, for all this happened long ago. Jane is now a common grown-up, with a daughter called Margaret; and every spring-cleaning time, except when he forgets, Peter comes for Margaret and takes her to the Neverland, where she tells him stories about himself, to which he listens eagerly. When Margaret grows up she will have a daughter, who is to be Peter's mother in turn; and thus it will go on, so long as children are gay and innocent and heartless.
>
> (226)

The final phrase has appeared four times before this, as we've noted, and the last word is crucial. To fly and to be a child and to stop time is to be heartless; the narrator knows this. He encompasses past, present, and future and calmly conveys his understanding that, as Nabokov's Humbert Humbert put it to Lolita, "the only immortality you and I may share" is "the refuge of art."[38]

J. D. SALINGER'S SAINTLY DROPOUT

Holden Caulfield

MID-TWENTIETH-CENTURY FICTION was full of odd children—sensitive young misfits and martyrs whose anxious vulnerability was a sign of their emotional, intellectual, and moral superiority to the conformists of the lonely crowd. In the Gothic South there was the tomboy of Carson McCullers's *Member of the Wedding* (1946) and the sissy of Truman Capote's *Other Voices, Other Rooms* (1948); in the West there was the tormented cowboy brother and sister of Jean Stafford's *Mountain Lion* (1947); and in the Midwest there was the blank abused Candide of James Purdy's *Malcolm* (1959). While demonic children were portrayed in William March's *Bad Seed* (1954) and William Golding's *Lord of the Flies* (1954), the most conspicuous angelic children and saintly adolescent misfits can be seen in the work of J. D. Salinger. In such blessed little girls as the four-year-old Sybil in "A Perfect Day for Bananafish" (1948), the thirteen-year-old heroine of "For Esmé—with Love and Squalor" (1950), and Holden Caulfield's ten-year-old sister, Phoebe, in *The Catcher in the Rye* (1951), Salinger portrays descendents of Little Nell, holy virgins who minister to the walking wounded traumatized by the aftershocks of World War II. Salinger's most famous character, sixteen-year-old Holden, is a holy rebel who combines elements of Oliver Twist and the Artful Dodger, Huckleberry Finn and Peter Pan. Like Oliver, Holden can be said to represent "the principle of Good surviving through every adverse circumstance, and triumphing at last."[1] Like the Artful Dodger, he is a quick-tongued urban trickster. Like Peter Pan, he mocks his own conventional (and comfortably affluent) society and wants to never grow up. But his most celebrated ancestor is Huckleberry Finn. Salinger transforms Huck the frontier fugitive into Holden the prep-school dropout: both boys' famously provocative colloquial voices embody their quests for American freedom and authenticity.

When *The Catcher in the Rye* was first published, it brought Salinger immediate celebrity (which he violently resisted and then famously escaped) and considerable wealth. Though the book was roundly criticized as false and sentimental, snobbish, and self-consciously cute by the mid-century literary establishment (Alfred Kazin, Mary McCarthy, and many others), it quickly became the object of fervent adolescent identification and much English department analysis (which George Steiner mocked as "the Salinger industry")[2] and soon achieved a double notoriety as one of the most often banned and most frequently assigned books in American high schools. In one of the great examples of cultural co-option, the foul-mouthed teenage rebel dropout became required reading. As Louis Menand put it, the boy who refused to be socialized became the instrument of socialization.[3]

Of all the many postwar novels of teenage saints and martyrs, only *The Catcher in the Rye* has become a popular classic, but Salinger's literary reputation is weak. It is only recently, in Morris Dickstein's excellent book on postwar American fiction, *Leopards in the Temple*, and in articles by Janet Malcolm and Louis Menand, that he seems to be getting a fair rereading. Perhaps we can now move beyond the more familiar mythic themes and symbols (the quest, the fall from innocence into experience, the hunting cap defiantly worn backward like a baseball catcher's hat) and beyond the symptomology of *The Catcher in the Rye* as a hegemonic agent of the American 1950s. The book's sentimentality and nostalgia for innocent (and highly affluent) childhood have long been well described, but the intricate workings of its voice, its finely calibrated structure, and its psychological precision and range are the qualities that have kept Holden alive as a seriocomic scourge, a pilgrim, and a secular redeemer, however morally compromised and culturally collusive such redemption may now seem to readers alert to the political unconscious. This literary child still generates impressive energy.

The two most famous loudmouths in American literature, Huckleberry Finn and Holden Caulfield, share many things. Both of them are intensely self-conscious about their literary efforts and about their auditors' rhetorical and moral expectations, which they belligerently defy in a transparently defensive way. Both of them have an urgent need to pit their idiosyncratic and energetic voices against the lies of conventional social speech and writing and against what they often portray as the dead or deadly adult world. Both are not as isolated as they seem: they're quick to refer to social and family circumstances, which they clearly feel are necessary constituents of their identities. Both of them are children living in extremis—Huck is fourteen and Holden seventeen as he narrates the story of his previous year—who launch themselves into extravagantly virtuosic monologues in an attempt to make sense of a recent personal crisis they've just barely managed to survive. And both of them realize that these crises are not merely private but conspicuously social and encompass large questions of freedom, authenticity, and civilization and its discontents. So Holden's and Huck's aggressively colloquial styles epitomize their personal and cultural survival. They wield them as magic weapons to cut away the lies of what Huck calls "sivilization" and what Holden calls the phonies' crap. These loud boys are agents of truth. They will deliver us from evil and restore us to life, or so they—and their creators—seem to suggest.

Huck begins his tale with a literary flourish that trumpets his connection to a famous predecessor and a trinity of female truth tellers:

> You don't know about me, without you have read a book by the name of "The Adventures of Tom Sawyer," but that ain't no matter. That book was made by Mr. Mark Twain, and he told the truth, mainly. There was things which he stretched, but mainly he told the truth. That is nothing. I never seen anybody but lied, one time or another, without it was aunt Polly, or the widow, or maybe Mary. Aunt Polly—Tom's Aunt Polly, she is—and Mary, and the widow Douglas, is all told about in that book—which is mostly a true book; with some stretchers, as I said before.[4]

Huck's voice is simultaneously proclaiming both its idiosyncratic superiority and its dependence on a written text, just as Huck himself is both proudly singular and part of a vividly specific social context. Huck also knowingly embodies another paradox: like the Cretan who tells us all Cretans are liars, Huck is telling us the truth, which is that he lies—particularly since he's not one of the exclusive triumvirate of female truth tellers. These many kinds of doubleness—speech and writing, truth and falsehood, male and female, universal and local—foreshadow many of the coming themes and conflicts.

Holden Caulfield's first sentences are just as rich:

> If you really want to hear about it, the first thing you'll probably want to know
> is where I was born, and what my lousy childhood was like, and how my
> parents were occupied and all before they had me, and all that David Cop-
> perfield kind of crap, but I don't feel like going into it, if you want to know
> the truth. In the first place, that stuff bores me, and in the second place, my
> parents would have about two hemorrhages apiece if I told anything pretty
> personal about them. They're quite touchy about anything like that, especially
> my father. They're *nice* and all—I'm not saying that—but they're also touchy
> as hell. Besides, I'm not going to tell you my whole goddam autobiography
> or anything. I'll just tell you about this madman stuff that happened to me
> around last Christmas just before I got pretty run-down and had to come out
> here and take it easy.[5]

From the first page of *The Catcher in the Rye* what's likely to strike us
today is how loudly Holden speaks, how intensely literary his famous
colloquial style is (like Twain's, like Hemingway's), and how many literary and cultural references come charging at us. He begins by declaring
the primacy of speech: "If you really want to hear about it"—if you want
to "hear," not "read," the truth this prophetic wise child will utter—"the
first thing you'll probably want to know is where I was born, and what
my lousy childhood was like, and how my parents were occupied and all
before they had me." All the usual determiners of identity—geographi-
cal, psychological, socioeconomic—are undermined by that "lousy" and
the deliberate jokey awkwardness of "occupied and all." All the conventional facts exerting their conventional absolute force are dismissed as
"all that David Copperfield kind of crap." And for Holden to conclude
this first sentence with "I don't feel like going into it, if you want to know
the truth" is to challenge the reader's expectations and even his desire "to
know the truth." We can also hear that Holden is projecting his anxiety
about his unconventionality into a challenge to the conventional reader's
tolerance.

The *David Copperfield* reference is loaded. Like many adolescents,
Holden often makes a show of dismissing what's most important to him;
in fact, he's similar to David Copperfield in his sensitivity, rebelliousness,
miserable family and school life, and moral concern. Dickens's book—
like this one—is a first-person inquiry into the narrator's psychological and moral status: it's the autobiography of a writer who has recovered from a childhood marked by abandonment and abuse to become

nothing less than a "Hero as Man of Letters," as Dickens's friend Carlyle put it. David Copperfield begins his autobiography by explicitly declaring its purpose: "Whether I shall turn out to be the hero of my own life, or whether that station will be held by anyone else, these pages must show" (must, not will).[6] Holden has a similar goal: he must grapple with the tale of "this madman stuff that happened to me." But Holden is speaking, not writing. His vantage point is only a few months after these events, not thirty years, and as a narrator he's also twenty years younger than David—not yet the famous writer he may or may not become, though he certainly displays in abundance a novelist's eye and ear.

While Holden's Christian name suggests, of course, the power to "hold on" (to people and the past and life itself), his surname intensifies the connection to Dickens. David Copperfield was born with a caul, a fetal membrane thought to be a good omen, a sign that he would see ghosts and spirits and be magically preserved from death by drowning (which is visited upon others in the book). "Caulfield" suggests not only David's caul and its signaling magic powers of sight and survival and good luck (the pun on "call" conveys personal vocal urgency and a sense of mission, a "calling) but also the "field" of rye in which Holden imagines imperiled children must be "caught" and saved from falling over a cliff into deadly adult life of time and change.

As Holden's first paragraph continues, he proclaims "that stuff"—conventional facts—"bores" him, but he also immediately confesses that he doesn't want his narrative to anger or injure his parents: "They're *nice* [pleasant, proper, fastidious] and all—I'm not saying that—but they're also touchy as hell." He clearly does care about them and needs them. He is also quick to reduce the scale of his project: "I'm not going to tell you my whole goddam autobiography or anything. I'll just tell you about this madman stuff that happened to me around last Christmas just before I got pretty run-down and had to come out here and take it easy." Although it turns out Holden is not in an insane asylum, as "madman" misleadingly suggests, but in a sanatorium that's testing him for tuberculosis (which he doesn't have—it's not the goddam nineteenth century), we sense that the urgency of his telling arises from his fear of "this madman stuff" and his belief that by telling it he can comprehend or control or exorcize it. To narrate his story is to prove he's recovered from it. Thus his book is a classic bildungsroman, a novel of education and development that demonstrates its central figure is a hero by showing how he got to be the person who could tell the tale.

Holden's strong belief in the heroic moral importance of literature is evident from his anger at his brother D.B., who "wrote this terrific book of short stories, *The Secret Goldfish*." (The animal reference is the first statement of what will become a recurrent theme of innocent wildlife—encompassing fish, horses, ducks, sea lions, deer, bears, dogs, a chimpanzee—that expresses Holden's anxiety about vulnerable natural goodness trapped in deadly civilization, an urban park, a zoo.) His brother is now "out in Hollywood . . . being a prostitute" by writing screenplays. "If there's one thing I hate, it's the movies. Don't even mention them to me," says our fervent literary purist (4). Nevertheless, in just a few pages he will do a Fred Astaire tap routine from *The Ziegfield Follies*, and later he'll tell us the entire plot of the sappy Ronald Coleman film *Random Harvest* and repeatedly imitate a gangster plugged in the guts in a film noir. He's part of the culture he resists. He has to come to terms with it without becoming a phony, a recluse, or a madman.

Literary works are crucial to this effort. They represent a usable inheritance and moral compass for this unmoored, mourning child. As the novel progresses there will be a wealth of literary references: to the passionate and rebellious Eustacia Vye of Hardy's *Return of the Native*, Isak Dinesen's *Out of Africa*, Ring Lardner's satires, the "smart and entertaining," innocent loudmouth Mercutio in *Romeo and Juliet* (145), Somerset Maugham, Rupert Brooke, and Emily Dickinson ("the best war poet," a brilliant observation), *The Great Gatsby* (which Holden adores), *A Farewell to Arms* ("phony," an excellent call in 1951) (182–83). Holden is also a merciless critic of the performing arts: he hates exhibitionistic virtuosity in jazz and in the snob-literary Broadway theater—the Lunts are slammed, and Olivier as Hamlet is "too much like a goddam general, instead of a sad, screwed-up type guy" (152). And though Holden hates the Rockettes, he loves to dance—both tap and ballroom, from jitterbug to tango.

The novel's most obvious literary reference is, of course, to Robert Burns's "Comin Thro' the Rye," in which a female speaker elliptically expresses her secret love and sorrow. Burns's use of Scottish dialect and folksong to authenticate demotic thoughts and feelings (and, implicitly, to rebuke conventional English usage and literary forms) is paralleled by Salinger's use of children's colloquial speech. Holden tellingly misquotes the poem (too tellingly—the slip typifies the Freudian 1950s). Burns wrote, "Gin a body meet a body / Comin thro' the rye," but Holden remembers it as "If a body catch a body comin' through the rye." His prescient sister Phoebe corrects him, but he says he thought it was "catch" because his defining ambition—and hence title of his book—is to be the "catcher in the rye" who stands at the edge of a cliff and saves the lives of "thousands of little kids" about to fall over (224). Holden is still mourning the death from leukemia of his eleven-year-old brother Allie three years before. He keeps Allie's left-handed outfielder's mitt, covered with lines of poetry, as a magic catch-all for his memories and love. Holden is also obsessed with the suicide of an abused boy at school who threw himself out of a window. Holden tells us when he himself is wildly upset that he feels "like jumping out the window" (63). He suffers a recurring sensation of falling—first, as he leaves the school he's just been thrown out of and, later, as he wanders drunkenly and then feverishly through sordid Manhattan. Such literary allusions and metaphoric webs may seem overdetermined and unironic today, but they are uncommonly well balanced by the loud and (apparently) loose diction of Holden's monologue, which moves with still-impressive ease and momentum.

Holden's language is famous—and infamous among school censors—for its keywords: "phony," "lousy," "crumby," "crap," and "crazy." Scholars have noted a hundred instances of slang in the book and catalogued Holden's frequent triteness, redundancy, vagueness, odd grammar and usage, and use of phrases like "if you want to know the truth." They also note that Holden can certainly draw on a large vocabulary, including "ostracized," "unscrupulous," "conversationalist" and "traveling incognito," and that he turns nouns into adjectives like "perverty" and "vomity" or even into adverbs, as in the wonderful "she sings it very Dixieland and whorehouse, and it doesn't sound at all mushy" (149). In addition to these lexicographical effects, Holden's monologue is conspicuously filled with references to being "sad," "depressed," "lonesome," and "sorry" for people, even his antagonists.[7]

These various kinds of verbal repetitions become refrains and produce an elegiac poetry. Holden lurches between cliché and originality, vagueness and precision, mixing all kinds of diction and usage from informal kid speech and teenage slang to upper- and lower-class and ethnic lingo to kitsch movie dialogue and advertising phrases to schoolteacher jargon, moving from the private or eccentric to the ostentatiously conventional or stilted. His often surprising juxtapositions are highly expressive of his inner state and character (and his class and culture) and produce not only comedy (both intended and accidental) or bathos (ditto) but also an ironic eloquence (ditto again) that comes from both Holden and, above him, the author.

One of the earliest examples of this comes when the decrepit history teacher Spencer reads out loud Holden's exam essay on the ancient Egyptians (who will figure throughout this book that is filled with tombs, cemeteries, and the fear of death, decay, and change): "Modern science would still like to know what the secret ingredients were that the Egyptians used when they wrapped up dead people so that their faces would not rot for innumerable centuries. This interesting riddle is still quite a challenge to modern science in the twentieth century" (16). Holden flunked history and loudly tells us his essay is "crap," but right in the heart of his cheap advertising lingo ("secret ingredients") and his anxious tautologies is the horrific precision of "they wrapped up dead people so that their faces would not rot." And the sentence ends with nothing less than the gorgeous Sir Thomas Browne effect of "innumerable centuries." Such sudden but graceful thematic and stylistic enlargements occur throughout the book. Just as Holden's actions refute postwar norms of masculine heroism and gray-flannel social success, his verbal style refutes both Hemingway's stoic minimalism and Faulkner's grandiloquence. As Salinger put it in a contributor's note in *Esquire* in 1945: "The men who have been in this war deserve some sort of trembling melody rendered without embarrassment or regret."[8]

Holden's style sounds spontaneous, free-associative, a rambling performance by a sloppy teenage saint of candor. His voice is so loud, repetitive, slangy, and obscene that it obscures the author's architectonic cunning, his feats of narrative and metaphoric construction. The narrative is composed of four sections of six or seven chapters that trace the events of forty-eight hours, from Saturday afternoon to Monday afternoon of Christmas week. Each section contains some kind of physical collapse and concludes with Holden bursting into tears. The first section is set in the school Holden has just been expelled from: we meet a teacher and two representative students, the gross loser Ackley and the slick bastard Stradlater (modeled on Dickens's glamorous, seductive Steerforth in *David Copperfield*). We learn that Holden is still mourning the death of his brother. After a transitional chapter in which Holden rides a late train into the dark night of Manhattan (accompanied by a loving mother figure), the second section portrays him in a sordid hotel and nightclub world of sexual predation, culminating in a visit from a prostitute "around my age" and a punch in the gut from her pimp (123).

The third section runs from Sunday morning to after midnight and provides a survey of New York City life. It takes us from a breakfast with two mendicant nuns at a Grand Central Station lunch counter to a Broadway theater date with the ultimate preppy glamour girl, Sally Hayes, which ends in a quarrel about escaping from the respectable adult world of their class; a hostile meeting with a former student advisor; a solitary drunken evening in a midtown bar; and a futile attempt to escape into the dark and wintry paradise lost of Central Park long after midnight. This third section ends with feverish, weeping Holden deciding to sneak back home to see his sister Phoebe before he dies of pneumonia.

The fourth section takes him into his dark apartment where "I felt swell, for a change. . . . I just felt good, for a change," visiting with his sister until his parents return and he has to escape lest they realize he's been expelled (207). He goes to the false refuge of his former prep school mentor, Antolini, who may or may not make a pass at him. In terror he flees to the waiting room of Grand Central Station. In the morning he makes a final pilgrimage back uptown to say good-bye to his sister before he hitchhikes out west. He leaves a note at her school for her to meet him at the nearby Metropolitan Museum, where he visits the mummies' tombs, collapses in the bathroom, but then begins to feel better. When Phoebe arrives and begs him to take her with him, he refuses—she must not be taken from the customary order of things—and he decides to abandon his westward escape. Instead of going to a Colorado ranch or getting a job pumping gas, he takes Phoebe to the Central Park Zoo, where she rides a wooden horse on the carrousel. Holden just watches: "I felt so damned happy all of a sudden, the way old Phoebe kept going around and around" (275). He understands that time and change cannot be stopped but the ceremony of innocence can be celebrated on the artful carrousel. A beneficent rain descends—not like the punishing rain on his dead brother's grave, but a baptism, a rebirth that leaves Holden in tears.

This plot clearly enacts the developing themes: Holden's mournful journey ends when he returns his sister to her childhood. He stops his active, linear wandering and contemplates her circular play. He returns to life. The sentimentality of this final affirmation and the author's evident endorsement of Holden's ostensibly enlightened embrace of the order of nature and culture are mitigated by the virtuoso voice and the wealth of structural details. The book is full of doublings and contrasts: there are two prep school brutes, two teachers, two dead boys, two mothers, two girlfriends, two cabbies, two "flits" (both of them flawed advisors), two bars, two virtuoso dancers (a "dopey" tourist and precocious Phoebe), two museums.

Holden is obsessed with death and change and treasures New York's two great complementary museums of nature and culture because in them "everything always stayed right where it was" (157). On the West Side there is the Museum of Natural History, "the only nice, dry, cozy place in the world" (156), with its displays of animal and primitive human life (including an ice-fishing Eskimo who is echoed in Holden's worry about the Central Park ducks and fish in winter). On the East Side is the Metropolitan Museum of Art with its displays of ancient Egyptian civilization, particularly the mummies' tombs, where it's "so nice and peaceful" (264) (unlike Allie's drenched cemetery)—until Holden discovers "fuck you" scrawled in red crayon (nothing is safe from rot) and collapses in the bathroom (a fortunate fall) before arising to meet Phoebe (260).

Perhaps the most memorable physical symbol in the book is Holden's red hunting cap, which he wears backward like a baseball catcher's hat and is significantly donning and doffing throughout the narrative. It signals his status as an eccentric hunter in the urban forest, and its color links him to his siblings—Allie and Phoebe have red hair while Holden has a shock of gray hair on one side of his head, a mark of his status as a wise child, a prophet, someone halfway old before his time. In the last section, in a series of Mozartian exchanges, Holden bestows the blessed hat on Phoebe, and she, in a gesture of beneficent role reversal, returns it to him and then puts it on his head as she mounts the carrousel horse.

The book's readers have always been quick to note Holden's identification with the ducks of the Central Park lagoon—he repeatedly asks what happens to them in winter, who takes care of them, and even goes to see for himself in the middle of night—but the horse theme is even more impressive. On the second page of the book Holden denounces his prep school's magazine ads of "some hot-shot guy on a horse jumping over a fence. Like as if all you ever did at Pencey was play polo all the time. I never even once saw a horse anywhere *near* the place" (4). In his Rockefeller Center denunciation to Sally Hayes of the consumer culture of ever-newer cars he bursts out, "I'd rather have a goddam horse. A horse is at least *human*, for God's sake" (170). When he tells clear-eyed Phoebe he's decided to go out west to work on a Colorado ranch, she immediately says, "You can't even ride a horse" (216). And in a final transformation, Phoebe herself rides a brown wooden carrousel horse as

Holden happily watches; nature and art are reconciled in a circular musical ceremony of child's play, affirming the beneficent order of memory and time.

Even the most casual details turn out to be loaded. For example, the book begins with Holden on a hill overlooking his prep school's football game. While the louts bray below, he stands by a cannon from the Revolutionary War, the sole relic of an authentic male heroic past. This historical reference will be echoed at the end of the book when Holden is restored to himself by his determination to return his kid sister to her starring role in the school play, which surveys American history for the benefit of a shamed and eventually redeemed Benedict Arnold. Holden's decaying and pompous history teacher lives on Anthony Wayne Avenue, which is named after an exceptionally vigorous general of the Revolutionary War known as "Mad Anthony Wayne." The slick make-out artist Stradlater seduces girls with his "Abraham Lincoln sincere" voice; the orator of Gettysburg getting it on in the back seat of a car is the legacy of American history (64). Other military references include Holden's depressed older brother lying on the bed during his army furloughs and Holden's losing the fencing team's equipment on the subway. These lost foils are recalled when Holden later regrets that his favorite character in *Romeo and Juliet*, "smart and entertaining" and innocent Mercutio, is killed in a pointless duel (145).

A more subtle but no less significant use of a literary allusion to war occurs as Holden tries to pick up three "dopey" tourist girls in a bar. Though Holden has been quick to denounce the Hemingway of *A Farewell to Arms*, he is thinking of Hemingway's story "Soldier's Home" (1925) when he tells us that one of the girls was "Bernice something—Crabs or Krebs" (95). Fitzgerald's story "Bernice Bobs Her Hair" is also referenced here, and we understand that Holden's fear of sexual contamination and death lies behind that "Crabs." But, more important, Harold Krebs is the depressed late-returning war veteran of Hemingway's story, which bears several thematic similarities to *The Catcher in the Rye*. Krebs's experience of the army, the war, and postwar Germany has made it impossible for him to resume normal, American, small-town Oklahoma life. He has come back too late for parades and war stories. Passive, numb, without friends or any energy to seek a girl or a job, he lives at home with his parents, who treat him like the high school boy he was before he left. Krebs's depression and schizoid alienation from other people and from conventional life and feeling are his war wound. He can't bear lies; he doesn't believe in God and won't join his intrusive, manipulative, and sanctimonious mother in prayer; he even briefly tells her he doesn't love her but then recants. Krebs is the original dropout, Holden's World War I progenitor. The one person he does respond to—and tells he loves—is his kid sister, a tomboy who wants him to be her "beau" and come down to the school to see her play baseball. Just as he can't fill the customary male roles, his sister achieves her palpable authenticity (her actions and speech are direct and uncontaminated) by violating customary gender roles—even her baseball game is a bit askew since it's played indoors. A candid, affectionate angel in a world of hypocrites and bores, this kid sister is a progenitrix of Phoebe.[9]

After years of feminist and queer studies, we're likely to be struck by Salinger's hostility and repugnance toward men and his sympathy and attraction to women. Men are depicted more reductively, and though women are verbally stereotyped and often function sentimentally as Holden's comforters, they exhibit greater human variety as well. The men and boys in the book are phonies, bullies, slobs, snobs, drunks, "flits," and "mean guys" (217). Their bodies are seen with Swiftian disgust. At school, the loser Ackley has "sinus trouble, pimples, lousy teeth, halitosis, crumby fingernails" (51); the yearbook Adonis Stradlater is a secret slob; and the pontificating history teacher Spencer has the grippe and picks his nose. In New York, the "pimpy elevator guy" in the Edmont hotel has "a big fat hairy stomach" (132–33). Even the ostensibly benevolent men are corrupt: Holden's former student advisor Carl Luce is an affected expert on perverts. Holden's mentor Antolini is highly intelligent, generous, perceptive, and admirable when he picks up the broken body of the boy suicide, but he's also an often sententious, self-pitying drunk—and his "petting" or "patting" Holden's head (249) is a self-indulgent bit of sentimental affection that terrifies Holden and leads him to bolt from this one adult refuge. (Holden never resolves the question of Antolini's possible homosexual feelings for him, and Salinger unfortunately leaves it unresolved in an awkward way.) As for Holden's father, we learn he's a corporate lawyer who wants Holden to go to Yale or Princeton, won't be going to Phoebe's school play, and will certainly "kill" Holden when he learns he's been expelled (224), but we never see or hear him: he's never more than a figure in the next room who's about to turn on the news as Holden sneaks out of the house.

But as Holden is trumped again and again by male bullies and phonies, he turns toward an impressive number and variety of women and
girls; as he says, "Women kill me. They really do. . . . I just like them, I
mean" (70). He makes it clear he needs to "*really* like" a girl to feel desire
for her, and he lets us know that unlike other boys he stops his advances
when girls ask him to: "I get to feeling sorry for them" (121). He worries
he's a "sex maniac" (81) but confesses, "If you want to know the truth,
I'm a virgin. I really am. I've had quite a few opportunities to lose my
virginity and all, but I've never got around to it yet. Something always
happens" (120).

It's in this context that *The Catcher in the Rye* can be seen as a child's-
eye feminist novel of the chauvinist 1940s and 1950s. The book abounds
in women and girls, old and young. There's the history teacher's wife,
Mrs. Spencer, who's so old she's deaf and has so little "dough" that she's
got to answer her own front doorbell. There's the attractive, observant,
and discreetly skeptical Mrs. Morrow on the New York–bound night
train, who is the mother of a towel-snapping bully that rivalrous, lying
Holden turns into a popular schoolboy Galahad in an attempt to gain
her attention and sympathy (she's the warm, responsive mother he
doesn't have). Holden completely misses how smart and tactful she is
as he suavely asks her if she'd like to join him for a cocktail and later
tells her he's got "this tiny little tumor on the brain" (75). Holden's own
mother—who's "nervous as hell" (206) and "isn't over" the death of her
middle child three years before—is just a voice that Holden hides from
in the closet, though, unlike his father, she at least comes into the room
and speaks to Phoebe.

Shy and teary Jane Gallagher had a "lousy childhood" just like Holden
and has a predatory "booze hound" of a stepfather (42). When she plays
checkers she always keeps her kings in the back row—refuses to enter
the fray, keeps her powers to herself, won't play the game—which profoundly attracts Holden. She's a great hand holder (the hand theme runs
throughout the book; Holden broke his hand in grief for Allie). Jane
is also one of the two girls Holden actually describes himself kissing,
but throughout his narrative he fears vulnerable innocent Jane may have
succumbed to the advances of the "sexy bastard" Stradlater. So Holden
keeps thinking of calling her but never gets her on the phone. The other
girl he kisses is Jane's opposite, Sally Hayes, who returns his embraces
and wants Holden to come trim her family's Christmas tree but is clearly

flourishing in the prep-school, Ivy League, "sophisticated" New York world (she's full of pretentious Broadway theater talk). Sally's a flirt in her "little blue butt-twitcher of a dress" in the Rockefeller Center skating rink (167). Sally may find school a "bore," but she's comfortable with the order of things in her snobbish, materialistic life, and she certainly won't leave Manhattan to run off to a cabin in the woods with Holden to play kid Thoreau.

At the other end of the social scale, there's the tough-talking former burlesque stripper, Faith Cavendish, whom Holden calls for a date in the middle of the night, and Sunny, the yawning prostitute about Holden's age, with her green "frock" and impatience with this talky "crumb-bum" who calls himself Jim Steele (127–28). There are the three movie-star-hunting tourists from Seattle whom Holden dances with in a seedy bar. There are the two young mendicant nuns Holden greatly admires when he meets them over breakfast at a sandwich shop near Grand Central Station and eagerly chats up about books and even "sexy" *Romeo and Juliet* (to his embarrassment) (144). And there are minor female characters who function as feminine grace notes, like the solicitous hat-check girl in the Wicker Bar who tries to get drunk Holden to put on his cap and go safely home or the careful schoolgirl on roller skates in Central Park whom Holden asks about his sister and wants to take for a hot chocolate, which she sensibly refuses (like the two cabbies who decline Holden's offer of a cocktail).

Of course, the most powerful moral and spiritual force in the novel is embodied in Holden's ten-year-old sister, Phoebe, the virgin princess and agent of grace, whose name alludes to the moon and to goodness, light, innocence—as in Hawthorne's Phoebe in *The House of the Seven Gables*. It is Phoebe's love and need for Holden's love that save him from a life of hitchhiking out west or working on Colorado ranch or pretending to be a deaf-mute working in a gas station and living in a cabin at the edge of the woods. Phoebe catches him from falling by making him take care of her instead of the imaginary children running through the rye.

Throughout his story Holden frequently uses the phrase "like a madman" (the subject of his narrative is "this madman stuff," of course), and he tells us: "If you want to know the truth, the guy I like best in the Bible, next to Jesus, was that lunatic and all, that lived in the tombs and kept cutting himself with stones. I like him ten times as much as the Disciples, that poor bastard. . . . All they did was keep letting Him down"

(130). Holden is remembering Mark, chapter 5, in which Jesus casts the self-destructive madman's many devils into the Gadarene swine and they, not the lunatic, perish by falling off a cliff into the sea:

There met him out of the tombs a man with an unclean spirit,

Who had his dwelling among the tombs; and no man could bind him, no, not with chains:

Because that he had been often bound with fetters and chains, and the chains had been plucked asunder by him, and the fetters broken in pieces: neither could any man tame him.

And always, night and day, he was in the mountains, and in the tombs, crying, and cutting himself with stones.

But when he saw Jesus afar off, he ran and worshipped him . . .

And the unclean spirits went out, and entered into the swine: and the herd ran violently down a steep place into the sea, (they were about two thousand,) and were choked in the sea.

Holden's destructive unclean spirits are exorcized by Phoebe's love and need for him. He becomes her catcher and returns her to the world of school and the play about a redeemed Benedict Arnold. But Phoebe has also become his catcher, for he now no longer needs to jump out a window or hitchhike to Colorado or become a deaf-mute gas jockey. He can return home with Phoebe, and then indeed go west, not to a fantasy wilderness or to corrupt Hollywood but to the sanitarium where, under the eye of his older brother, he can recover his health and then return home to continue at some eastern school.

So at the end of the novel, Holden has become profoundly conservative and reconciled to his (privileged) place in the conventional order of things. He will not attempt to erase the scrawled "fuck you's" that fill the world and that he thinks may eventually adorn his grave (like a curse on his mourners and the motto of his life). Holden's narrative demonstrates his recovery, and the act of telling it has enlarged his sympathies. Through this social act of speech and literary art he has rejoined what was soon to be called "the family of man" and finds he "misses" everyone he has described, even "old Stradlater and Ackley" and that "goddam Maurice" (the pimp who slugged him), as well as dead Allie and the schoolboy who jumped out of the window and his own lousy childhood (277). Holden's art links past and present, the living and dead.

Salinger portrays such aesthetic salvation as consubstantial with moral and psychological deliverance. All's well that ends well: there is

not a flicker of political or social concern. Women are a graceful, civilizing force, and brutal men can be defeated by sensitive but firmly heterosexual boys. Once again, a child will lead us. Holden is a conservative
enforcer disguised as a teenage loudmouth. And for all its extraordinary
flexibility, responsiveness, invention, and power, Holden's justly famous
verbal style never opens magic casements or ever threatens the reader. In
the end—after all the comic patter and the lyric pathos—the worst thing
that can happen to Holden is that "Daddy's going to kill you" (224).

VLADIMIR NABOKOV'S ABUSED NYMPH

Lolita

THE MOST EXTRAORDINARY USE of a child in twentieth-century American literature can be found in Vladimir Nabokov's *Lolita*. When the novel appeared in America in 1958—three years after its first publication in the Traveler's Companion series of the Paris pornographer Maurice Girodias, whom Nabokov knew only as the publisher of art books—*Lolita* sold more quickly than any book since *Gone With the Wind*. There were endless cartoons and talk-show jokes and a brilliant if crucially altered movie version by Stanley Kubrick, and within a few years the concept and indeed the word "Lolita" had pervaded international culture. (I was once assured by a Japanese student that I could already speak at least one word of Japanese, "Lolita.") It is a cruel irony that in popular usage a "Lolita" is a corrupt young girl inviting violation. Nabokov's character Dolores Haze has been eclipsed by the fantasy Lolita created by Nabokov's narrator, Humbert Humbert.

The reader has to struggle to keep in focus that Dolly Haze is not Lolita, that the narrator not only has "deprived [her] of her childhood," as he says,[1] but also, by delivering one gorgeous threnody after another, has shifted the emphasis from her story to his, from her erasure or occlusion to his own redemption through art—his own bildungsroman, which runs from his sunlit Riviera childhood (culminating in rapturous first love but a traumatic coitus interruptus) to his shady American adulthood that ends in the prison cell from which he is writing this confession of murder and last will and testament. Just as James challenged the reader to examine the governess's perplexing testimony, Nabokov is challenging us to free Dolly from Humbert's self-justifying, self-advertising narrative by scrutinizing his strategies and arguments. There's no other way to recover the child, to resurrect her from the narrator's fatal embrace. But Nabokov is also using the story of the death of this child as a way of leading us to heaven, a world of transcendental "concord" (308) and "aesthetic bliss" that far exceeds Humbert's narcissistic declarations of faith.[2] Humbert's lip service serves Nabokov's fervent affirmation.

Over the past half-century, the literary stature of *Lolita* has grown. It was rejected by five American publishers, and when it finally appeared, the *New York Times* reviewer memorably denounced it as "bad news . . . it is dull, dull, dull in a pretentious, florid and archly fatuous fashion [and] it is repulsive."[3] But a flurry of distinguished essays by such critics as Lionel Trilling and F. W. Dupee was followed by some twenty years of postmodernist explication and argument that flourished in the shadow of Alfred Appel's exemplary *Annotated Lolita* (1970; revised 1991). Such critics as John Updike, Michael Wood, David Rampton, Ellen Pifer, Vladimir Alexandrov, and Brian Boyd, Nabokov's excellent biographer, have significantly increased our understanding of what now looks like one of the supreme works of twentieth-century literature.

The first generation of scholars of *Lolita* enabled readers not only to negotiate the literary allusions (to Poe's "Annabel Lee," Mérimée's novel *Carmen*, Shakespeare, Joyce, Chateaubriand, Verlaine, Proust, etc.) but also to appreciate Nabokov's cornucopia of American and European cultural artifacts—poems, songs, ads, movies, motels—and descriptions (out of Chateaubriand) of the glorious American landscape that looms unnoticed beyond the neon. The early scholars documented Nabokov's ear for rhymes and puns in English, French, German, and Russian and scrupulously traced his careful patterns of sights, sounds, words, objects, characters, and events. They have shown us how the book is a symphony of literary parodies and pastiches of slang and commercial lingo, a confessional sex novel, a psychiatric case study, a fairytale, and a hard-boiled tough-guy detective novel: a mixture of Gogol, Dostoyevsky, and Dick Tracy (who appears as "Jutting Chin") topped off with echoes of French romanticism and symbolism. They have shown how it is a novel of prisons, doubles, grotesques, images of sun and shade, predatory artists—Humbert and his darker shadow Quilty, the celebrity playwright and pornographer who takes Lolita away from him. Throughout the novel, the details are so precisely constructed and deployed that one can, for example, follow Humbert's unconscious (or pseudo-unconscious) associations (and slips of the pen) as they lead to surprising revelations he may never catch but that the reader can and must.

But the book is considerably more than a self-referential literary game, more than a Fabergé egg constructed by an imperial imagination delighting in its ingenuity. *Lolita* is famously a novel of Europe and America, a love story and product of the author's self-proclaimed "love affair" with the "English language."[4] Though Nabokov derided Henry James as "that pale porpoise," Lolita is a younger sister of that scandalous representative American girl, Daisy Miller, of 1878.[5] *Lolita* may not be the portrait of a lady, but it is certainly the portrait of a nymph; the word refers to a divine spirit or bride in Greek and also to "the young of an insect undergoing incomplete metamorphosis" (we should note that "incomplete").[6] Humbert declares the book is his attempt to recapture time, "to fix once for all the perilous magic of nymphets" (as one might "fix" a butterfly on a cork board) (134), but as I've said it is also a self-portrait, a confession, a self-accusation, a bildungsroman—a novel about the narrator's growth and development proven by his ability to write the book we're reading. To possess or "fix" childhood is to pervert it, destroy it, kill it. The book describes a doomed attempt to stop time, growth, transformation—and the final renunciation of that attempt except in the form of memory preserved in an immortal work of art. Says Humbert.

So *Lolita* is about metamorphosis, but not only of Lolita from girl of twelve to pregnant woman of seventeen but also of Humbert Humbert, from child to adolescent, husband in Paris, American exile, husband of Charlotte Haze, lover and father of Lolita—a state of bliss and torment that leads to his vengeful pursuit of his rival, Quilty, and his final remorse, renunciation, and regret. It most urgently narrates a transformation of lust to love. Says Humbert.

In Nabokov's fake foreword, a parodic mid-century psychologist ("John Ray, Jr.") calls it "a tragic tale tending unswervingly to nothing less than a moral apotheosis" (5). In the genuine author's note written after the original American publication, Nabokov is anxious to proclaim the independence and originality of a work of art and so announces that there is no lesson or moral or sociological or journalistic information to be found in the book. But this is a polemical overstatement. In the text he inserts the gnomic verse "the moral sense in mortals is the duty / We have to pay on mortal sense of beauty" (283); that is, morality arises from our sense of the mortality of our sense of beauty (and beauty itself). Art is a "refuge" from outrageous fortune, melancholy, exile, guilt; art affords "bliss," a momentary balance of body and mind, a peaceful perception of the pattern of life, a brief suspension of time itself. But—despite Nabokov's disclaimers, which in McCarthyite 1950s America were a form of protective coloration—art for Nabokov is not moralistic but moral. David Rampton has unearthed a 1964 interview in which Nabokov says, "I don't think *Lolita* is a religious book, but I do think it is a moral one. And I do think that Humbert Humbert in his last stage is a moral man because he realizes that he loves Lolita like any woman should be loved. But it is too late, he has destroyed her childhood. There is certainly this kind of morality in it."[7] And in another interview that Nabokov himself reprinted in *Strong Opinions*, a late collection of pronunciamentos and obiter dicta, he declared Humbert "a vain and cruel wretch who manages to appear 'touching.'"[8]

The crucial issue is Humbert's "reliability": Does his lust really change to love? Does he finally love Lolita as a father, as he claims? Or is this just something for the "ladies and gentlemen of the jury" (9), as he calls us? Should he be pardoned for Quilty's murder—and for the murder of Lolita's childhood? There's plenty of tricky evidence to consider and admire. But the most extraordinary achievement of the novel—and one that makes its use of the child of inestimable historical importance—is that Nabokov has constructed it so that we become accomplices in aestheticizing a physical and moral crime: child abuse, rape. Our intellectual, literary, and moral vanity seduces us. Thanks to Humbert's creamy (and comic) crooning, we are transformed into his collaborators, tracing hidden patterns that flatter our acumen, wit, and sensitivity, all too easily adept (like H.H.) in thereby neglecting and thus destroying the child whose independent existence we barely see, though we praise her endlessly. We're appallingly ready to perceive a pretty pattern and ignore that beauty is (for Nabokov) not only moral but also a glimpse of eternal life. The story of Lolita's death (which is ultimately what we're reading) is, for Nabokov, a "benediction and a promise" of a metaphysical, indeed, religious order beyond time and space.[9] Every artist, for Nabokov, discovers and portrays the traces of a greater Artist at work; the intricately constructed story of the sacrifice of this child proves it.

From Humbert's first page, we know this will be a song of praise and sorrow that "a murderer" (of whom? of what?) is singing in his own defense to the "ladies and gentlemen of the jury" (9). The entire book is a literary embrace of Lolita. The first words—"Lolita, light of my life, fire of my loins"—introduce her to us, the jury, and the last words are addressed to her: "the refuge of art . . . is the only immortality you and I may share, my Lolita" (9, 309). Humbert's change of focus from jury to girl is presumably a proof of his self-proclaimed evolution from criminal to lover. But Nabokov immediately establishes that "Lolita" is Humbert's nickname for a child primarily known to all others and to herself as Dolores or Dolly Haze. So from the very start we see she has been enfolded or trapped within an ostentatiously literary appellation. This pet name is her cage and her tomb (which is suggested by the first paragraph's allusions to the dead bride in Poe's "Annabel Lee").

We ladies and gentlemen of the jury must struggle to keep our eyes on the facts of rape and murder (though Nabokov says in the afterword that "reality" is a word that can only be used within quotation marks).[10] It's not easy since the only information we get is from the accused. But let's "look at this tangle of thorns" (9), this testimony by a fairytale's enchanted hunter or a saint or savior with a crown of thorns.

Humbert bluntly declares, "It was she who seduced me" (132), but after much expert literary foreplay (to keep the reader panting, too) he tucks in the remark that "she was not quite prepared for certain discrepancies between a kid's life and mine. Pride alone prevented her from giving up" (134)—meaning full penetration by what he boasts elsewhere is "a foot of engorged brawn" (283) was difficult for her and painful. He concludes his narrative of their first night with an ekphrastic prose poem imagining the commemorative mural he could paint on the walls of the Enchanted Hunters hotel where they're staying: "There would have been a fire opal dissolving within a ripple-ringed pool, a last throb, a last dab of color, stinging red, smarting pink, a sigh, a wincing child" (134–35). The "wincing child" is almost buried in Humbert's wave of words, but not Nabokov's.

Not that Humbert delays his defense. Four pages later we learn that although she's not really human—he's "anointed and ringed with the feel of her body—the body of some immortal daemon disguised as a female child" (139)—he does feels guilt, "an oppressive, hideous constraint as if I were sitting with the small ghost of somebody I had just killed" (140). This defensive double move—a depersonalized, highly literary description and a preemptive declaration of guilt—will run through the entire book. Five lines later she's clearly in pain and calls him "you brute."

"Cold spiders of panic crawled down my back. This was an orphan. This was a lone child, an absolute waif, with whom a heavy-limbed, foul-smelling adult had had strenuous intercourse three times that very morning" (140). He is panicked about detection, not her pain.

He feels "pangs of guilt" but also the "agonizing thought" that her "mood might prevent me from making love to her again as soon as I found a nice country road where to park in peace. In other words, poor Humbert Humbert was dreadfully unhappy, and while steadily and inanely driving toward Lepingville ["butterfly-hunting town"] he kept racking his brains for some quip, under the bright wing of which [the wing of a butterfly, of a predator, and of Poe's deadly "noble-winged seraphs"] he might dare to turn to his seatmate. It was she, however, who broke the silence: 'Oh, a squashed squirrel,' she said, 'what a shame.' 'Yes, isn't it?' (eager, hopeful Hum)" (140): hopeful for sex, not her welfare.

Though she is "sweetly smiling" as she says, "You chump . . . you revolting creature. I was a daisy-fresh girl, and look what you've done to me. I ought to call the police and tell them you raped me. Oh, you dirty, dirty old man" (141), Humbert notes that "an ominous hysterical note ran through her silly words." We understand that her "smile" and thin, flirty irony are her attempts at gaining some control and minimizing her physical pain, but soon she is telling him that "I had torn something inside her." She wants to call her mother, but he drives on: "Why can't I call my mother if I want to?" "'Because,' I answered, 'your mother is dead'" (141). And with this the chapter abruptly ends. There's no response, no reaction, no scene. Just silence—and then a jump to the famous last chapter of the first half of the book, which begins with forced cheer:

> In the gay town of Lepingville I bought her four books of comics, a box of candy, a box of sanitary pads [no comment], two cokes, a manicure set, a travel clock with a luminous dial, a ring with a real topaz [homage to their intercourse], a tennis racket, roller skates with white high shoes, field glasses, a portable radio set, chewing gum, a transparent raincoat [a magic fetish], sunglasses [recurrent symbol throughout the entire novel], some more garments—swooners, shorts, all kinds of summer frocks.
>
> (141–42)

This consumer culture buy-out embeds her in commercial creature comforts and fantasies. We have yet to see or hear anything to do with people and their actions, just a heap of commodities. And then the paragraph springs into active life in the two great concluding sentences: "At the hotel we had separate rooms, but in the middle of the night she came sobbing into mine, and we made it up very gently. You see, she had absolutely nowhere else to go" (142). Made up the death of her mother? Made up the horrific scene Humbert never shows us? Made up her rape? We should also pause and admire Nabokov's architectural genius in ending the first part of the book with "to go"—which propels us into the cross-country trips of the second half and also, by ending so resoundingly and conclusively, conveys that she "absolutely" can't escape and that mere motion is no escape anyway.

It's in the second half of the book that the facts of Dolly's abuse really accumulate. Even though Humbert has sex with her every day and is always advertising his feelings for her, he also has a roving eye for other nymphets (about a dozen are mentioned casually, en passant). He has Dolly masturbate him while he looks at pretty children leaving school (161). Some thirty pages later he finds her in a school room:

> All was very quiet, and there was another girl with a very naked, porcelain-white neck and wonderful platinum hair, who sat in front reading too, absolutely lost to the world and interminably winding a soft curl around one finger, and I sat beside Dolly [not Lolita here] just behind that neck and that hair [depersonalized fragments], and unbuttoned my overcoat and for sixty-five cents plus the permission to participate in the school play, had Dolly put her inky, chalky, red-knuckled hand under the desk. [And here comes the fancy move:] Oh, stupid and reckless of me, no doubt, but after the torture I had been subjected to, I simply had to take advantage of a combination that I knew would never occur again
>
> (198)

Humbert is always seeking new pleasures: he copulates with Dolly when she runs a fever, for "I could not resist the exquisite caloricity of unexpected delights—Venus febriculosa—though it was a very languid Lolita that moaned and coughed and shivered in my embrace" (198).

But on a daily basis he denies her coffee till she does "her morning duty" (165), and he frequently refers to her "basic obligations" as well as fellatio. The sex gets pretty loud and violent—"whose cat has scratched poor you?" a woman asks Dolly—and Humbert feels free to grab her hair and push her into bed (164). He also resorts to bribes and negotiations: "I had brought prices down drastically by having her earn the hard and nauseous way permission to participate in the school's theatrical program" (184–85). He terrorizes her with threats of being sent to a reformatory if she doesn't do his will or if she denounces him. He isolates her as best as he can without arousing suspicion. As his rival Quilty slowly closes in, Humbert gets more violently jealous: "I pushed her softness back into the room and went in after her. I ripped her shirt off. I unzipped the rest of her. I tore off her sandals. Wildly, I pursued the shadow of her infidelity; but the scent I traveled upon was so slight as to be practically undistinguishable from a madman's fancy" (215). As ever, we note his strategy of swerving away from her to himself.

A few pages later, "without a word I delivered a tremendous backhand cut that caught her smack on her hot hard little cheekbone. And then the remorse, the poignant sweetness of sobbing atonement, groveling love, the hopelessness of sensual reconciliation" (227). That recognition of the hopelessness of their embraces to effect a reconciliation is morally and psychologically astute but ultimately cynical and self-pitying. He calls her a "poor fierce-eyed child [with] everything soiled, torn, dead" (185). He notes that "something in her had been broken by me" (232). She may resemble "a little patient . . . after a major operation," but soon his tenderness turns to lust and she cries out, "Oh, *no*," and once again "all would be shattered" (285).

The year-long cross-country tour of America in all its glorious natural and glitzy cultural splendor does not transform paradise lost into paradise regained: "We had been everywhere. We had really seen nothing. And I catch myself thinking today that our long journey had only defiled with a sinuous trail of slime the lovely, trustful, dreamy, enormous country that by then, in retrospect, was no more to us than a collection of dog-eared maps, ruined tour books, old tires, and her sobs in the night—every night, every night—the moment I feigned sleep" (175–76). Humbert does note that although this child "seduced" him, she feels no pleasure in their intercourse—indeed, quite the contrary—but he manages to turn her sorrow (and pain) into a cultural critique and another occasion for his own seductive self-pity:

> She had entered my world, umber and black Humberland, with rash curiosity; she surveyed it with a shrug of amused distaste; and it seemed to me now that she was ready to turn away from it with something akin to plain repulsion. Never did she vibrate under my touch, and a strident 'what d'you think you are doing?' was all I got for my pains. To the wonderland I had to

offer, my fool preferred the corniest movies, the most cloying fudge. To think that between a Hamburger and a Humburger, she would—invariably, with icy precision—plump for the former. There is nothing more atrociously cruel than an adored child. Did I mention the name of that milk bar I visited a moment ago? It was, of all things, The Frigid Queen. Smiling a little sadly, I dubbed her My Frigid Princess. She did not see the wistful joke.

(166)

Humbert can bring himself to admit, "I simply did not know a thing about my darling's mind" (284) and explain, "it was always my habit and method to ignore Lolita's states of mind while comforting my own base self" (287). He can even expostulate, "Charlotte, I begin to understand you," about her daughter (159) and describe Dolly as the twelve-year-old kid she really is: "A combination of naiveté and deception, of charm and vulgarity, of blue sulks and rosy mirth, Lolita, when she chose, could be a most exasperating brat. I was not really quite prepared for her fits of disorganized boredom, intense and vehement griping, her sprawling, droopy, dopey-eyed style, and what is called goofing off—a kind of diffused clowning which she thought was tough in a boyish hoodlum way. Mentally, I found her to be a disgustingly conventional little girl" (147–48).

But in the most famously erotic scene in the book, when he masturbates against Dolly's legs to the tune of a pop song about Carmen and the barman (presumably a ditty of doomed pop-verismo passion), he completely misses her real sexual response to his frottage: "'Oh, it's nothing at all,' she cried with a sudden shrill note in her voice, and she wiggled, and squirmed, and threw her head back, and her teeth rested on her glistening underlip as she half turned away . . . while I crushed out against her left buttock the last throb of the longest ecstasy man or monster had ever known. . . . There she stood and blinked, cheeks aflame, hair awry . . . Blessed be the Lord, she had noticed nothing!" Triumphantly, he declares, "Lolita had been safely solipsized" (60–61). (This is even clearer in Nabokov's Russian translation of *Lolita*, where it's "Lolita's reality was successfully cancelled," as Vladimir Alexandrov has noted.)[11] In one of the most candid moments in his testimony, Humbert goes on to explain:

> What I had madly possessed was not she, but my own creation, another, fanciful Lolita—perhaps, more real than Lolita; overlapping, encasing her; float-

ing between me and her, and having no will, no consciousness—indeed, no life of her own.

The child knew nothing. I had done nothing to her. And nothing prevented me from repeating a performance that affected her as little as if she were a photographic image rippling upon a screen and I a humble hunchback abusing myself in the dark.

(62)

This is indeed pure Berkeleyan solipsism: all being is perceiving and if she hasn't perceived it, it doesn't exist. He's free to do it again! Ignorance is bliss.

And just to cover his tracks with the jury, he can always launch into a sorrowful aria: "Oh my poor, bruised child. I loved you. I was a pentapod monster, but I loved you. I was despicable and brutal, and turpid, and everything, *mais je t'aimais, je t'aimais!* And there were times when I knew how you felt, and it was hell to know it, my little one. Lolita girl, brave Dolly Schiller" (284–85). Clever to use her married name here, just to prove to us he knows who's who. But after the Don José in *Carmen* riff of *"mais je t'aimais,"* the sheer American tough-guy-sentimental blarney of "there were times when I knew how you felt, and it was hell to know it, my little one. Lolita girl, brave Dolly Schiller," is patently a pitch to the jury.

There are two moments when he does manage to see her clearly: when she bursts into tears at the sight of a dull school friend casually embracing a dull loving father and when he first sees her at camp, where he's come to get her after her mother has died:

> She was thinner and taller, and for a second it seemed to me her face was less pretty than the mental imprint I had cherished for more than a month: her cheeks looked hollowed and too much lentigo camouflaged her rosy rustic features; and that first impression (a very narrow human interval between two tiger heartbeats) carried the clear implication that all widower Humbert had to do, wanted to do, or would do, was to give this wan-looking though sun-colored little orphan *aux yeux battus* (and even those plumbaceous umbrae under her eyes bore freckles) a sound education, a healthy and happy girlhood, a clean home, nice girl-friends of her age among whom (if the fates decided to repay me) I might find, perhaps, a pretty little *Mägdlein* for Herr Doktor Humbert alone. But 'in a wink,' as the Germans say, the angelic line of conduct was erased, and I overtook my prey (time moves ahead of our

fancies!), and she was my Lolita again—in fact, more of my Lolita than ever. . . . We sped though the striped and speckled forest.

(111)

In this extraordinary performance we see a clear-eyed, realistic description of an exhausted, allergenic twelve-year-old (with circles round her eyes, which in French ["*yeux battus*"] literally means "black and blue beaten eyes"), "erased" by a narcissistic, multilingual, parodic, Grimm-Freudian fairytale. It amounts to literary cannibalism.

As the book draws to a close, Humbert produces four proofs of his moral reclamation and the transformation of his lust to love. One, which he doesn't stress and is seldom remarked upon, is his two-year affair with Rita, a woman of his own age whom he picks up in a bar and cares for tenderly and lustfully enough, given their steady sleazy inebriation. Rita is no nymphet; Humbert has changed. The other three proofs comprise some of the most celebrated moments in the entire novel.

Shortly after Dolly escapes from Humbert with Quilty (on Independence Day) and Humbert embarks on his revengeful grand tour in reverse in the hope of finding them and killing Quilty, Humbert approaches the "friendly abyss" below a roadside precipice overlooking a small mining town from which arises the "melody of children at play. . . . I stood listening to that musical vibration from my lofty slope, to those flashes of separate cries with a kind of demure murmur for background, and then I knew that the hopelessly poignant thing was not Lolita's absence from my side, but the absence of her voice from that concord" (307–8). The French and English word "concord" suggests a transcendental revelation of natural and supernatural order—via the name of Emerson and Thoreau's hometown in Massachusetts. Humbert presumably wants us to see that he finally gets it. But Nabokov no doubt wants us to spot—in the midst of this great aria merging nature and culture, the "geometry" of streets and the pastoral "serpentine stream" and "behind it all, great timbered mountains"—that there's also "the crazy quilt of dark and pale fields." *(Et in Arcadia Quilty.)* Brian Boyd emphasizes that for all this transcendental concord, Humbert will still go off to avenge himself on Quilty, will maintain his rage for three years and then achieve what he calls the "intolerable bliss" of killing him. So as Boyd says, this hardly seems a moral apotheosis that transforms his feelings or actions. Just because it comes at the end of the book doesn't mean it's his final feeling or belief or action.

A far better proof of Humbert's love occurs in the chapter that follows the description of his last interview with seventeen-year-old, pregnant, and married Dolly in Coalmont: "With the utmost simplicity and clarity I now saw myself and my love. Previous attempts seemed out of focus in comparison" (282). Humbert tells us he had sought Roman Catholic absolution but realized that though he might find "spiritual solace" in confession, "nothing could make my Lolita forget the foul lust I had inflicted upon her" (283). Whereupon he really revs things up:

> Unless it can be proven to me—to me as I am now, today, with my heart and my beard, and my putrefaction—that in the infinite run it does not matter a jot that a North American girl-child named Dolores Haze had been deprived of her childhood by a maniac, unless this can be proven (and if it can, then life is a joke), I see nothing for the treatment of my misery but the melancholy and very local palliative of articulate art.
>
> (283)

The focus here is ultimately on his misery, of course: It needs treatment, so he provides a transparently fictitious "old poet" to furnish a clinching quote: "The moral sense in mortals is the duty / We have to pay on mortal sense of beauty" (283). Which is to say—as noted earlier—that morality is the necessary consequence and price of sensing beauty and knowing it must die. Humbert is telling us he hasn't paid this "duty." Knowing this—or writing this—ostensibly makes him a moral man, transformed, a true lover. But Nabokov no doubt expects us to register how very often Humbert pirouettes into such self-exculpating remorse and insight. The elaborate rhetoric of this declaration undermines its authenticity.

But the best and most tricky proof of Humbert's love is in his account of his final interview with Dolly Haze Schiller in Coalmont (269–80). Dolly has just told him her sad tale of Quilty's kicking her out and her drifting for two years and doing restaurant work (which she'd feared when she was younger) and then meeting her husband, the deaf vet Dick. "It was so *strange*, so *strange*," she says (277), as if referring to a sad twist at the end of a fairy tale about a "strange mushroom" (the title of one of Quilty's plays).

"She closed her eyes and opened her mouth, leaning back on the cushion, one felted foot on the floor. The wooden floor slanted, a little steel ball would have rolled into the kitchen. I knew all I wanted to know. I had no intention of torturing my darling" (277). The house is a wreck but conforms to the natural order of decline and decay. Humbert at last understands the way things fall into place. But that "little steel ball" also suggests he's thinking of bullets and revenge, though not upon her. So he imagines that perhaps there's another way to understand all this: "Somewhere beyond Bill's shack an afterwork radio had begun singing of folly and fate"—a country-and-western tearjerker (instead of *Carmen*) may provide an aesthetic and moral context. "And there she was with her ruined looks and her adult, rope-veined narrow hands and her gooseflesh white arms, and her shallow ears, and her unkempt armpits"—unblinking, unromantic description—"there she was (my Lolita!)"—the parenthesis is a gasp of surprised recognition and an embrace—"hopelessly worn at seventeen, with that baby, dreaming already in her of becoming a big shot and retiring around 2020 A.D."—far away from the magical enchanted past—"and I looked and looked at her, and knew as clearly as I know I am to die, that I loved her more than anything I had ever seen or imagined on earth, or hoped for anywhere else" (277).

This sounds as authentic as it gets—Humbert is affirming his love of this real girl, not the imaginary nymphet. To emphasize the contrast he conjures up the past: "She was only the faint violet whiff and dead leaf echo of the nymphet I had rolled myself upon with such cries in the past." But there's a suspiciously decadent gleam in this memory of his disastrous *en plein air* copulation with her on a hillside, and suddenly things start to get worse: she's "an echo on the brink of a russet ravine, with a far wood under a white sky, and brown leaves choking the brook, and one last cricket in the crisp weeds." The autumnal imagery is a shot at pathos, but even more disturbing is the echo of an earlier memory of a luxurious pornographic work of art praising "the russet ravine." The allusion to fin-de-siècle obscenity brings Europe back with a jolt that undercuts the all-American declaration of love.

Sensing this, Humbert tries to recover himself: "But thank God it was not that echo alone that I worshipped." And then he loses it: "What I used to pamper among the tangled vines of my heart, *mon grand péché radieux*"—Verlaine's destructive but "radiant" "sinful" affair with Rimbaud—"had dwindled to its essence: sterile and selfish vice, all *that* I cancelled and cursed. You may jeer at me"—addressing the jury now, not Dolly, and clearly launching into a narcissistic tirade—"and threaten to clear the court, but until I am gagged and half-throttled, I will shout my poor truth. I insist the world know how much I loved my Lolita, *this* Lolita"—here he recovers a bit—"pale and polluted, and big with another's

child, but still gray-eyed, still sooty-lashed, still auburn and almond."
We're sold. But an allusion to *Carmen* and masturbating with her legs
on the couch bursts out of him: "still Carmencita, still mine." He starts
quoting Don José begging Carmen to come back to him (just before he
kills her): "*Changeons de vie, ma Carmen, allons vivre quelque part où nous
ne serons jamais séparés*; Ohio? The wilds of Massachusetts?" (277–78).

Mérimée's melodramatic French outburst is juxtaposed—on the
other side of a devastating, insurmountable semicolon—to the river-roll-
ing American name of a Midwestern state, Ohio, and the even more dis-
sonant sound of the American Indian name of an Eastern state, Massachusetts. Europe versus America, art versus geography, romantic speech
versus plain place names: all express the impossibility of their "living
somewhere where we'll never be separated."

To conclude his aria, Humbert launches into the mounting arc of a
dramatic soliloquy filled with a deliberately grotesque and then lovingly
pornographic inventory of his beloved: "No matter, even if those eyes
of hers would fade to myopic fish and her nipples swell and crack and
her lovely young velvety delicate delta be tainted and torn [as it was by
Humbert and may be by childbirth]—even then I would go mad with
tenderness at the mere sight of your dear wan face, at the mere sound of
your raucous young voice, my Lolita" (278). Again, embracing her and
possessing her by using her pet name at the end.

The narrative then resumes. Humbert asks her to come away with
him as if in a fairy tale or romantic melodrama—"'And we shall live happily ever after.' *Carmen, voulez-vous venir avec moi?*" She asks if he's saying he will give her the money she needs only if she goes to a motel with
him, and he replies with ostentatiously American tough-guy speech,
"No . . . you got it all wrong. I want you to leave your incidental Dick
[who's angry?], and this awful hole [ditto], and come to live with me, and
die with me, and everything with me (words to that effect)." Again, the
cutting parenthesis gives it all away.

And then comes an even more extraordinary sequence as Humbert
continues: "'Anyway, if you refuse you will still get your . . . *trousseau*.'
'No kidding?' asked Dolly" (278). Humbert uses his native French here to
prove his authenticity—he is her true loving father, providing the traditional marriage gift of linen that blesses her departure from his paternal
realm to the bed and board of her new husband. Her reply affirms her
colloquial American freedom and declares she's not a kid any more. This

would then seem to be the ultimate proof of Humbert's transformation. He is her father at last. But then there's a swerve: "Gingerly, uncertainly, she received *mon petit cadeau*" (279). The phrase occurred earlier in the scene with the young Paris prostitute Monique (22). "*Petit cadeau*" is old-time slang for the payment to a prostitute. So is Humbert giving her a father's "*trousseau*" or a john's "gift" to a whore for services rendered? It's impossible to say which—or is it both? And what does this tell us about Humbert's proof of love?

There's no doubt about Dolly's response: she tells him she won't go off with him but (with casual tenderness and generosity) calls him "honey," and "she had never called me honey before" (279). Her banal endearment welcomes Humbert into the good old normal world of family affection. Earlier she had cried out to her husband, "Dick, this is my Dad" (273), which had strongly, even preemptively affirmed their conventional roles. This is stronger because it's so calmly and tenderly affectionate. "Oh, don't cry," she says, "I'm so sorry I cheated so much, but that's the way things are" (279). And then she "exults" in the money he's giving her to start a new life in Alaska with Dick and their baby.

Humbert concludes the chapter by interweaving memories of "a radiant child of twelve, sitting on a threshold, 'pinging' pebbles at an empty can" (279) with mounting rage and determination to avenge himself on Quilty: "Yes, I was quite sure I had to go. I had to go, and find him, and destroy him" (280). His awareness that he's speaking to the jury increases: "I was surprised (this is a rhetorical figure, I was not) that the sight of the old car in which she had ridden as a child and a nymphet left her so very indifferent. All she remarked was it was getting sort of purplish around the gills" (280). Dolly's intelligence and wit, which we had glimpsed when she was twelve—whenever Humbert permitted her to speak on the page—has clearly survived. The fish imagery recalls earlier seaside and lakeside scenes (including the near murder of her mother), and the purple recalls royal Humbert's robe (and anticipates Quilty's final purple bathrobe).

His longing and anger at Dolly are conveyed by repetitions of the Carmen theme, complete with a wild flourish "then I pulled out my automatic—I mean, this is the kind of fool thing a reader might suppose I did." Humbert launches into a last plea—will you "not come to live with me? I will create a brand new God and thank him with piercing cries, if you give me that microscopic hope"—but he immediately undercuts it with the comment "(to that effect)." He then reminds the reader of the legal arrangements about the publication of the manuscript, and trots out a dog (a double of the fatal Ramsdale pooch) who "lope[s] alongside my car like a fat dolphin [seaside, fish, and resurrection symbol], but he was too heavy and old, and very soon gave up," just like pathetic old Humbert, we're supposed to feel. For it is certainly pathos that he goes for at the end of this altogether extraordinary chapter: "And presently I was driving through the drizzle of the dying day with the windshield wipers in full action but unable to cope with my tears" (280). This is his story, not Lolita's. So off we go to murder Quilty. Some moral apotheosis.

The remaining pages will contain several notable expressions of remorse and moral and philosophical illumination. As I've noted, the book ends with the transcendental revelation on the "friendly abyss" of "the absence of Lolita's voice from the concord" (307–8). A bit earlier, after Humbert confesses that "it was always my habit and method to ignore Lolita's states of mind while comforting my own base self," he goes on to acknowledge the depth of her understanding and her growth: "It had become gradually clear to my conventional Lolita ["conventional" is censorious, of course] during our singular and bestial cohabitation [arch, indeed] that even the most miserable of family lives was better than the parody of incest which, in the long run, was the best I could offer the waif" (287). The irony here barely impedes the Dickensian moral and emotional momentum of "waif."

Dolly Haze is indeed a descendent of Oliver Twist and David Copperfield and Little Nell and the motherless children that moved Nabokov so much in *Bleak House*. Nabokov's challenge to the reader is to see through Humbert's performance and glimpse the child. The dramatic point of the book is to startle the reader into a horrific "moral apotheosis" of his own—a comprehension and acknowledgment of his own moral and intellectual vanity and literary sensitivity that foster collaboration with ever-ingenious, seductive Humbert, the "vain and cruel wretch who manages to appear 'touching.'"

But Nabokov's ironic presentation of Humbert still causes trouble for readers. Fifty years ago the book was often condemned (and banned in Paris) or misread even by so strong a critic as Leslie Fiedler, who thought the little girl was "Annabel Lee as nymphomaniac, demonic rapist of the soul."[12] Upon rereading *Lolita* amidst the pedophilic scandals of the 1990s, Norman Podhoretz denounced it as insidiously seducing its readers into 'thinking about the unthinkable.' . . . the way [Nabokov] treated [pedophilia] was emphatically not calculated to deepen our horror over it. Just the opposite. . . . The very brilliance of his language, the very sharpness of his wit, the very artfulness of his treatment all help to shatter the taboo and thereby to rob pedophilia of its horror. In other words, in aestheticizing the hideous, Nabokov—as I can now clearly see—comes very close to prettifying it. Worse yet, he comes very close to excusing it. [13]

This completely neglects the distance between author and character.

For a postmodern admirer of Nabokov like Alfred Appel, "What is extraordinary about *Lolita* is . . . the way in which Nabokov enlists us, against our will, on Humbert's side. . . . Humbert has figuratively made the reader his accomplice in both statutory rape and murder."[14] For Appel in 1974 this proved the power of art over conventional morality, not the corruption of civilization by amoral aesthetes.

Still, even from the beginning, there were readers and critics who responded to Nabokov's irony much more sensitively. As early as 1957 F. W. Dupee spotted the "strained" tone of Humbert's "belated love cries for his Lolita, which seem to be dictated by some principle of compensation and ring a little false (to me)."[15] In 1958 Lionel Trilling described how "we find ourselves the more shocked when we realize that, in the course of reading the novel, we have come virtually to condone the violation it presents . . . we have been seduced into conniving in the violation, because we have permitted our fantasies to accept what we know to be revolting." For Trilling, "another reason for being shocked [is] that in recent fiction no lover has thought of his beloved with so much tenderness, that no woman has been so charmingly evoked, in such grace and delicacy, as Lolita. The description of her tennis game . . . is one of the few examples of rapture in modern writing." Trilling strongly admires the novel's "ability to arouse uneasiness, to throw the reader off balance, to require him to change his stance and shift his position and move on." He is even "not sure that Nabokov has not laid an emotional trap for the reader" at the end and that there is irony (as Dupee thought, too) about the "culmination of H.H.'s moral evolution."[16]

By 1984 David Rampton could note that "the book cries out for a condemnation, a defense, a judgment, yet for various reasons it actively subverts the judgment-making capacity of the reader," and he goes on to argue that *Lolita* thereby "dramatizes the potential inhumanity of the kind of aesthetic attitude to experience that fails to make this kind of [emotional and moral] commitment."[17] In 1989 Leona Toker would go even further: "The cathartic effect of *Lolita* derives from its promotion of our temporary sympathy for Humbert and inattentiveness to Dolly Haze and then in its making us modify our attitudes. . . . Eventually . . . the audience is entrapped: it begins to derive a pleasure from the account of the pursuit of ecstasy and to ignore the price of this pursuit, the suffering that Humbert causes to others."[18] This is also part of the case Nabokov's biographer Brian Boyd advances against Humbert.

Michael Wood, one of the most perceptive contemporary critics of Nabokov, writes, "I can't believe in his repentance because the language of his renunciation is the language of gloating—as indeed his language throughout, however guilty he feels or says he felt, is full of relished remembrance." Wood describes Humbert's final claim that Lolita's "absence from that concord" is "the most poignant thing" as "mawkish and self-regarding, altogether too good to be true, 'dictated by some principle of compensation,' as Dupee says. Humbert's fussy prose, elsewhere so resourceful and acrobatic, here manages to seem both artful and hackneyed." For Wood, Humbert often "ends on *his* misery, and is still glamorizing his misdemeanors. . . . What we question is not his passion but its supposed new respectability."[19]

Humbert's artful and at times even hysterical exaggerations and intricate games (as well as his outbursts or solemn candor) not only serve to distract and defend him against sorrow and guilt and longing but also— as he well knows—serve to win the jury's sympathy and, he hopes, ultimate forgiveness. What Humbert doesn't know is that there is a higher power at work on, through, and above him: the author.

Nabokov uses Humbert to dramatize—with extraordinary literary legerdemain—how fatally our intellectual and moral pride, our sensitivity, our sentimentality, our preening erudition and articulate powers lead us to destroy the children we feel—or claim—we love. Nabokov uses the figure of a child to demonstrate our willing misperceptions and fatal neglect. Dolly Haze, far more than Lolita, is the index of our moral life and the perilous health of our culture and society—which is not to say, of course, that the importance of *Lolita* is that it "should make all of us—parents, social workers, educators—apply ourselves with still greater vigilance and vision to the task of bringing up a better generation in a safer world," as John Ray, Ph.D., so memorably puts it in Nabokov's foreplaying foreword (6). The importance of *Lolita* lies in the way its "aesthetic bliss" encompasses moral and, for some, religious or philosophical questions in a way that is ever renewing. A little child shall lead them.

7

PHILIP ROTH'S PERFORMING LOUDMOUTH

Alexander Portnoy

THE THREE UNDISPUTED MASTERS of Jewish American fiction—Henry Roth, Saul Bellow, and Philip Roth—combine the drama of Eastern European immigrant loss and American assimilation with the childhood family romance at its most operatically Oedipal. All three are heirs of Dickens and Joyce, virtuoso verbal performers and mimics, masters of deep structures and improvisatory riffs, bursting with anthropological and psychological detail, nostalgia, anger, jokes, and jeremiads. And all three magnificently evoke childhood, for through a child's eyes the many conflicts that obsess, delight, and torment them can be most vividly described and dramatized.

Henry Roth's *Call It Sleep* (1934) follows a boy from six to nine as he struggles heroically with his monstrously violent father and angelically compassionate and smothering mother and makes his desperate and trembling way through the polyglot Lower East Side of New York just before the First World War. The book is now universally—and justly—recognized one of the classic novels of childhood. In its self-defining and self-liberating arc from darkness to light and its Verdian interplay of ethnic voices, it anticipates and strongly resembles the equivalent African American novel, *Invisible Man*. In both, a minority child's progress is portrayed as the representative American experience: *e pluribus unum*.

Children and childhood are also crucial to Saul Bellow's *Herzog* (1964)—a neoconservative bildungsroman and cultural satire of debased romanticism among anxious, hustling intellectuals and talk-show stars that uses the narrator's memories of his impoverished Russian Jewish immigrant family and scruffy neighborhood as an index of virtue and source of ultimate redemption. As our manic hero writes in one of dozens of unsent letters to the living and dead, today "we love apocalypses too much, and crisis ethics and florid extremism with its thrilling language. Excuse me, no, I've had all the monstrosity I want. . . . no, no! I am simply a human being, more or less." In the old neighborhood there was "a wider range of human feelings than he had ever again been able to find. . . . All he ever wanted was there."[1] His horror at a child abuse case in New York's Family Court and his own jumpy visit with his six-year-old daughter are major turning points in this "bouncy" and "melancholy" narrative of growth and development.[2]

Like *Herzog*, Philip Roth's *Portnoy's Complaint* (1969) is an often comic howl of pain and pride, but Herzog loves his boyhood family while Portnoy wants out because he wants in—to America, to women, to all-American women. The Jewish immigrant past that Herzog has to recover is, for Portnoy, nothing but a source of guilt, restraint, and self-righteousness. Masturbation and narcissistic sex are the only exit. But the trap is precisely narcissism. As he lies on a New York psychoanalyst's couch (much as Herzog tells all from a scruffy country hammock), Portnoy wrestles with his past in bursts of untrammeled hysterical rage, rant, and randy boasting: "She puts the id back in Yid, I put the *oy* back in *Goy!*"[3] But this guilty onanist is also filled with biting nostalgia for his childhood momma and papa even as he exhibitionistically violates their every taboo—an effort that binds him to them all the more tightly. In *Portnoy's Complaint* the nonlinear, free-associative psychoanalytic monologue achieves a most adroit variation on the usually linear novel of childhood and adolescence. The style and structure vividly convey how the raucously static and impotent narrator is at once reluctant and desperate to escape being a jerk-off Peter Pan.

As we've seen, Holden Caulfield calls his narrative "this madman stuff," but he's a privileged character, a superior soul, who only appears to be a victim. All this drove Philip Roth up the wall. In 1960 he wrote that Salinger "by reputation at least, is *the* writer of the age. . . . [but] for all his loving handling of the world's objects there seems to me . . . a spurning of life as it is lived in the immediate world—this place and time is viewed as unworthy of those few precious people who have been set down in it only to be maddened and destroyed."[4] The last thing Roth wanted to read was a covertly sentimental, morally and intellectually arrogant Jewish writer presenting WASP self-pity as if it were saintly martyrdom, particularly if that imagined WASP self-pity was really Jewish moral vanity in disguise, an unacknowledged form of narcissism, less a barbaric yawp than a star turn.

In 1974, in a wonderful autobiographical essay, "In Response to Those Who Have Asked Me 'How Did You Come to Write That Book, Anyway?'" Roth describes the process by which *Portnoy's Complaint* arose from the "wreckage of four abandoned projects" between 1962 and 1967. The first was *The Jewboy*, which focused on a "Dickensian orphan hero" and "treated growing up in Newark as a species of folklore": "charming," "dreamy," "fantastic." The second was *The Nice Jewish Boy*, a conventional, realistic play that sank under its own caution. The third was an untitled monologue "beside which the fetid indiscretions of *Portnoy's Complaint* would appear to be the work of Louisa May Alcott." It was an obscene slideshow lecture about the private parts of the famous that was "blasphemous, mean, bizarre, scatological, tasteless, spirited," and, "largely out of timidity," unfinished. The fourth project was *Portrait of the Artist*, a factual autobiography into which he introduced some imaginary relatives living upstairs—the Portnoys.

Elements from these four abandoned projects were then picked up in a short story entitled "A Jewish Patient Begins His Analysis" narrated by a "'watched-over' Jewish son with his sexual dream of The Other." The resulting psychoanalytic monologue combined the fantastic, the realistic, and the obscene. "The writing of *Portnoy's Complaint* began with discovering Portnoy's voice—more accurately, his mouth—and discovering along with it, the listening ear: the silent Dr. Spielvogel." And Portnoy's mouth—far more than Holden's or Huck Finn's—expresses "brash, shameful, masochistic, euphoric, vengeful, conscience-ridden exhibitionism."[5] We are not being asked to endorse a voice "speaking truth to power" but to listen critically, analytically.

Alexander Portnoy is not a wise child so much as a wised-up child, a comic performer who gets us to laugh at what he sees and how he sees it and who he is—a super-virtuosic unreliable narrator who finally just gives up and screams like an enraged schoolboy, "the Temper Tantrum Kid," "Mr. Conniption-Fit," as his mother calls him (229–30). Here at the end of the novel, the doctor, in the voice of a stage-comic Viennese Jewish shrink, invites Portnoy (and us) "to begin"—because all we've been reading is Portnoy's defense against self-knowledge and self-transformation.

His "complaint" is indeed a "sickness," a "lament," a "confession," and a "song." And we recognize Portnoy is an index of personal, social, and cultural health and virtue—as much as Oliver Twist or David Copperfield or Pip. For Portnoy is as enthralled as David Copperfield with a destructive erotic ideal—not a "child wife" but a forbidden gentile *shikse*—and is as broken on the wheel of conventional psychological, social, and moral categories as Pip.

Pip's expectations were social and romantic and brought him criminal grief and lonely exile. Portnoy's expectations are social and erotic and bring him to lonely, howling impotence and a doctor's care. Both novels expose official manners and morals as frauds. Both employ a model child who harbors a guilty secret. Both use the first person to follow that child from provincial infancy and adolescence to cosmopolitan life as a man about town. Both demonstrate how the protagonist's delusive expectations have destroyed him—tragically in the case of Pip, comically in the case of Portnoy.

Of course, the two narratives are cast in very different literary forms. Both are variations of the classic bildungsroman (such as *David Copperfield*), but Pip conceives his life as a chronological history, a progress toward grim enlightenment. Portnoy has no such secure teleological pattern to rely on. Instead he delivers what Roth has called "blocks of consciousness": free-associative memories, anecdotes, fragments, and riffs that jump around from the age of four or five to his present (christological) thirty-three.[6] Dickens's narrative builds on the Victorian historical works of Carlyle; Roth's, on the modernist collages of Joyce, Woolf, Kafka, Faulkner, and, of course, Freud, whose psychoanalytic method promised to unearth the latent coherent tale beneath the manifest bricolage of free association. Dickens delivers a Victorian narrative, a written document, while Roth gives us a modernist performance, a spoken and then animal emission. Pip finally acknowledges and conforms to Victorian humanistic truths, but Portnoy can only howl. It's up to the analyst and the reader to understand the conservative moral and psychological context in which all this Sturm und Drang take place. Beneath the antinomian anarchy lies latent order; despite appearances, the comedy is deeply conservative. Yet, in a gleeful recursive paradox, despite its conservatism, the comedy is also profoundly antinomian. To convey this novelistically (not declaratively), Roth employs a panoply of literary methods and devices: as he says in another essay on the book, his own, authorial "view of life . . . [is] imbedded in parody, burlesque, slapstick, ridicule, insult, invective, lampoon, wisecrack, in nonsense, in levity, in *play*."[7]

But let's not exaggerate the surface difficulties and distractions of *Portnoy's Complaint*. Amidst the swirl of free associations it's pretty easy to discern what recent events have led Portnoy to the doctor: on a trip to Europe with his girlfriend (whom he usually calls the Monkey, lest he mistake her for a human being), Portnoy took a Roman prostitute into their bed for a threesome. This occasioned such guilt in them both that a few days later in Athens, his girlfriend threatened to commit suicide unless he married her, and he walked out saying, "Look, you want to jump, jump" (106). He then flew to the third source of the Judeo-Christian tradition, Israel, where instead of finding a promised homeland he discovered himself in lonely exile, impotent in Israel where everybody looks like Mom and the incest taboo is universal. So, having degraded and abandoned his lover (possibly fatally), and reduced by guilt to impotence, he returns to New York, where he lives alone and without children, to start analysis, read Freud, masturbate, and complain. The novel ends with the analyst's suggestion that they can now begin the interpretive work that can lead to a cure.

Portnoy's problem is clear: "How have I come to be such an enemy and flayer of myself? And so alone! *Oh*, so alone! Nothing but *self!* Locked up in *me!*" (248). We catch the suggestion in that word "flayer" that masturbation is a form of skinning himself alive. "LET MY PETER GO" (251) he cries to his parents and their Jewish community of "censorious small-mindedness and shame-ridden xenophobia."[8] But he's the one who's holding on, which he sort of knows (or says he does): "My endless childhood! Which I won't relinquish—or which won't relinquish me!" (271) It's enough to make you howl. Portnoy is king of the culture of narcissism, a representative man—or, rather, a little prince.

The first and last thing people remember about the book is the masturbation, which is described by one of the loudest and most obscene mouths in English and American literature. The unprecedented subject and the sheer comic noise distract us from any need to follow a chronological plot or any anxiety about postmodern aesthetic structure. Who can think about form when this is coming at you: "I tear off my pants, furiously I grasp that battered battering ram to freedom, my adolescent cock, even as my mother begins to call from the other side of the bathroom door. 'Now this time don't flush. Do you hear me, Alex? I have to see what's in that bowl!' Doctor, do you understand what I was up against? My wang was all I really had that I could call my own" (33)? And: "Doctor Spielvogel, this is my life, my only life, and I'm living it in the middle of a Jewish joke! I am the son in the Jewish joke—*only it ain't no joke!* Please, who crippled us like this? Who made us so morbid and hysterical and weak? . . . Why am I still hopelessly beating my meat? . . . Bless me with manhood! Make me brave! Make me strong! Make me *whole!* Enough being a nice Jewish boy, publicly pleasing my parents while privately pulling my putz! Enough!" (36–37).

Portnoy famously uses an apple, a milk bottle, a piece of raw liver: "So. Now you know the worst thing I have ever done. I fucked my own family's dinner" (134). Few novels (of serious literary ambition) provide chapter titles such as "Whacking Off" or "Cunt Crazy," which memorably begins, "Did I mention that when I was fifteen I took it out of my pants and whacked off on the 107 bus from New York?" (78).

But at the other rhetorical extreme are memories of childhood filled with "pleasure—I mean a rapturous, biting sense of loss" (27). Consider the following Flaubertian extravaganza about his father's visit to their "furnished room at the seashore":

> He arrives after we have already eaten, but his own dinner waits while he unpeels the soggy city clothes in which he has been making the rounds of his debit all day, and changes into his swimsuit. I carry his towel for him as he clops down the street to the beach in his unlaced shoes. I am dressed in clean short pants and a spotless polo shirt, the salt is showered off me, and my hair—still my little boy's pre-steel wool hair, soft and combable—is beautifully parted and slicked down. There is a weathered iron rail that runs the length of the boardwalk, and I seat myself upon it; below me, in his shoes, my father crosses the empty beach. I watch him neatly set down his towel near the shore. He places his watch in one shoe, his eyeglasses in the other, and then he is ready to make his entrance into the sea. To this day I got into the water as he advised: plunge the wrists in first, then splash the underarms, then a handful to the temples and the back of the neck . . . ah, but slowly, always slowly. This way you get to refresh yourself, while avoiding a shock to the system. Refreshed, unshocked, he turns to face me, comically waves farewell up to where he thinks I'm standing, and drops backward to float with his arms outstretched. Oh he floats so still—he works, he works so hard, and for whom if not for me?—and then at last, after turning on his belly and making with a few choppy strokes that carry him nowhere, he comes wading back to

shore, his streaming compact torso glowing from the last pure spikes of light driving in, over my shoulder, out of stifling inland New Jersey, from which I am being spared.

And there are a lot more memories like this one, Doctor. A lot more. This is my mother and father I'm talking about.

(29–30)

The spatial and narrative geometry of this glorious scene conveys the rich emotional and psychoanalytic meaning. The father is exhausted, soiled, and awkward with his "unlaced" city shoes and "choppy strokes" but he is also a godlike figure, with echoes of Neptune, or a heroic martyred saint or Christ himself, striding out of the sea with his "streaming compact torso glowing from the last pure spikes of light driving in" from behind the little boy, whom he is sparing from the "stifling" mosquito-ridden world of adult duty. The son's rivalry, guilt, identification, pride, gratitude, and love are smoothly interwoven.

A similar cluster of feelings and themes arises from the boy's visit with his father to the *shvitz* bath, an all-male preserve where they are safe from women and gentiles. The men's powerful naked bodies, their "wet meaty flanks and steaming torsos" (49) make them look like prehistoric figures groaning with relief and pleasure (not complaint). A powerful example for little Alex. But his identification with his father also extends beyond the physical to the verbal and the comic. Jack Portnoy suffers from constipation and can spend an hour falling asleep on the toilet before he has to rocket himself up and out to work:

> Zoom, he's dressed, and in his hat and coat, and with his big black collection book in one hand he bolts his stewed prunes and his bran flakes standing up, and fills a pocket with a handful of dried fruits that would bring on in an ordinary human being something resembling dysentery. "I ought to stick a hand grenade up my ass, if you want the truth," he whispers privately to me . . . "I got enough All-Bran in me to launch a battleship. It's backed up to my throat, for Christ's sake." Here, because he has got me snickering, and is amusing himself too in his own mordant way, he opens his mouth and points downward inside himself with a thumb. "Take a look. See where it starts to get dark? That ain't just dark—that's all those prunes rising up where my tonsils used to be. Thank God I had those things out, otherwise there wouldn't be room."

"Very nice talk," my mother calls from the bathroom. "Very nice talk to a child."

(115)

Clearly, young Alex has learned his stuff from a master. Like father, like son. Even more than it may at first appear: "But all catharses were in vain for that man: his *kishkas* [guts] were gripped by the iron hand of outrage and frustration. Among his other misfortunes, I was his wife's favorite" (5). The prissy last sentence of Oedipal triumph comes right after the grandiose thematic statement "gripped by the iron hand of outrage and frustration." That "iron hand" will move from the father's guts to the son's own penis as one immigrant Jewish generation follows another in "outrage and frustration."

One of the boy's earliest guilty memories is of seeing that his father can't even hold a baseball bat correctly. For baseball soon becomes the boy's protected realm as a more assimilated Jew. Unlike the men's steambath, where he feels awe, the softball field is where Alex feels "nice and calm—nothing trembling, everything serene—standing there in the sunshine. . . . Oh, the unruffled nonchalance of that game. . . . Oh, to be a center fielder, a center fielder—and nothing more!" (70–72). (In a kid's game a center fielder doesn't often see a lot of action, doesn't have to play with others very much, and can dream of imperial preeminence in solitary glory.) But there's one step more in the baseball theme, when Alex remembers the neighborhood men playing their weekly softball game ("I'm going up the field . . . *to watch the men!*" Alex calls to his mother [245]). Here is a masculine ideal to remember: "Why leave, why go, when there is everything here that I will ever want. . . . Fierce as the competition is, they cannot resist clowning and kibbitzing around. Putting on a show! How I am going to love growing up to be a Jewish man!" (243–44).

But first he has to resolve the family romance, which is far more complicated than dealing with a conventional seductive mother and castrating father. The book begins with an opposition between a flying mother and a sitting father. On the one hand, there is the powerful, ubiquitous, active mother (who the little boy thinks is also his teacher at school), with her crooning praise of the best little boy in the world, her magic ability to suspend peaches in Jell-o, and her glamorous teenage years as "*Sophie Ginsky the boys call 'Red,' / She'll go far with her big brown eyes and her clever head*" (31). On the other hand is the eternally constipated, immobile, grumpy, exhausted, clumsy father chained to the toilet (as his guilty son thirty years later imagines he will be chained to a toilet in hell), working six days a week until late at night selling insurance to Newark blacks "in that ferocious and self-annihilating way in which so many Jewish men of his generation served their families" (8). Though Jack Portnoy can't fly, perhaps his son can take off: "Where he had been imprisoned, I would fly: that was his dream. Mine was its corollary: in my liberation would be his—from ignorance, from exploitation, from anonymity" (8–9).

What prevents this is Sophie's incestuous idolization of her son, her anxious rage, self-righteousness, and narcissism, both physical—rolling up her stockings in front of her son even now as a "sixty-year-old beauty queen" (47)— and moral: "You know what my biggest fault is, Rose? I hate to say it about myself, but I'm too good" (123). And though she extravagantly praises her son as "Albert Einstein the Second" and the "best little boy a mommy ever had" (4, 45), she can also suddenly lock him out of the house or whip out a bread knife and point it right at his seven-year-old heart for not eating his vegetables, which leads to the final twist: "And why doesn't my father stop her?" (17): because, gripped by the "iron hand of outrage and frustration," he's stuck on the toilet.

To which his son repairs for ejaculations that fly all over the place: at least one part of the boy is as magically powerful as his mother. The most brilliant use of this imagery of flying is when he refuses to marry the Monkey, the only woman who could match him for energy, wit, mouth, and (we see) intelligence, and tells her to jump out the Athens hotel window. If she's as good as his mother, she'll fly. And "the Monkey's Revenge" is that he "couldn't get it up in the state of Israel" (271, 257). So in outrage and frustration he reverts to immobility, lies down on the analytic couch, and lets his words fly.

What about the Jews? For Portnoy the 5,000-year, three-generation immigrant tradition has shrunk to the lesson that life is boundaries and restrictions: renunciation is all, and guilt and suffering, superstitious rules and regulations, parochial fear, insufferable moral self-righteousness, and atavistic ethnic pride are all that remains. The American Jewish heritage that runs from the genius of Henry Roth, Malamud, and Bellow to the kitsch of Harry Golden and *Fiddler on the Roof* is portrayed as a source not of strength but of paralysis and hypocrisy. From the time of the publication of two of his earliest stories—"Epstein" in 1958 and "Defender of the Faith" in 1959, which were both collected in his first book *Goodbye, Columbus* (1959)—Roth has been denounced and even hated for his satire: the great scholar Gershom Scholem called *Portnoy's Complaint* "the book for which all anti-Semites have been praying," and Irving Howe, the preeminent literary critic of the immigrant Jewish tradition, attacked Roth and his novel with such ferocity that the aftershocks could be felt in Roth's literary work for the next ten years or more.[9] Which is not to say that Roth's art didn't thrive under such provocations. In fact, the violence of Portnoy's rants against his Newark Jewish community are carefully contextualized not only as local anthropology but as psychoanalytic performances.

Consider the way Portnoy's memories of his father's constipation are linked to the sanctimonious self-pity and pride of the Jewish neighborhood: "Jew Jew Jew Jew Jew Jew! It is coming out of my ears already, the saga of the suffering Jews! Do me a favor, my people, and stick your suffering heritage up your suffering ass—*I happen also to be a human being!*" (76). So, in this boy, adolescent rebellion meets universal human rights (don't forget that Portnoy will become assistant commissioner of human opportunity for the City of New York) and the history of the Jews in America becomes a saga pointing toward sex with forbidden gentile girls, *shikses*: "O America! America! it may have been gold in the streets to my grandparents, it may have been a chicken in every pot to my father and mother, but to me, a child whose earliest movie memories are of Ann Rutherford and Alice Faye, America is a *shikse* nestling under your arm whispering love love love love love!" (146).

So off he runs after ice-skating blond beauties and college sweethearts like Kay Campbell of Davenport, Iowa (whom he calls the Pumpkin to make sure she's more fat Thanksgiving treat than person) or Sarah Abbott Maulsby of New Canaan, Foxcroft, and Vassar (whom he calls the Pilgrim to make sure her Mayflower prudery won't escape notice). That the goal and the excitement of all this is imperial assimilation couldn't be clearer to him: "What I'm saying, Doctor, is that I don't seem to stick my dick up these girls, as much as I stick it up their backgrounds—as though through fucking I will discover America. *Conquer* America" (235). Once again the deeper structure can be seen: the reference to Columbus reminds us (not Portnoy) that one of his happiest childhood memories was of playing Columbus to his mother's Queen Isabella. So maybe he's still a nice Jewish boy after all, though not as nice as Ronald Nimkin, who hangs himself in the shower. And not all his feelings for *shikses* are longings for WASP American beauties. One of the most sordid episodes in the book dramatizes the rage and self-hatred behind his adolescent lust. At sixteen, with two gross friends, he visits eighteen-year-old Bubbles Girardi, a lower-class loser doing the ironing in a slip with a picture tacked on the wall of the kitchen sink of Jesus in a pink nightie ascending to Heaven, "the Pansy of Palestine" (168). After negotiations she agrees to give Portnoy a hand-job, but despite her "fist tearing away at me" he can't come until he touches himself and explodes all over the couch, the doilies, the lamp, the walls. "Sheeny!" she screams, "Hebe! You can't even come off unless you pull your own pudding, cheap bastard fairy Jew!" And Portnoy is a terrified pint-sized polluted Oedipus: "I'm going blind! A *shikse* has touched my dick with her bare hand, and now I'll be blind forever!" (180–81). Sex with *shikses* is violent, dangerous, degrading (to this woman of the people as well as to Portnoy), shameful, and medically risky, too. Some Columbus!

Of course, the "sexual triumph of [Portnoy's] life" (214) is his two-year affair with Mary Jane Reed (the Monkey), a West Virginia coalminer's daughter and fashion model he picked up on the street as she was getting into a cab. She's smart, sensitive, generous, adventurous, loving, and ready to take the risk and marry him. For Portnoy they're "the perfect couple" (209). She is as witty and can be as violently obscene and angry as he, but we also see what he can't see (and certainly can't abide): she is capable of self-transformation, growth, self-education, the free expression of both tenderness and lust.

Portnoy knows all about Freud's classic essay "The Most Prevalent Form of Degradation of the Erotic Life"—one of the three "Contributions to the Psychology of Love" from 1912—which describes how in a "fully normal attitude in love, two currents of feeling have to unite . . . the tender, affectionate feelings and the sensual feelings." The failure to combine these produces the "degradation" not of masturbation but impotence: "Where such men love they have no desire and where they desire they cannot love."[10] It's all the result of the incest taboo. In pop culture shorthand this is known as the Madonna/whore complex. Portnoy can quote Freud and ask, "What do you think, Doc? Has a restriction so pathetic been laid upon my object choice? . . . Listen, does that explain the preoccupation with *shikses*?" (186). But that doesn't mean he gets it. The novelistically rich account of his weekend in Vermont with the

Monkey makes it abundantly clear that he's much too threatened by her loving and sexual responsiveness and needs. Even his veiled attempt to intimidate her by quoting Yeats's "Leda and the Swan" (divine sex, power, and knowledge) leads to her opening up and actually understanding the poem and declaring her love and lust for him. But as they drive back to New York, his defensive contempt kicks in and all is lost. Later she'll participate in the threesome in Rome (to please and excite him), but the sight of the prostitute's little boy and the knowledge that even she has a husband are too much to bear—particularly when she feels Portnoy's own guilt turn into scorn. And then he tells her to jump out the window.

The fifth section, "In Exile," greatly enlarges the cultural, historical, and psychological context. Portnoy's humiliating impotence with "Naomi, The Jewish Pumpkin"—that "hardy, red-headed, freckled, ideological hunk of a girl" (258) who even he realizes looks like his mother—permits Roth to place him in the "culture of the Diaspora" with its "ghetto humor" (265) and thereby to distinguish between Jewish history, Israeli Jews, and Jewish America, Newark style. The volume increases as Portnoy imagines an irate judge sentencing him to a "limp dick" for "degrading another human being" (272). And after a page of moralistic waffling he asks the doctor's permission to howl (such a nice well-behaved boy) and imagines himself surrounded by the police in a Hollywood gangster film: "You're surrounded, Portnoy. You better come on out and pay your debt to society." "Up society's ass, Copper!" "Three to come out with those hands of yours up in the air, Mad Dog, or else we come in after you, guns blazing. One." "Blaze, you bastard cop, what do I give a shit? I tore the tag off my mattress—" "Two." "—But at least while I lived, *I lived big!*" (273–74). This is followed by five lines of "aaaahhhh" and the one-sentence sixth section of the novel: "PUNCH LINE. So [*said the doctor*]. Now vee may perhaps to begin. Yes?" (274).

The boyish pop-culture bad-guy braggadocio puts Portnoy right back in Newark (seeing something like *White Heat*, with James Cagney blowing up after boasting, "Top of the world, Ma!"). The anal imagery brings him back to his father, and "*I lived big*" is pure infantile male narcissism. The PUNCH LINE (with boxing reference and borscht-belt humor intended) permits us to hear the even more cartoonish voice of the stereotype Viennese Jewish shrink and—for three words "[*said the doctor*]"—to sense the author (hitherto invisible and paring his nails) in charge of the whole show.

What Roth has achieved is the comic culmination of the novel of childhood—a bildungsroman in which failure to grow and develop is the point of the whole extravaganza. In 130 years, we have gone from genteel, well-spoken Oliver Twist, the principle of Good, a deliberately cardboard allegorical figure whose tale is told in the third person, to Portnoy, the obscene infant who wants to be Bad, a first-person depth-psychology performance artist. No longer trailing clouds of glory but grandiose infantile delusions. No longer a victim of society in need of reform but an example of the unsocialized, culturally damaged, neurotic self that requires not a proper, nominally Christian change of heart but psychoanalysis, a modernist cure. Not that we really believe the shrink will ever get Portnoy to shut up. And don't we—like complaining Portnoy himself—also admire the recalcitrant, infantile brio of it all?[11] With this iconic child, it's not regression but a bold, ferocious, solipsistic stasis that becomes a form of redemption. So we've circled back to Wordsworth's *Ode* with a vengeance: "Heaven lies about us in our infancy! / Shades of the prison-house begin to close/ Upon the growing Boy." If "the Child is Father of the Man," the ultimate victory is to stop time in its tracks or, even better, to step out of time and dwell in the unchanging realm of "the glory and the dream." Sublime, antinomian, transcendent bliss. Paradise regained—in grandiose solitary confinement.

ACKNOWLEDGMENTS

———

I'M GRATEFUL TO Jennifer Crewe, Philip Leventhal, and Michael Haskell of Columbia University Press and to my friend and agent, Georges Borchardt.

Lis Harris, Richard Howard, Patty O'Toole, and Alan Ziegler of the Writing Program of the Columbia University School of the Arts have been wonderful friends and colleagues.

Morris Dickstein, Lore Dickstein, Peter Winn, and Sue Gronewold have be immensely helpful and encouraging friends.

My daughters Sarah and Rebecca, my stepson Nicholas, my son-in-law Eric, and my wife Wendy have immeasurably enriched and supported my life and work.

NOTES

INTRODUCTION

1 Mark Twain, *Adventures of Huckleberry Finn*, ed. Thomas Cooley (New York: Norton, 1999), 120.

2 Peter Coveney, *The Image of Childhood: The Individual and Society: A Study of the Theme in English Literature* (Harmondsworth: Penguin, 1967), 127; Michael Mason, in *Jane Eyre* by Charlotte Brontë, ed., intro., and notes Michael Mason (London: Penguin, 1996), 505.

3 Vladimir Nabokov, "On a Book Entitled *Lolita*," in Nabokov, *The Annotated Lolita*, ed., preface, intro., and notes Alfred Appel Jr (New York: Vintage, 1991), 312.

4 Philip Roth, "On *Portnoy's Complaint*," in Roth, *Reading Myself and Others* (New York: Vintage, 2001), 13.

5 See, for example, James Baldwin, *Go Tell It on the Mountain* (New York: Universal Library/Grosset and Dunlap, 1953); Ralph Ellison, *Invisible Man* (New York: Vintage, 1995); Jamaica Kincaid, *At the Bottom of the River* (New York: Vintage, 1985), and *Annie John* (Plume/New American Library, 1986); and Toni Morrison, *The Bluest Eye* (New York: Knopf, 2000).

6 John Locke, *Some Thoughts Concerning Education*, quoted in Cunningham, *Children and Childhood in Western Society Since 1500* (Harlow, U.K.: Pearson, 2005), 60, 61.

7 Allan Bloom, introduction to Jean-Jacques Rousseau, *Emile, or On Education*, intro., trans., and notes Allan Bloom (New York: Basic Books, 1979), 4.

8   William Blake, "The Chimney Sweeper" and "London," in *Blake's Poetry and Designs*, ed. Mary Lynn Johnson and John E. Grant (New York: Norton, 1979), 25, 53.

9   William Wordsworth, "Ode: Intimations of Immortality from Recollections of Early Childhood," in *William Wordsworth: The Poems*, vol. 1, ed. John O. Hayden (New Haven, Conn.: Yale University Press, 1981), 523, 525.

10   Lionel Trilling, "The Immortality Ode," in *The Liberal Imagination: Essays on Literature and Society* (New York: Viking, 1950), 129–59.

11   Ralph Waldo Emerson, *Nature*, in *Essays and Lectures* (New York: Library of America, 1983), 46; quoted in Cunningham, *Children and Childhood*, 69.

12   Mark Twain, "Brief Biographical Sketch of George Washington," in *The Celebrated Jumping Frog of Calaveras County, and Other Sketches*, the Classical Library, http://www.classicallibrary.org/twain/celebrated/15-brief.htm.

1. CHARLES DICKENS'S HEROIC VICTIMS

1   Lionel Trilling, "Little Dorrit," in *The Opposing Self: Nine Essays in Criticism* (New York: Viking, 1955), 50–65; Edmund Wilson, "Dickens: The Two Scrooges," in *The Wound and the Bow: Seven Studies in Literature* (New York: Oxford University Press, 1970), 3–85.

2   Charles Dickens, *David Copperfield*, intro. and notes Jeremy Tambling (London: Penguin, 1996), 358, 594–95.

3   Charles Dickens, *Oliver Twist*, ed. Fred Kaplan (New York: Norton, 1993), 5–6.

4   Steven Marcus, *Dickens: From Pickwick to Dombey* (New York: Basic Books, 1965), 78.

5   See Fred Kaplan's footnote on the echo of Milton in this line (Dickens, *Oliver Twist*, 20n).

6   Robert Tracy, "'The Old Story' and Inside Stories: Modish Fiction and Fictional Modes in *Oliver Twist*," in *Oliver Twist*, by Charles Dickens, ed. Fred Kaplan (New York: Norton, 1993), 558.

7   John Forster, from *The Examiner*, September 10, 1837, in *Oliver Twist*, by Charles Dickens, ed. Fred Kaplan (New York: Norton, 1993), 400.

8   Anonymous, "Charles Dickens and His Works," in *Oliver Twist*, by Charles Dickens, ed. Fred Kaplan (New York: Norton, 1993), 411.

9   Anonymous review of *Oliver Twist* in *Quarterly Review* 64 (June 1839), quoted in Philip Collins, ed., *Charles Dickens: The Critical Heritage* (London: Routledge, 1971), 92.

10 Thomas Carlyle, *On Heroes, Hero-Worship, and the Heroic in History*, Project Gutenberg e-book 1091 (1997), http://www.gutenberg.org/ebooks/1091.

11 Martha Nussbaum, "Steerforth's Arm: Love and the Moral Point of View," in *Love's Knowledge: Essays on Philosophy and Literature* (New York: Oxford University Press, 1990), 335–64.

12 William Wordsworth, "We are Seven," in *William Wordsworth: The Poems*, vol. 1, ed. John O. Hayden (New Haven, Conn.: Yale University Press, 1981), 298.

13 Charles Dickens, *Great Expectations*, ed. Edgar Rosenberg (New York: Norton, 1999), 533.

14 Q. D. Leavis, "How We Must Read Great Expectations," in *Dickens the Novelist*, by F. R. Leavis and Q. D. Leavis (New York: Pantheon, 1970), 290.

2. MARK TWAIN'S FREE SPIRITS AND SLAVES

1 Mark Twain, *The Adventures of Tom Sawyer*, intro. and notes John C. Gerber (Berkeley: University of California Press, 1982), 3.

2 Jonathan Arac, *Huckleberry Finn as Idol and Target: The Functions of Criticism in Our Time* (Madison: University of Wisconsin Press, 1997), 23.

3 Mark Twain, *Adventures of Huckleberry Finn*, ed. Thomas Cooley (New York: Norton, 1999), 296.

4 T. S. Eliot, "Introduction to *Adventures of Huckleberry Finn*," in *Huckleberry Finn*, by Mark Twain, ed. Thomas Cooley (New York: Norton, 1999), 348–54; Lionel Trilling, "*Huckleberry Finn*," in *The Liberal Imagination: Essays on Literature and Society* (New York: Viking, 1950), 104–17.

5 John Keats, "On First Looking into Chapman's Homer," in *The Poems of John Keats*, ed. Jack Stillinger (Cambridge, Mass.: Belknap Press/Harvard University Press, 1978), 64.

6 Trilling, "*Huckleberry Finn*," 108.

7 Leslie Fiedler, "Come Back to the Raft Ag'in, Huck Honey," *Partisan Review* (June 1948), reprint, in *A New Fiedler Reader* (Amherst, New York: Prometheus, 1999), 3–12.

8 Arac, *Huckleberry Finn as Idol and Target*, 52–62.

9 Trilling, "*Huckleberry Finn*," 112–13.

10 Arthur M. Schlesinger Jr., "The Opening of the American Mind," quoted in Arac, *Huckleberry Finn as Idol and Target*, 18.

11 Toni Morrison, "This Amazing, Troubling Book," in *Adventures of Huckleberry Finn*, by Mark Twain, ed. Thomas Cooley (New York: Norton, 1999), 385–92.

12   W. H. Auden, "Oliver and Huck," quoted in *Mark Twain: Tom Sawyer and Huckleberry Finn*, ed. Stuart Hutchinson (New York: Columbia University Press, 1998), 75–76.

13   Perry Miller, *Nature's Nation*, quoted in Arac, *Huckleberry Finn as Idol and Target*, 34.

14   Arac, *Huckleberry Finn as Idol and Target*, 34.

15   Arac, *Huckleberry Finn as Idol and Target*, 52–62.

16   Mark Twain, *Notebook*, quoted in Hutchinson, *Mark Twain*, 115.

17   Toni Morrison, *Playing in the Dark: Whiteness and the Literary Imagination*, quoted in Hutchinson, *Mark Twain*, 90.

18   Leo Marx, "Mr. Eliot, Mr. Trilling, and Huckleberry Finn," quoted in Hutchinson, *Mark Twain*, 103.

19   Trilling, "*Huckleberry Finn*," 115.

20   Arac, *Huckleberry Finn as Idol and Target*, 20.

21   Arac, *Huckleberry Finn as Idol and Target*, 16, 62, 31.

22   Ernest Hemingway, "The Green Hills of Africa," quoted in Hutchinson, *Mark Twain*, 79.

23   Ralph Ellison, "Twentieth-Century Fiction and the Black Mask of Humanity," in *The Collected Essays of Ralph Ellison,* ed. and intro. John F. Callahan (New York: Modern Library, 2003), 90.

24   Vladimir Nabokov, "On a Book Entitled *Lolita*," in *The Annotated Lolita*, ed., intro., and notes Alfred Appel Jr. (New York: Vintage, 1991), 311.

25   William Dean Howells, *My Mark Twain*, quoted in Hutchinson, *Mark Twain*, 5.

3. HENRY JAMES'S DEMONIC LAMBS

1   Henry James, *The Turn of the Screw*, ed. Deborah Esch and Jonathan Warren (New York: Norton, 1999), 151, 153; unless noted otherwise, all references are to this edition.

2   Millicent Bell, "Class, Sex, and the Victorian Governess: James's *The Turn of the Screw*," in *New Essays on* Daisy Miller *and* The Turn of the Screw, ed. Vivian R. Pollak (Cambridge: Cambridge University Press, 1993), 119.

3   Peter G. Beidler's edition of *The Turn of the Screw* (Boston: Bedford Books, 1995) provides a useful survey of the critical history.

4   Millicent Bell, *Meaning in Henry James* (Cambridge, Mass.: Harvard University Press, 1991), 225.

5   M. Jeanne Peterson, "The Victorian Governess: Status Incongruity in the Family and Society," in *Suffer and Be Still*, ed. Martha Vicinus, quoted in Bell, "Class, Sex, and the Victorian Governess," 115.

6   Walter Benjamin, "The Storyteller: Reflections on the Works of Nikolai Leskov," in *Illuminations*, ed. Hannah Arendt (New York, Schocken, 1969), 101.

7   Oscar Wilde to Robert Ross, January 12, 1899, in *The Complete Letters of Oscar Wilde*, ed. Merlin Holland and Rupert Hart-Davis (New York: Holt, 2000), 1118.

8   Henry James to H. G. Wells, July 10, 1915, in *Selected Letters*, by Henry James, ed. Leon Edel (Cambridge, Mass.: Belknap Press/Harvard University Press, 1987), 431.

9   Henry James, "Alphonse Daudet," in *Henry James: Literary Criticism: French Writers, Other European Writers, the Prefaces to the New York Edition*, ed. Leon Edel (New York: Library of America, 1984), 242.

4. J. M. BARRIE'S ETERNAL NARCISSIST

1   Quoted in Andrew Birkin, *J. M. Barrie and the Lost Boys* (New Haven, Conn.: Yale University Press, 2003), 126.

2   R. D. S. Jack, *The Road to the Never Land: A Reassessment of J. M. Barrie's Dramatic Art* (Aberdeen, U.K.: Aberdeen University Press, 1991), 3, 234.

3. Quoted in Jack, *The Road to the Never Land*, 4.

4   Lisa Chaney, *Hide-and-Seek with Angels: A Life of J. M. Barrie* (London: Hutchinson, 2005), 372; Birkin, *J. M. Barrie and the Lost Boys*, 157.

5   Anonymous, "Barrie as Dramatist: A Divided Mind," *Times Literary Supplement*, June 26, 1937.

6   Jack, *The Road to the Never Land*, 158.

7   Jack, *The Road to the Never Land*, 11–13.

8   Peter Coveney, *The Image of Childhood: The Individual and Society: A Study of the Theme in English Literature* (Harmondsworth: Penguin, 1967), 240–41.

9   Jack, *The Road to the Never Land*, 154.

10 Jacqueline Rose, *The Case of Peter Pan; Or, The Impossibility of Children's Fiction* (Philadelphia: University of Pennsylvania Press, 1993), xii.

11 Ann Yeoman, *Now or Neverland: Peter Pan and the Myth of Eternal Youth, a Psychological Perspective on a Cultural Icon* (Toronto: Inner City Books, 1998), 152.

12 Birkin, *J. M. Barrie and the Lost Boys*, 202.

13   Humphrey Carpenter, *Secret Gardens: A Study of the Golden Age of Children's Literature* (London: Allen & Unwin, 1985), 186.

14   J. M. Barrie, *Peter Pan and Other Plays,* ed., intro., and notes Peter Hollindale (Oxford: Oxford University Press, 1999), 98, 125, 137.

15   Chaney, *Hide-and-Seek with Angels,* 310

16   J. M. Barrie, *Tommy and Grizel,* quoted in Birkin, *J. M. Barrie and the Lost Boys,* 65.

17   Quoted in Chaney, *Hide-and-Seek with Angels,* 207.

18   Birkin, *J. M. Barrie and the Lost Boys,* 63.

19   Barrie, *Tommy and Grizel,* quoted in Coveney, *The Image of Childhood,* 255.

20   Quoted in Chaney, *Hide-and-Seek with Angels,* 174.

21   Quoted in Birkin, *J. M. Barrie and the Lost Boys,* 22.

22   Jack, *The Road to the Never Land,* 164–65.

23   Rose, *The Case of Peter Pan,* 103.

24   *New York Times,* August 28, 2006.

25   Quoted in Chaney, *Hide-and-Seek with Angels,* 138.

26   Chaney, *Hide-and-Seek with Angels,* 139.

27   J. M. Barrie, *Margaret Ogilvy* (New York: Charles Scribner's Sons, 1896; reprint, St. Clair Shores, Mich.: Scholarly Press, n.d), 204, 205.

28   J. M. Barrie, *The Little White Bird,* Project Gutenberg e-book no. 1376 (1998), http://www.gutenberg.org/ebooks/1376.

29   J. M. Barrie, *Peter Pan in Kensington Gardens and Peter and Wendy,* ed., intro, and notes Peter Hollindale (Oxford: Oxford University Press, 1999), 3, 4.

30   Barrie, *The Little White Bird,* 129.

31   R. D. S. Jack goes into admirable detail about these issues in *The Road to the Never Land.*

32   Quoted in Birkin, *J. M. Barrie and the Lost Boys,* 95.

33   Quoted in Birkin, *J. M. Barrie and the Lost Boys,* 130.

34   Barrie, *Peter and Wendy,* 89. The cited volume contains the two prose works *Peter Pan in Kensington Gardens* and *Peter and Wendy.* For clarity's sake, when quoting the latter in the text, I will use only its title, *Peter and Wendy.*

35   Barrie, *Peter Pan in Kensington Gardens,* 77; *Peter Pan and Other Plays,* 97; *Peter and Wendy,* 203.

36   Quoted in Jack, *The Road to the Never Land,* 171.

37   Quoted in Birkin, *J. M. Barrie and the Lost Boys,* 110, 118.

38   Vladimir Nabokov, *The Annotated Lolita,* ed., intro., and notes Alfred Appel Jr. (New York: Vintage, 1991), 309.

5. J. D. SALINGER'S SAINTLY DROPOUT

1   Charles Dickens, *Oliver Twist*, ed. Fred Kaplan (New York: Norton, 1993), 3.

2   George Steiner, "The Salinger Industry," *The Nation*, November 14, 1959, 360–63.

3   Louis Menand, "Holden at Fifty," *New Yorker*, October 1, 2001, 82–87.

4   Mark Twain, *Adventures of Huckleberry Finn*, ed. Thomas Cooley (New York: Norton, 1999), 13.

5   J. D. Salinger, *The Catcher in the Rye* (Boston: Little, Brown, 1951), 3.

6   Charles Dickens, *David Copperfield*, intro. and notes Jeremy Tambling (London: Penguin, 1996), 11.

7   Donald P. Costello, "The Language of *The Catcher in the Rye*," in *Critical Essays on Salinger's* The Catcher in the Rye, ed. Joel Salzberg (Boston: G. K. Hall, 1990), 44–53.

8   J. D. Salinger, "Backstage with Esquire," *Esquire*, October 1945, http://www.esquire.com/the-side/feature/young-jd-salinger-letter-012810.

9   Ernest Hemingway, "Soldier's Home," in *In Our Time* (1925; New York: Scribner, 2003), 69–77.

6. VLADIMIR NABOKOV'S ABUSED NYMPH

1   Vladimir Nabokov, *The Annotated Lolita,* ed., intro., and notes Alfred Appel Jr. (New York: Vintage, 1991), 283. Further references will be made in the text.

2   Vladimir Nabokov, "On a Book Entitled *Lolita*," in *The Annotated Lolita*, ed., intro., and notes Alfred Appel Jr. (New York: Vintage Books, 1991), 314.

3   Orville Prescott, "Books of The Times," *New York Times*, August 18, 1958, quoted in Brian Boyd, *Vladimir Nabokov: The American Years* (Princeton, N.J.: Princeton University Press, 1991), 364.

4   Nabokov, "On a Book Entitled *Lolita*," 316.

5   Vladimir Nabokov, in Nabokov and Edmund Wilson, *Dear Bunny, Dear Volodya: The Nabokov-Wilson Letters, 1940–1971*, ed., annot., and intro. Simon Karlinsky (Berkeley: University of California Press, 2001), 308.

6   Nabokov, *The Annotated Lolita*, 338–39 (note to p. 16).

7   Douglas M. Davis, *The National Observer*, June 29, 1964, quoted in David Rampton, *Vladimir Nabokov: A Critical Study of the Novels* (Cambridge: Cambridge University Press, 1984), 202.

8   Vladimir Nabokov, *Strong Opinions* (New York: McGraw-Hill, 1973), 94.

9   Vladimir Nabokov, *Selected Letters, 1940–1977*, ed. Dmitri Nabokov and Matthew J. Bruccoli (New York: Harcourt Brace Jovanovich, 1989), 355.

10   Nabokov, "On a Book Entitled *Lolita*," 312.

11   Vladimir E. Alexandrov, *Nabokov's Otherworld* (Princeton, N.J.: Princeton University Press, 1991), 171.

12   Leslie Fiedler, *Love and Death in the American Novel*, 326–27, quoted in Ellen Pifer, *Demon or Doll: Images of the Child in Contemporary Writing and Culture* (Charlottesville: University Press of Virginia, 2000), 69.

13   Norman Podhoretz, "'Lolita,' My Mother-in-Law, the Marquis de Sade, and Larry Flynt," *Commentary* 103, no. 4 (April 1997): 29.

14   Alfred Appel Jr., "*Lolita*: The Springboard of Parody," quoted in Nomi Tamir-Ghez, "The Art of Persuasion in Nabokov's *Lolita*," in *Vladimir Nabokov's Lolita: A Casebook*, ed. Ellen Pifer (New York: Oxford University Press, 2003), 18.

15   F. W. Dupee, "A Preface to *Lolita*," in *"The King of the Cats" and Other Remarks on Writers and Writing* (Chicago: University of Chicago Press, 1984), 125.

16   Lionel Trilling, "The Last Lover," in *Speaking of Literature and Society*, ed. Diana Trilling, (New York: Harcourt Brace Jovanovich, 1980), 322–42.

17   Rampton, *Vladimir Nabokov*, 107, 119.

18   Leona Toker, *Nabokov: The Mystery of Literary Structures* (Ithaca, N.Y.: Cornell University Press, 1989), 202.

19   Wood, *The Magician's Doubts*, 139–41.

7. PHILIP ROTH'S PERFORMING LOUDMOUTH

1   Saul Bellow, *Herzog*, ed. Irving Howe (New York: Viking, 1976), 345, 153–54.

2   Irving Howe, "Down and Out in New York and Chicago," in *Herzog*, by Saul Bellow, ed. Irving Howe (New York: Viking, 1976), 397.

3   Philip Roth, *Portnoy's Complaint* (New York: Random House, 1969), 209. Further references will be made in the text.

4   Philip Roth, *Reading Myself and Others* (New York: Vintage, 2001), 172, 174.

5   Ibid., 29–36.

6   Ibid., 13.

7   Ibid., 28.

8   Ibid., 135.

9   Ross Posnock, *Philip Roth's Rude Truth: The Art of Immaturity* (Princeton, N.J.: Princeton University Press, 2006), 41. Irving Howe, "Philip Roth Reconsidered," *Commentary* 54, no. 6 (December 1972): 69–77.

10 Sigmund Freud, "The Most Prevalent Form of Degradation in Erotic Life,"
    in *Sexuality and the Psychology of Love*, ed. and intro. Philip Rieff (New York:
    Collier, 1972), 59, 62.
11 See Posnock, *Philip Roth's Rude Truth*, for a rich critical and historical discus-
    sion of these themes.

SELECTED BIBLIOGRAPHY

Alexandrov, Vladimir E. *Nabokov's Otherworld*. Princeton, N.J.: Princeton University Press, 1991.

Arac, Jonathan. *Huckleberry Finn as Idol and Target: The Functions of Criticism in Our Time*. Madison: University of Wisconsin Press, 1997.

Baldwin, James. *Go Tell It on the Mountain*. New York: Universal Library/Grosset and Dunlap, 1953.

Barrie, J. M. *The Little White Bird*. Project Gutenberg e-book no. 1376. 1998. http://www.gutenberg.org/ebooks/1376.

———. *Margaret Ogilvy*. New York: Charles Scribner's Sons, 1896. Reprint, St. Clair Shores, Mich.: Scholarly Press, n.d.

———. *Peter Pan and Other Plays*. Ed., intro., and notes Peter Hollindale. Oxford: Oxford University Press, 1999.

———. *Peter Pan in Kensington Gardens and Peter and Wendy*. Ed., intro, and notes Peter Hollindale. Oxford: Oxford University Press, 1999.

Bayley, John. "*Oliver Twist*: Things as They Really Are." In *Oliver Twist*, by Charles Dickens, ed. Fred Kaplan, 461–69. New York: Norton, 1993.

Bell, Millicent. "Class, Sex, and the Victorian Governess: James's *The Turn of the Screw*." In *New Essays on* Daisy Miller *and* The Turn of the Screw, ed. Vivian R. Pollak, 91–119. Cambridge: Cambridge University Press, 1993.

———. *Meaning in Henry James*. Cambridge, Mass.: Harvard University Press, 1991.

Bellow, Saul. *Herzog*. Ed. Irving Howe. New York: Viking, 1976.

Benjamin, Walter. "The Storyteller: Reflections on the Work of Nikolai Leskov." In *Illuminations*, ed. Hannah Arendt, 83–109. New York, Schocken, 1969.

Birkin, Andrew. *J. M. Barrie and the Lost Boys*. New Haven: Yale University Press, 2005.

Blake, William. *Blake's Poetry and Designs*. Ed. Mary Lynn Johnson and John E. Grant. New York: Norton, 1979.

Bloom, Allan. Introduction to Jean-Jacques Rousseau, *Emile, or On Education*, intro., trans., and notes Allan Bloom. New York: Basic Books, 1979.

Bloom, Harold, ed. *Holden Caulfield*. New York: Chelsea House, 1990.

——, ed. *J. D. Salinger*. New York: Chelsea House, 1987.

Boyd, Brian. *Vladimir Nabokov: The American Years*. Princeton, N.J.: Princeton University Press, 1991.

Britten, Benjamin. *The Turn of the Screw*. Ed. Patricia Howard. Cambridge: Cambridge University Press, 1985.

Brontë, Charlotte. *Jane Eyre*. Ed. Michael Mason. London: Penguin, 1996.

Brooks, Peter. *The Melodramatic Imagination: Balzac, Henry James, Melodrama, and the Mode of Excess*. New Haven, Conn.: Yale University Press, 1976.

——. "Repetition, Repression, and Return: The Plotting of *Great Expectations*." In *Great Expectations*, by Charles Dickens, ed. Edgar Rosenberg, 679–89. New York: Norton, 1999.

Capote, Truman. *Other Voices, Other Rooms*. 1948. New York: Vintage, 1994.

Carey, Peter. *His Illegal Self*. New York: Knopf, 2008.

——. *The Unusual Life of Tristan Smith*. New York: Vintage, 1994.

Carlyle, Thomas. *On Heroes, Hero-Worship, and the Heroic in History*. Project Gutenberg e-book no. 1091, 1997. http://www.gutenberg.org/ebooks/1091.

Carpenter, Humphrey. *Secret Gardens: A Study of the Golden Age of Children's Literature*. London: Allen & Unwin, 1985.

Chaney, Lisa. *Hide-and-Seek with Angels: A Life of J. M. Barrie*. London: Hutchinson, 2005.

Collins, Philip, ed. *Charles Dickens: The Critical Heritage*. London: Routledge, 1971.

Connolly, Julian W., ed. *Nabokov and His Fiction: New Perspectives*. Cambridge: Cambridge University Press, 1999.

Conroy, Frank. *Stop-Time*. New York: Penguin, 1977.

Costello, Donald P. "The Language of *The Catcher in the Rye*." In *Critical Essays on Salinger's* The Catcher in the Rye, ed. Joel Salzberg, 44–53. Boston: G. K. Hall, 1990.

Coveney, Peter. *The Image of Childhood: The Individual and Society: A Study of the Theme in English Literature*. Harmondsworth: Penguin, 1967.

Crawford, Catherine, ed. *If You Really Want to Hear About It: Writers on J. D. Salinger and His Work*. New York: Thunder's Mouth Press, 2006.

Cunningham, Hugh. *Children and Childhood in Western Society Since 1500*. Harlow, U.K.: Pearson, 2005.

DeLillo, Don. *White Noise*. New York: Elisabeth Sifton/Viking, 1985.

Dickens, Charles. *David Copperfield*. Intro. and notes Jeremy Tambling. London: Penguin, 1996.

——. *Great Expectations*. Ed. Edgar Rosenberg. New York: Norton, 1999.

——. *Oliver Twist*. Ed. Fred Kaplan. New York: Norton, 1993.

Dickstein, Morris. *Leopards in the Temple: The Transformation of American Fiction, 1945–1970*. Cambridge, Mass.: Harvard University Press, 2002.

——. *A Mirror in the Roadway: Literature and the Real World*. Princeton, N.J.: Princeton University Press, 2005.

Donoghue, Emma. *Room*. New York: Little, Brown, 2010.

Doyle, Roddy. *Paddy Clarke Ha Ha Ha*. New York: Penguin, 1995.

Dupee, F. W. *Henry James*. New York: Morrow, 1974.

——. "A Preface to *Lolita*." In *The King of the Cats" and Other Remarks on Writers and Writing*, 111–25. Chicago: University of Chicago Press, 1984.

Eliot, T. S. "Introduction to *Adventures of Huckleberry Finn*." In *Adventures of Huckleberry Finn*, by Mark Twain, ed. Thomas Cooley, 348–54. New York: Norton, 1999.

Ellison, Ralph. *Invisible Man*. New York: Vintage, 1995.

——. "Twentieth-Century Fiction and the Black Mask of Humanity." In *The Collected Essays of Ralph Ellison*, ed. John F. Callahan, 81–99. New York: Modern Library, 2003.

Felman, Shoshana. "Turning the Screw of Interpretation." In *Literature and Psychoanalysis: The Question of Reading: Otherwise*, ed. Shoshana Felman, 94–207. Baltimore, Md.: Johns Hopkins University Press, 1982.

Fiedler, Leslie A. "Come Back to the Raft Ag'in, Huck Honey!" *Partisan Review* (June 1948). Reprint, in *A New Fiedler Reader*, 3–12. Amherst, N.Y.: Prometheus, 1999.

Foer, Jonathan Safran. *Extremely Loud and Incredibly Close*. New York: Houghton Mifflin, 2005.

Forster, John. From *The Examiner*, September 10, 1837. In *Oliver Twist*, by Charles Dickens, ed. Fred Kaplan. New York: Norton, 1993.

French, Warren. *J. D. Salinger*. New York: Twayne, 1985.

——. *J. D. Salinger, Revisited*. New York: Twayne, 1988.

Freud, Sigmund. "The Most Prevalent Form of Degradation in Erotic Life." In *Sexuality and the Psychology of Love*, ed. and intro. Philip Rieff, 58–70. New York: Collier, 1972.

Geduld, Harry M. *Sir James Barrie*. New York: Twayne, 1971.

Golding, William. *Lord of the Flies*. New York: Penguin, 1999.

Gosse, Edmund. *Father and Son*. Ed., intro., and notes Michael Newton. Oxford: Oxford University Press, 2009.

Gross, John, and Gabriel Pearson, eds. *Dickens and the Twentieth Century*. Toronto: University of Toronto Press, 1966.

Hamilton, Ian. *In Search of J. D. Salinger*. New York: Random House, 1988.

Hemingway, Ernest. "Soldier's Home." In *In Our Time*, 69–77. 1925. New York: Scribner, 2003.

Higonnet, Anne. *Pictures of Innocence: The History and Crisis of Ideal Childhood*. New York: Thames and Hudson, 1998.

Homes, A. M. *The End of Alice*. New York: Scribner, 1996.

Howe, Irving. "Down and Out in New York and Chicago." In *Herzog*, by Saul Bellow, ed. Irving Howe, 391–400. New York: Viking, 1976.

——. "Philip Roth Reconsidered." *Commentary* 54, no. 6 (December 1972): 69–77.

Hughes, Richard. *A High Wind in Jamaica*. New York: New York Review, 1999.

Hutchinson, Stuart, ed. *Mark Twain: Tom Sawyer and Huckleberry Finn*. New York: Columbia University Press, 1998.

Hyde, G. M. *Vladimir Nabokov: America's Russian Novelist*. London: Boyars, 1977.

Ishiguro, Kazuo. *Never Let Me Go*. New York: Knopf, 2005.

Jack, R. D. S. *The Road to the Never Land: A Reassessment of J. M. Barrie's Dramatic Art*. Aberdeen, U.K.: Aberdeen University Press, 1991.

James, Henry. "Alphonse Daudet." In *Henry James: Literary Criticism: French Writers, Other European Writers, the Prefaces to the New York Edition*. Ed. Leon Edel. New York: Library of America, 1984.

——. *Selected Letters*. Ed. Leon Edel. Cambridge, Mass.: Belknap Press/Harvard University Press, 1987

——. *The Turn of the Screw*. Ed. Peter G. Beidler. Boston: Bedford Books, 1995.

——. *The Turn of the Screw*. Ed. Deborah Esch and Jonathan Warren. New York: Norton, 1999.

Jordan, John O. "The Purloined Handkerchief." In *Oliver Twist*, by Charles Dickens, ed. Fred Kaplan, 580–93. New York: Norton, 1993.

Kaplan, Fred. *Dickens: A Biography*. New York: Morrow, 1998.

Karr, Mary. *The Liar's Club: A Memoir*. New York: Penguin, 1996.

Kazin, Alfred. *Bright Book of Life: American Novelists and Storytellers from Hemingway to Mailer*. Boston: Little, Brown, 1973.

——. "J.D. Salinger: 'Everybody's Favorite.'" In *Contemporaries*. Boston: Little, Brown, 1962.

Keats, John. *The Poems of John Keats*. Ed. Jack Stillinger. Cambridge, Mass.: Belknap Press of Harvard University Press, 1978.

Kincaid, Jamaica. *Annie John*. Plume/New American Library, 1986.

———. *At the Bottom of the River*. New York: Vintage, 1985.

Kingston, Maxine Hong. *The Woman Warrior: Memoirs of a Girlhood Among Ghosts*. New York: Vintage, 1989.

Leavis, Q. D. "How We Must Read *Great Expectations*." In *Dickens the Novelist*, by F. R. Leavis and Q. D. Leavis, 277–331. New York: Pantheon, 1970.

Lethem, Jonathan. *The Fortress of Solitude*. New York: Doubleday, 2003.

———. *Girl in Landscape*. New York: Vintage, 1998.

Lerer, Seth. *Children's Literature: A Reader's History, From Aesop to Harry Potter*. Chicago: University of Chicago Press, 2008.

Lurie, Alison. *Don't Tell the Grown-ups: The Subversive Power of Children's Literature*. Boston: Little, Brown, 1990.

Maar, Michael. *Speak, Nabokov*. London: Verso, 2009.

———. *The Two Lolitas*. London: Verso, 2005.

Malcolm, Janet. "Justice to J. D. Salinger." *New York Review of Books*, June 21, 2001, 16–21.

March, William. *The Bad Seed*. New York: Ecco, 1997.

Marcus, Steven. *Dickens: From Pickwick to Dombey*. New York: Basic Books, 1965.

McCarthy, Mary. "J. D. Salinger's Closed Circuit." In *The Writing on the Wall and Other Literary Essays*, 35–41. New York: Harcourt Brace Jovanovich, 1970.

———. *Memories of a Catholic Girlhood*. New York: Harcourt Brace Jovanovich, 1974.

McCourt, Frank. *Angela's Ashes*. New York: Scribner, 1996.

McCullers, Carson. *The Member of the Wedding*. New York: Mariner/Houghton Mifflin, 2004.

McEwan, Ian. *The Child in Time*. Boston: Houghton Mifflin, 1987.

———. *Atonement*. New York: Nan A. Talese/Doubleday, 2002.

Menand, Louis. "Holden at Fifty." *New Yorker*, October 1, 2001, 82–87.

Miller, D. A. *The Novel and the Police*. Berkeley: University of California Press, 1988.

Miller, J. Hillis. "*Oliver Twist*." In *Oliver Twist*, by Charles Dickens, ed. Fred Kaplan, 432–48. New York: Norton, 1993.

Millhauser, Steven. *Edwin Mulhouse: The Life and Death of an American Writer, 1943–1954, by Jeffrey Cartwright*. New York: Knopf, 1972.

Mintz, Steven. *Huck's Raft: A History of American Childhood*. Cambridge, Mass.: Belknap/Harvard University Press, 2004.

Morrison, Toni. *The Bluest Eye*. New York: Knopf, 2000.

———. "This Amazing, Troubling Book." In *Adventures of Huckleberry Finn*, by Mark Twain, ed. Thomas Cooley, 385–92. New York: Norton, 1999.

Moynahan, Julian. "The Hero's Guilt: The Case of *Great Expectations.*" In *Great Expectations* by Charles Dickens, ed. Edgar Rosenberg, 654–63. New York: Norton, 1999.

Nabokov, Vladimir. *The Annotated Lolita.* Ed., intro., and notes Alfred Appel Jr. New York: Vintage, 1991.

——. *Lectures on Literature.* Ed. Fredson Bowers, intro. John Updike. New York: Harcourt Brace Jovanovich, 1980.

——. "On a Book Entitled *Lolita.*" In *The Annotated Lolita*, ed., intro., and notes Alfred Appel Jr., 311–17. New York: Vintage, 1991.

——. *Selected Letters, 1940–1977.* Ed. Dmitri Nabokov and Matthew J. Bruccoli. New York: Harcourt Brace Jovanovich, 1989.

——. *Strong Opinions.* New York: McGraw-Hill, 1973.

Nabokov, Vladimir, and Edmund Wilson. *Dear Bunny, Dear Volodya: The Nabokov-Wilson Letters, 1940–1971.* Ed., annot., and intro. Simon Karlinsky. Berkeley: University of California Press, 2001.

Nussbaum, Martha. "Steerforth's Arm: Love and the Moral Point of View." In *Love's Knowledge: Essays on Philosophy and Literature,* 335–64. New York: Oxford University Press, 1992.

Oates, Joyce Carol. "Accursed Inhabitants of the House of Bly." In *Haunted: Tales of the Grotesque,* 254–83. New York: Plume/Penguin, 1995.

Okri, Ben. *The Famished Road.* New York: Nan A. Talese/Doubleday, 1992.

Orwell, George. "Charles Dickens." In *A Collection of Essays by George Orwell,* 48–104. New York: Harcourt Brace Jovanovich, 1953.

Paroissien, David. *The Companion to Oliver Twist.* Edinburgh: Edinburgh University Press, 1992.

Pifer, Ellen. *Demon or Doll: Images of the Child in Contemporary Writing and Culture.* Charlottesville: University Press of Virginia, 2000.

——. *Nabokov and the Novel.* Cambridge, Mass.: Harvard University Press, 1981.

——, ed. *Vladimir Nabokov's Lolita: A Casebook.* New York: Oxford University Press, 2003.

Podhoretz, Norman. "'Lolita,' My Mother-in-Law, the Marquis de Sade, and Larry Flynt." *Commentary* 103, no. 4 (April 1997): 23–36.

Pollak, Vivian R., ed. *New Essays on* Daisy Miller *and* The Turn of the Screw. Cambridge: Cambridge University Press, 1993.

Posnock, Ross. *Philip Roth's Rude Truth: The Art of Immaturity.* Princeton, N.J.: Princeton University Press, 2006.

Proffer, Carl R. *Keys to Lolita.* Bloomington: Indiana University Press, 1968.

Prose, Francine. *Blue Angel.* New York: HarperCollins, 2000.

Purdy, James. *Malcolm*. New York: Farrar, Straus & Cudahy, 1959. New York: Avon, n.d.

Quennell, Peter, ed. *Vladimir Nabokov: A Tribute: His Life, His Work, His World*. New York: Morrow, 1980.

Rampton, David. *Vladimir Nabokov: A Critical Study of the Novels*. Cambridge: Cambridge University Press, 1984.

Ricks, Christopher. "*Great Expectations*." In *Great Expectations*, by Charles Dickens, ed. Edgar Rosenberg, 668–74. New York: Norton, 1999.

Robinson, Marilynne. *Housekeeping*. New York: Picador/ Farrar, Straus and Giroux, 1981.

Rodriguez, Richard. *Hunger of Memory: The Education of Richard Rodriguez*. New York: Dial, 2004.

Rose, Jacqueline. *The Case of Peter Pan; Or, The Impossibility of Children's Fiction*. Philadelphia: University of Pennsylvania Press, 1993.

Roth, Henry. *Call It Sleep*. New York: Equinox/Avon, 1976.

Roth, Philip. *Portnoy's Complaint*. New York: Random House, 1969.

——. *Reading Myself and Others*. New York: Vintage Books, 2001.

Rushdie, Salman. *Midnight's Children*. New York: Penguin, 1991.

Salinger, J. D. "Backstage with Esquire." *Esquire*, October 1945. http://www.esquire.com/the-side/feature/young-jd-salinger-letter-012810.

——. *The Catcher in the Rye*. Boston: Little, Brown, 1951.

Salzberg, Joel, ed. *Critical Essays on Salinger's* The Catcher in the Rye. Boston: G. K. Hall, 1990.

Salzman, Jack, ed. *New Essays on* The Catcher in the Rye. Cambridge: Cambridge University Press, 1991.

Schlicke, Paul, ed. *Oxford Reader's Companion to Charles Dickens*. New York: Oxford University Press, 1999.

Smiley, Jane. "Say It Ain't So, Huck: Second Thoughts on Mark Twain's 'Masterpiece.'" In *Adventures of Huckleberry Finn*, by Mark Twain, ed. Thomas Cooley, 354–62. New York: Norton, 1999.

Stafford, Jean. *The Mountain Lion*. New York: Dutton, 1983.

Steed, J. P., ed. *The Catcher in the Rye: New Essays*. New York: Peter Lang, 2002.

Steiner, George. "The Salinger Industry," *The Nation*, November 14, 1959, 360–63.

Tamir-Ghez, Nomi. "The Art of Persuasion in Nabokov's *Lolita*." In *Vladimir Nabokov's Lolita: A Casebook*, ed. Ellen Pifer, 17–37. New York: Oxford University Press, 2003.

Todorov, Tzvetan. *The Fantastic: A Structural Approach to a Literary Genre*. Cleveland, Ohio: The Press of Case Western Reserve University, 1973.

——. *The Poetics of Prose*. Ithaca, N.Y.: Cornell University Press, 1995.

Toker, Leona. *Nabokov: The Mystery of Literary Structures*. Ithaca, N.Y.: Cornell University Press, 1989.

Tracy, Robert. "'The Old Story' and Inside Stories: Modish Fiction and Fictional Modes in *Oliver Twist*." In *Oliver Twist*, by Charles Dickens, ed. Fred Kaplan, 557–74. New York: Norton, 1993.

Tredell, Nicolas, ed. *Charles Dickens: Great Expectations*. New York: Columbia University Press, 1998.

Trilling, Lionel. "*Huckleberry Finn*." In *The Liberal Imagination: Essays on Literature and Society*, 104–17. New York: Viking, 1950.

——. "Little Dorrit." In *The Opposing Self: Nine Essays in Criticism*, 50–65. New York: Viking, 1955.

——. "The Immortality Ode." In *The Liberal Imagination: Essays on Literature and Society*, 129–59. New York: Viking, 1950.

——. "The Last Lover." In *Speaking of Literature and Society*, ed. Diana Trilling, 322–42. New York: Harcourt Brace Jovanovich, 1980.

Twain, Mark. *Adventures of Huckleberry Finn*. Ed. Thomas Cooley. New York: Norton, 1999.

——. *The Adventures of Tom Sawyer*. Intro. and notes John C. Gerber. Berkeley: University of California Press, 1982.

——. *The Annotated Huckleberry Finn*. Ed., intro, notes, and biblio. Michael Patrick Hearn. New York: Clarkson N. Potter, 1981.

——. "Brief Biographical Sketch of George Washington." In *The Celebrated Jumping Frog of Calaveras County, and Other Sketches*. The Classical Library. http://www.classicallibrary.org/twain/celebrated/15-brief.htm.

Updike, John. "Grandmaster Nabokov." In *Assorted Prose*, 318–27. New York: Knopf, 1965.

——. "Vale, VN." In *Hugging the Shore: Essays and Criticism*, 244–46. New York: Knopf, 1983.

Wilde, Oscar. *The Complete Letters of Oscar Wilde*. Ed. Merlin Holland and Rupert Hart-Davis. New York: Holt, 2000.

Wills, Gary. "The Loves of Oliver Twist." In *Oliver Twist*, by Charles Dickens, ed. Fred Kaplan, 593–608. New York: Norton, 1993.

Wilson, Edmund. "The Ambiguity of Henry James." In *The Triple Thinkers: Twelve Essays on Literary Subjects*, 88–132. New York: Oxford University Press, 1963.

——. "Dickens: The Two Scrooges." In *The Wound and the Bow: Seven Studies in Literature*, 3–85. New York: Oxford University Press, 1970.

Wood, Michael. *The Magician's Doubts: Nabokov and the Risks of Fiction.* Princeton, N.J.: Princeton University Press, 1995.

Wordsworth, William. *William Wordsworth: The Poems.* Ed. John O. Hayden. Vol. 1. New Haven, Conn.: Yale University Press, 1981.

Wright, Richard. *Black Boy.* New York: Harper, 2008.

Yeoman, Ann. *Now or Neverland: Peter Pan and the Myth of Eternal Youth, a Psychological Perspective on a Cultural Icon.* Toronto: Inner City Books, 1999.

INDEX